THE MYSTERIES OF THE ISLANDS OF BUTON

ACCORDING TO THE OLD MEN AND ME

By

Caleb Coppenger

Aventine Press

Published by Aventine Press
750 State St. #319
San Diego CA, 92101
www.aventinepress.com

ISBN: 1-59330-701-2

Library of Congress Control Number: 2010919560
Library of Congress Cataloging-in-Publication Data
The Mysteries of the Islands of Buton

Printed in the United States of America

TABLE OF CONTENTS

Part II – The Land and Sea of Buton

Part III – The Neighbors of Buton

ACKNOWLEDGEMENTS

The number of people that contributed to this book is too large to count. Due to the fact that my initial explorations throughout these islands were not taken with writing a book in mind, most of the names of the individuals I spoke with remain a mystery to me. Everywhere I went, there were always friendly people willing to share their stories and their perspective on things. If we did not have a place to stay, many opened up their homes to my family and me. If we did not know where to get food, many provided meals for us. As well as being a challenge, it was also a delight to meet such a variety of people and see so many new and interesting things. I want to say "terima kasih" to everyone throughout Southeast Sulawesi that befriended my family and me and shared their stories and lives with us.

One friend in particular, Harisun, stands above the rest when it comes to sparking my interest in the people and history of the people groups of Buton. Harisun loves his culture and people so much that his desire to share it with others is infectious. The events in Lapandewa were my first look at what goes on out in the villages of these islands, and our trip to the top of Mt. Siontapina together is what ultimately convinced me that I needed to make a record of what goes on here. His openness to share the knowledge he has gleaned over his life as well as his willingness to let me take part in several cultural events is something I will never forget. The hospitality of his family in Lapandewa is a highlight of every visit.

Once I really started writing things down and the book started to take shape I asked a number of people to look it over and provide whatever suggestions or criticisms they had. I want to say thanks to Mom, Dad, and Chesed for taking the time to read it over and provide grammatical and clarification suggestions to make it more readable and understandable. I want to thank Rene and Jonathan for giving the typescript a quick read and providing some helpful suggestions. Thanks to La Ode Dini who was always available to answer any random questions I had as the book neared completion. Finally, I am indebted to David Mead for providing a detailed look regarding its accuracy pertaining to all matters Indonesian, especially on Sulawesi, along with the extra information provided regarding sources and background for several topics I touched upon. This being said, I accept full responsibility for any mistakes or deficiencies within this book.

I hope that this book can help develop a more complete picture for those interested in the islands that composed the former kingdom and sultanate of Buton. My family's traveling safety while exploring these islands as well as the key relationships we have made in Southeast Sulawesi are ultimately due to the grace of God. I have been blessed in many ways. One of the greatest blessings I have is my lovely wife, Tiffany, and my two awesome children, Alethia and Asher. They help make my life full and always keep it interesting!

INTRODUCTION

The islands of Buton are full of enough natural wonders, beauty, and natural resources to warrant a visit. Add to that the culture and history that has developed from a sultanate and kingdom that thrived for hundreds of years in Southeast Sulawesi, and you have what should be considered a prime tourist destination. The land is unexplored and undocumented enough (by outsiders taking notes) to make each trip out into the jungle, ocean, and outlying villages an adventure. Not only does this fairly large island demand a closer look, but also the surrounding islands each reflect the influence of the former kingdom of Buton, with their own unique expressions of each of the traditions. The history of each of these islands is tightly woven together with the past era in which pirates and armies at sea would sail across the East Indies to spread the influence of their kingdoms and to obtain spices and booty from their neighbors. It was an era that we may have a tough time imagining, but one whose mystery is enchanting. While things may not still be quite as dangerous and exciting in Buton, this island welcomes visitors with open arms. It invites them to explore the past and the present in a land that most Westerners only imagined after reading of the great world explorers of the past. Those explorers, as well as those who have visited this area more recently, have only scratched the surface of the mysteries that lie in the mountains, caves, and seas of these islands.

While mystery is exciting, so is unveiling it to reveal the sources of the narrative. In Buton, it is time that we try to find out the truth about who these people are and how their life came to be as it is now. If you go into the smaller villages and ask historical questions or want to know, "Why?" you will usually be told to ask the older people in the village. After posing one of these questions to a man who is locally guessed to be a hundred years old (probably closer to 70), he replied with the common, "You would have to ask the older men." That caught me off guard, because there was no one else older. So either that means nobody knows, or maybe he was implying we should talk with the deceased ancestors (which are said to make appearances). Either way, it is time to start writing things down.

Several things have been written on Buton, mainly within Indonesia, but also in the Netherlands and Japan, along with several resources about the variety of local languages. Each of these pieces clarifies certain aspects of Buton, but I would like to help bring them together and add a good deal of information from local interviews and traveling. While interviews themselves are not always reliable (especially when wandering around remote villages), true or not, they do give insight into how people perceive themselves and their history, which affects how they live today. It is also very important in this part of the world to get firsthand knowledge of places and events when possible. Having traveled extensively throughout the islands of Buton, I have tried to make the information in this book as accurate as possible.

The stories that are still told throughout these islands touch on all aspects of life: social, religious, cultural, and historical. Within this book I have done the same, bringing all the information I have obtained on Buton and trying to synthesize it. This is meant to be an ethnography of the people groups that live on Buton and the surrounding islands. At the same time, I have included stories of how the people have been impacted religiously and politically throughout the years. Buton's position as a major crossroads in the shipping routes to east Indonesia has led to outside influence touching all aspects of life on Buton.

None of these areas has been completely explored, but in each of the areas, there is some research available as well as plenty of local stories that give insight into how things might have been in the past. The most recognized symbol of the Sultanate of Buton is the pineapple. Of the several possible explanations I have heard of how this symbol came to be, the most prevalent is that the pineapple symbolizes the people of Buton: they are very rough on the outside, but once you open the pineapple, and get to the inside, you will be surprised by how sweet and rich it is. So this is how we will seek to understand the people of Buton, by working open the pineapple and getting to the part that has the most value, the inside. We will begin with what has been recorded of Buton by those on the outside, and the reputation Buton has built in the world. We will then look a little closer at the internal workings of the sultanate, how it did business and how it worked with the villages under its power. As we explore the core of Buton, we will get to know the different people groups, what they believe, and where they live. We will learn about these people from what they say and do today, and what they believe about the past. To complete our attempt at understanding Buton we will learn about some of the lesser known nearby mainland Sulawesi kingdoms along with the well known people groups from other lands that have moved to Buton and made it their home. I hope this book can provide a starting point to further explore the history and people of Buton as well as provide a handbook for getting around the islands and knowing what to expect experientially along the way. We now embark on a journey to clear up some of the mysteries and get the conversation started on the islands of Buton, according to the old men and me.

Part 1 – THE PEOPLE OF BUTON

I

In the Shadow of Two Powers

Many kingdoms rose and fell in the islands of the East Indies (later Indonesia), with their empires reaching as far as the Southeast Asia mainland. The ones that had the most lasting impression in the region and currently in the history books were those of the Sriwijaya and Majapahit. Throughout modern day Indonesia these are household names which can be seen on the names of businesses and establishments throughout the archipelago. Hundreds of years ago their influence was much more profound.

The majority of the time the Sriwijaya kingdom (683-1288 AD) had its center on the island of Sumatra, in the cities of Palembang and Jambi. The capital frequently moved as wars were fought and new dynasties took power. The capital was even moved to the Isthmus of Kra on the Malay Peninsula at one point. This kingdom also had control over the city of Jakarta (formerly Batavia) on the island of Java. The power of Sriwijaya was long and far-reaching, though it was eventually overshadowed by that of the Majapahit kingdom further east.

In eastern Java was the heart of the Majapahit kingdom (1293-1500 AD). This kingdom (and those related to it) left such great monuments as Prambanan and Borobudur, which have become the best known ancient sites in Indonesia today. Though the kingdoms in this area were not always known as Majapahit, that name is now used predominately. These two kingdoms overshadow all the others. The prevailing religion in these kingdoms and throughout the archipelago was a mix of Hinduism and Buddhism. This can be seen in the structures that have been left behind, as well as in the traditions found throughout the islands that are still practiced today. While the centers of these kingdoms were established in western Indonesia, eastern Indonesia had different dominant kingdoms.

Two of the kingdoms that loom large in the history of eastern Indonesia are those of Gowa (GO-wah) and Ternate (tur-NAH-tey). Sulawesi and its surrounding islands were right in the middle of their power struggle.[1] These kingdoms underwent many transformations, especially the kingdoms of South Sulawesi, as new powers appeared and sought to overthrow the domination of Gowa. While much less is written about these two kingdoms than those of Sumatra and Java, they wielded great power and had a dominant influence over major sea lanes in the East Indies. In between these two kingdoms was one that emerged that would not be destroyed by its larger neighbors. The kingdom of Buton arose among a group of islands with a variety of languages, cultures, and histories. It sought to bring these diverse people together and protect them from the attacks to which they often fell prey as Gowa and Ternate sought to expand their borders.

GOWA

The kingdoms of Gowa and Talloq were centered just south of the the present-day city of Makassar (also called Ujung Pandang), which is the home of the Makasar people.[2] The two Makasar kingdoms of Gowa and Talloq were unified, even though they were autonomous kingdoms.[3] The name of Gowa

---

[1] See map of Sulawesi.

[2] In this book the city will be spelled "Makassar" and the people group will be spelled "Makasar."

[3] J. Noorduyn, "The manuscripts of the Makasarese chronicle of Goa and Talloq; An evaluation," in *Bijdragen tot de Taal-, Land- en Volkenkunde* 147 (1991): 454.

is more prominent in the minds of people today, so references to Gowa usually also include the kingdom of Talloq. Gowa's hold over this land was tentative as their formidable Bugis neighbors vied for power in the region. The number of kingdoms that could be found throughout Sulawesi and the islands surrounding it is staggering. By the fourteenth century, when historical records begin, Luwuq and Soppeng were the dominant powers in their respective regions. Two other Bugis kingdoms, Bone and Wajoq, and the Makasar kingdoms of Gowa and Talloq, also do not seem to have become major powers until the sixteenth century, though their rise can be traced back to about 1400s.[4] While there were many small kingdoms associated with these larger powers that may have been significant at the time, usually only the larger names remain in the collective memory of the people today. In 1586 Gowa was strong enough to challenge the triple alliance of the Bugis kingdoms of Bone (BO-nay), Soppeng (SO-pang), and Wajoq (WAH-jo)[5], and during this time Gowa then became the preeminent power and commercial center in South Sulawesi.[6]

Even today South Sulawesi is often referred to as the gateway to East Indonesia, and it yields a great amount of influence because of its position between major sea lanes passing through Indonesia. Bone's economic power was based on its control, together with its allies Wajoq and Soppeng, of the rice basin in the central plain. Makassar's power came increasingly to rely on its position as a major port in the spice trade. To play a significant role as a power in the archipelago it was necessary to have both a supply of rice to feed one's population (and one's warriors), and to be able to participate in trade, either through transshipment

---

[4] Ian Caldwell, "Power, State and Society Among the Pre-Islamic Bugis," in *Bijdragen tot de Taal-, Land- en Volkenkunde* 151, no.3 (1995): 402.

[5] See map of South Sulawesi kingdoms.

[6] William Patrick Cummings, *A Chain of Kings: the Makassarese Chronicles of Gowa and Talloq* (Leiden: KITLV (Royal Institute of Linguistics and Anthropology or Koninklijk Instituut voor Taal-, Land- en Volkenkunde) Press, 2007), 4.

of goods from more remote islands, or through exporting prod-
ucts from one's own land. The competition between Makassar
and Bone was in part a competition to merge and control the
resources of the peninsula in order to participate in the profitable
trade of the archipelago.[7] While Gowa was dominant during
this timeframe, the role of the Bugis people and their influence
throughout Indonesia and neighboring countries cannot be over-
looked. The Bugis have left their mark throughout Singapore,
Malaysia, and other parts of Southeast Asia because of their skill
at sea and their exploits abroad in search of wealth.[8] But even
the Bugis were at one point under the sway of Gowa in Sulawesi.

Conflicts between Gowa and the Bugis continued despite intermarriage. It was like two brothers fighting. But when Gowa
subdued the Bugis in 1586 things started to change. Islam spread
through Sulawesi. Gowa also had recognition outside of the islands of modern day Indonesia. The reign of the 15th king of
Gowa, Sultan Malikussaid, was marked by friendly relations
with the Spanish in the Philippines, the king of Coromandel, the
English and the Arab consul in Mecca. The supremacy of Gowa
grew and it expanded its control over East Kalimantan, Bima,
Sumbawa, West Flores, Solor, and the island of Buton.[9] Regarding trade, the Portuguese held a particularly privileged position
in Makassar in the years 1615-1665, although traders from all
nations were welcomed. The Dutch, however, who began to
appear on the scene during this same period, demanded an end
to Makassar's participation in the spice trade.[10] The VOC (*Ver-
eenigde Oost-Indische Compagnie*, Dutch East India Company)
was intent on establishing a trade monopoly.

[7] Barbara Sillars Harvey, "Tradition, Islam, and Rebellion: South Sulawesi
1950-1965" (PhD diss., Cornell University, June 1974), 42.

[8] R.O. Winstedt, *A History of Johore* including the work by Professor Dato'
Ismail Hussein, *Hikayat Negeri Johor: A Nineteenth Century Bugis Histo-
ry relating events in Riau & Selangor* (Selangor, Malaysia: The Malaysian
Branch of the Royal Asiatic Society, 1992).

[9] J. Noorduyn, "Makasar and the Islamization of Bima," in *Bijdragen tot de
Taal-, Land- en Volkenkunde* 143, no.2/3 (1987): 327.

[10] Harvey, 44.

Buton during this time was not exactly a peer of these other kingdoms. Instead, it was a place from which to take resources and send exiles. Buton does, however, have the distinction of being the only other kingdom on Sulawesi, other than Gowa, to have written records that still survive to this day. The only time Buton appears in Gowa's records is when it was defeated or when a king was sent there in exile. In the late 16th century one of the rulers of Gowa (Tunipasuluq, ruled 1590-1593) was deposed and exiled to the "distant" island of Buton where he would later die.[11] King Matoaya of Gowa (also called Sultan Abdullah) converted to Islam on Sept. 22, 1605, and exerted his power throughout the islands. He conquered Buton, including the land of Pancana, Wawonio, Tubungku, Banggea, and Sula three times.[12] Later Sultan Hasanuddin (also called Tumamenang ri Ballaq Pangkana) went eastwards to Buton and then conquered Tobea.[13] Buton was a place to send people where they would not be bothered or bother anyone again. It was far enough away to provide assurance that they wouldn't affect what was going on in Gowa. Little did Gowa's rulers know that the remoteness and independent nature of Buton would be one piece in the puzzle of Gowa's eventual downfall later in the century. During this time of Gowa's supremacy the only other kingdom that would have been in a place to challenge its borders was the kingdom of Ternate.

TERNATE

Far to the northeast was a kingdom, Ternate, which pressured Buton from the east. As was the case with its equally small neighboring island, Tidore (tee-DOR-ey), the sultanate of Ternate wielded power disproportionate to its geographical size and controlled the spice trade before the Portuguese came. It

---

[11] Cummings, 4.
[12] Ibid., Talloq Chronicle, 87-88.
[13] Ibid., Gowa Chronicle, 49.

was then the center of Portuguese power among the Spice Islands, an area which they more or less dominated for most of the 16th century (1512-1575). During the seventeenth century Ternate ruled a vast colonial empire of islands in southern Maluku (including Buru) where it exacted tribute and demanded obedience to its rule.[14]

The kingdom of Ternate was centered on the island of Ternate. That is in the North Maluku (also Moluccas) islands off the western coast of the island of Halmahera, and to the east of the northern tip of Sulawesi.[15] The relationship they had with the Portugese in the early years of the spice trade eventually soured, and Sultan Baabullah of Ternate (1570-1583) expelled the Portugese after they murdered his father in 1570. Buton was mentioned in the records of when the Portuguese made their exit from Ternate on July 15, 1575 (because of Sultan Baabullah). Several days after their departure, the Portuguese cargo ship on which most of the castle company had departed was wrecked off Buton Island. There was no loss of life, and the crew used local boats to eventually reach Malacca.[16] Once again, Buton was a remote place but one that caused trouble to those who passed her way.

The removal of the Portuguese gave the sultan of Ternate momentum for further Islamization in Maluku and in Buton, Selayar, even the coast of east and north Sulawesi and southern Mindanao in the Philippines.[17] These visits from Ternate were not usually based on friendly terms. There are stories told to this day of raiding parties and pirates from Ternate and Tobelo that would drive the people of the islands of Buton to fortresses

---

[14] Beb Vuyk, *The Last House in the World in Two Tales of the East Indies* (Singapore: Periplus (HK) Ltd, 2000), 182, footnote 22.

[15] See map of Maluku Islands.

[16] Willard A. Hanna and Des Alwi, *Turbulent Times Past in Ternate & Tidore* (Moluccas: Yayasan Warisan dan Budaya Banda Naira, 1990), 93.

[17] Azyumardi Azra, *Islam in the Indonesian World: An Account of Institutional Formation* (Bandung: Mizan Pustaka, 2006), 41.

that they had built at the tops of mountains.[18] Buton fell under the sway of each of these kingdoms for hundreds of years, and the residents could tell from the prevailing winds which of these kingdoms would begin raiding their islands. The winds from the west brought Gowa, and the winds from the east brought Ternate.[19] Eventually the people were convinced that the dominance of these kingdoms had lasted for too long and someone needed to do something.

There was Buton, right in the middle of these two kingdoms, right in the middle of the major sea lane that led to the Spice Islands and Papua. To these two kingdoms Buton was a place to send their unwanted people, a place to be conquered, and a remote place where no one spent much time if they could help it. The people of Buton knew that they were just a pawn in the game of the larger kingdoms vying for their land and waters. As a result of this realization, they joined together to fight for a place in their world. Each of the islands had at least one fortress, but without an integrated defense with the other islands they were at the mercy of the roving bands of warriors. They were too spread out among islands and divided by cultures to really fight and win in the traditional way. So they analyzed their situation, decided whom they wanted to support, and offered the one thing that they had, remoteness and mystery.

BUGIS

Finally, the opportunity arose for the Butonese to free themselves from the power of Gowa and Ternate, and it involved hiding someone. In order to defend themselves and balance the power in the region the Butonese developed an alliance with the Bugis, the influential rivals of Gowa in South Sulawesi. According to one Dutch source, "the Bugis were a martial people

[18] Esther Velthoen, "Sailing in dangerous waters: piracy and raiding in historical context" *IIAS Newsletter*, no. 36 (March 2005): 8.
[19] Susanto Zuhdi, *Sejarah Buton yang Terabaikan: Labu Rope Labu Wana* (Jakarta: RajaGrafindo Persada, 2010).

as well as renowned mariners. Robbery and other feats of daring were once considered socially acceptable activities particularly by Bugis nobility. Because of their martial nature, the Bugis were often recruited by the colonial government for troops, but they were notorious for creating mayhem and murdering."[20] To add to the lore of the Bugis, the term "boogie man" also could have come from what the Dutch used to tell their children to scare them into behaving, that they would be visited by the "Bugis" of Sulawesi.[21] As back then, the Bugis have a big reputation today, though it is not as infamous. Still some fear remains.

A phenomenon identified with the Bugis will shed more light on just how they got their reputation. "Individuals induce themselves into a state of psychological immunity to either prudence or fear, one that is coupled with a homicidal mania knowing neither quarter nor discrimination." It is called running *amok*, and has been described as a "way of committing suicide in public." The condition of running *amok* was associated with the Malay peoples, wherever they lived, but at one point the Bugis were the best known for it. According to one source, in the nineteenth century the Bugis were considered "by far the most addicted to run amok. I should think three-fourths of all the cases I have seen have been by persons of this nation." Another author declared "Makassar is the most celebrated place in the East for 'running a muck.'" One should remember that this condition is affective and is not necessarily the result of opium or alcohol.[22] Even today Makassar is famous for its fervent demonstrations and violence anytime an issue arises in Indonesia. This may be the modern version of running *amok*.

The history of the Bugis is much better documented than that of Buton, and you can learn something about the people of

---

[20] P.A. Daum, *Ups and Downs of Life in the Indies* (Hong Kong: Periplus Editions Ltd., 1999), 147-148, footnote.

[21] Wikipedia, "Bogeyman," http://en.wikipedia.org/wiki/Bogeyman (accessed on 23 April 2010).

[22] H.F. Friedericy, *The Counselor in Two Tales of the East Indies* (Singapore: Periplus (HK) Ltd, 2000), 116.

Buton by those with which they associated. I have heard it said that the Bugis were seen as "brothers," and one man told me this was because the famous Bugis leader Arung Palakka had a father from Buton and a mother from Bone. This same Bugis leader is the one that Buton agreed to hide. The story of how Arung Palakka fled to Buton and was protected by Sultan Awu (1654-1664) looms large in the history of Buton. This is a classic example of how Buton is not only a mysterious and remote place, but it can also be considered a place of refuge for those that may be in trouble in other parts of Indonesia. Arung Palakka's refuge was sought at a pivotal time in the history of eastern Indonesia. Though Buton was not exactly the major player in what happened, it did play a very important role.

ARUNG PALAKKA

The people of Buton provided asylum for the Bugis Prince Arung Palakka and would not surrender him to Gowa. The Kingdom of Gowa (primarily Makasar people) had been the dominant force in Southern Sulawesi for hundreds of years, up until 1641. Their primary rival and enemy were the Bugis, who had several kingdoms farther to the north and around the Bay of Bone. Among these Bugis kingdoms Luwuq was the most ancient kingdom, Soppeng was moderately powerful, and Bone was the most powerful. It came about that in 1640 a young prince named Arung Palakka rose to power and led a rebellion against the kingdom of Gowa. He was defeated and forced to flee his land. He sought refuge in the city of Bau-Bau under the Sultan of Buton. The Sultan accepted him, and even when the powerful ships of Gowa arrived and started to attack the fortress of the Sultan from the nearby island of Kadatua, he did not relent. Buton was eventually included in an alliance between the Bugis and the Dutch. The Dutch by themselves had not been successful in overpowering the kingdom of Gowa and its powerbase in the city of Makassar, so they allied themselves with

the Bugis. Throughout the archipelago the Dutch formed alliances and pitted the local kingdoms against each other in order
to maintain their power. Arung Palakka and the Bugis were es-
sential to this strategy in Sulawesi.[23] One sultan of Buton told
a Dutch leader that visited his island that "Arung Palakka was
so greatly esteemed in the Makassar lands that...his assistance
would be sufficient to cause most of the Bugis lands to fall away
[from Gowa]."[24]

Arung Palakka spent two years in exile in Bau-Bau, within
the fortress walls that housed the sultanate. He eventually felt
secure enough to leave the island. He was escorted to Jakarta
(Batavia), where his alliance with the Dutch was cemented for
a future war with Gowa. The Bugis in Jakarta were kept fit and
in a state of readiness by Arung Palakka, as much for reasons of
morale as to prepare them for the hoped for war against Gowa.
The first hazardous but exciting years of exile on Buton within
easy reach of Gowa's fleets gave way to a period of inactivity
while exiled in Jakarta. He did have the opportunity to take part
in a military campaign against Minangkabau "rebels" in west
coast Sumatra, to further convince the Dutch of Bugis fighting
skill and that it would be worthwhile to support them in a war
against Gowa. So valiant and well-known did Arung Palakka
become in this campaign that after one of his victories in Sumatra the local people appointed him the king of their land.[25]

The Dutch had also been busy to the east of Buton. Ternate had already become an ally of the Dutch VOC in the mid-
seventeenth century, so no longer posed a threat. It was the de-
structive rivalry between Ternate and Tidore that allowed the
Europeans to play one against the other and insinuate their own
authority. The ruthless monopoly policy of the Dutch eventually
reduced Ternate, Tidore, and other Moluccan islands to indigent

[23] A. Sultan Kasim, *Aru Palakka Dalam Perjuangan Kemerdekaan Kerajaan Bone* (Makassar: CV. Walanae, 2002).
[24] Leonard Y. Andaya, *The Heritage of Arung Palakka: A History of South Sulawesi (Celebes) in the Seventeenth Century* (Leiden: KITLV, 1981), 66.
[25] Ibid., 66-67.

vassal states.[26] Because of Buton's alliance with the Dutch they no longer had to fear their neighbor to the east. To keep Gowa from bothering Buton a treaty was signed between the Dutch VOC and Gowa in Batavia on 19 August 1660 in which Gowa was forced to acknowledge that Buton and Manado belonged to Sultan Mandar Syah of Ternate. This treaty was subsequently ignored by Sultan Hasanuddin who continued to have pretensions over these lands.[27]

Gowa continued to have power over Buton up until the moment they were subdued in the 1660's. Even as rumors were spreading about a Buton-Bugis-Ternate invasion, Gowa was compiling their own force in Makassar composed of men from Gowa's vassal kingdoms of Bima, Sumbawa and Buton.[28] Buton had to provide troops for both sides, though the sultanate actually supported the Bugis. In April 1666 Sultan Hasanuddin was planning an expedition to Buton, Muna and other islands of Eastern Indonesia so Gowa could reaffirm its overlordship of the lands inherited from previous rulers. The Sultan of Buton was busily preparing his defenses in April 1666 because a Makasar fleet that had just captured some 5,000 Sula Islanders was rumored to attack Buton at the end of the Muslim fasting month. In spite of Gowa's preparations, troops from Ternate, Buton, and the kingdoms of the Bugis overpowered the kingdom of Gowa. This attack was only carried out after the Bugis had received confirmation that the Dutch would come to their aid, otherwise the Bugis believed they would be totally destroyed by Gowa.[29]

The 16th king of Gowa, Hasmaldi, eventually signed the treaty of Bungaya in 1667 after the Dutch Admiral Cornelius Speelman attacked with 21 ships, filled with Dutch soldiers and native soldiers from Ternate.[30] The treaty of Bungaya (18 Nov

[26] Vuyk, 182, footnote 22.
[27] Andaya, 65.
[28] Ibid., 60-61.
[29] Ibid., 64-66.
[30] Wicarawati, "Gowa, on the Crossroads to the Spice Islands," *Garuda Magazine* 9, no. 3 (1989): 18, 20.

1667) required Gowa to give up all claims to territory outside the kingdom itself, to have no further contact with other foreign powers, and to accept the VOC's monopoly of trade. It was basically a multilateral treaty of peace, friendship, and alliance, which included not only Gowa, Bone and the Company, but also Ternate, Tidore, Bacan, Buton, Soppeng, and Luwuq, and was open to any others who might wish to join. Wajoq did accede to the agreement in 1670. A mid-eighteenth century resistance to the Dutch was later led by Wajoq, and Gowa repeatedly tried to have the treaty revoked, but failed.[31] This was also the time that Gowa's Sultan Hasanuddin was made famous for his opposition to the Dutch. He is one of the more prominent figures in Makassar today with the International airport and the city's state university named after him. By exalting this Gowa sultanate they are thumbing their noses at the Bugis who teamed up with the Dutch to bring him down. This is significant because the Bugis have a dominant presence in Makassar today.

Even though the Bugis kingdom of Bone gained supremacy during this time, there were still later uprisings from some of the smaller Bugis kingdoms. Buton was actively involved in some of these later fights. Wajoq (a Bugis state located approximately 100 miles NE of Makassar) was one of the most loyal allies of the Makasar kings of Gowa. It refused to submit even after Makassar fell. The Wajoq resisted Dutch and Bugis rule under Arung Palakka of Bone for more than a year until their capital, Tosora, fell in December 1670 after a three month siege.[32] Later in 1736 the state of Wajoq again fought against Bone and a number of its allies. During this fight Bone was assisted by the Dutch, people from Buton, Mandar, the kingdom of Bitu-Babana-Minanga (Mamasa), the union of the six kingdoms of Masserempulu' (Enrekang), Tellu-Lembana (Tanah Toraja), the union of the five kingdoms of Ajatappareng, Tanete, Luwuq,

[31] Harvey, 45-46.

[32] J. Noorduyn, "The Wajorese merchants' community in Makassar," in *Authority and Enterprise Among the Peoples of South Sulawesi* ed. Roger Tol, Kees van Dijk and Greg Acciaioli (Leiden: KITLV Press, 2000), 95.

Soppeng, and Sidenreng. A man called Patola La Tombong attacked the combined Mandar, Ajatappareng, Luwuq and Buton
forces and drove them back to Paselloreng. The Luwuq and Buton forces fled to Jalang and Peneki. After the queen of Bone,
who also acted as the sovereign of Soppeng, learned of the Bone
forces defeat she immediately left Bone and fled to Makassar,
seeking refuge with Dutch Admiral Smout.[33] This is just one
example of the continued presence of the several smaller kingdoms, along with their rebellions and alliances that make the
history of the East Indies at times very complicated. One thing
that is clear, that the Bugis and Buton have always had a good
relationship, and are marked by their willingness to work with
the Dutch. It is also clear from conversations in Buton today
that the Butonese have a history of being kind and having a willingness to work with "the people of white skin." This willingness to work with others is not always apparent to those that are
looking in from the outside.

DUTCH

There were several efforts to work with the Dutch. Western
writers take the position that Buton was in a strategic position
in the route from Java to Makassar to Maluku, which was the
center for the production of spices for Indonesia.[34] When Buton had particular difficulty defending its independence from the
struggle for power between the two sultanates in Makassar and
Ternate in the first part of the 17th century, the VOC played an
important role.

The walls of the fortress (or *keraton*) of Buton (or Wolio)
were built in 1613 following clashes with the VOC. Rusty cannon can still be found at various points along the 3km (1.8 mile)

[33] Abidin, A.Z. "LA MA'DUKELLENG: Precursor of South Sulawesi Unification Against the Dutch VOC" *Prisma: The Indonesian Indicator* 22 (Sept.
1981): 36-37.
[34] David Henley, *The idea of Celebes in history*, Working Papers on Southeast
Asia, 59 (Victoria: Monash Asia Institute, 1989).

perimeter of the fortress, many with the blazon of VOC. In 1613 the Dutch general Anthony van Diemen tried to take the *keraton* with 700 soldiers, but relented because of the "terrible steepness" of the mountain, on top of which lay the city.[35] As an aside, Anthony van Diemen was the same Van Diemen that sent Abel Tasman (where the island Tasmania got its name) out three times to the South Seas from Batavia (Jakarta) in search of a passage through to Australia.[36] As a result of the attack on the *keraton*, in 1613 Buton made the first covenant with the VOC when conducting a meeting between the 4th sultan, La Elangi, and the first governor general of Holland, Pieter Both. This covenant was made by Buton to guard their independence against Makassar and Ternate. Later in 1650 there was a tragedy that ended up further strengthening the relationship between Buton and the VOC. A Dutch armada wrecked on the west side of the island of Kabaena and the sultanate was eager to help. This may have been one of the reasons that Speelman came to the aid of Buton when they were attacked by Gowa in 1667. This may have also been where Buton obtained some of their cannon.[37]

Only after the sultanate in Makassar was conquered by the VOC between 1667 and 1669 was Buton free from their role in this power struggle. After that, Buton became a part of the area of *Pax Neerlandica*.[38] For the 17th, 18th, and 19th centuries the sultanate of Buton was an independent kingdom. Although in the 19th century the Netherlands Indies government was not strong enough to control this kingdom effectively, that changed in the early 20th century. The Dutch had won the Bone wars, and were finally bringing government control to many areas of

---

[35] Kal Muller and Dinah Bergink, *Sulawesi: Island Crossroads of Indonesia* (Singapore: Passport Books, 1995), 213.

[36] Holly S. Smith, *Adventuring in Indonesia: Exploring the Natural Areas of the Pacific's Ring of Fire* (San Francisco: Sierra Club Books, 1997), 321.

[37] Horst H. Liebner, "Sebuah Naskah Belanda tentang Kecelakaan Armada VOC di Pulau Kabaena, Maret-Mei 1650," in *Naskah Buton, Naskah Dunia*, ed. M. Yusran Darmawan (Bau-Bau: Respect, 2009), 100.

[38] The Netherlands Peace was the transition from a Dutch military government to a civilian one in Indonesia, primarily administered from 1908-1942.

Sulawesi which had up until this point been left on their own. In 1906 a new agreement was made that said the Netherlands government could become involved in the internal affairs of the sultanate. At that time Buton formed a part of the colonized area. This was the foundation for socioeconomic and cultural development throughout the islands, primarily in the connection with government, education, health services, and economy. This is one more step which eventually led to full integration into the sociopolitical system of the Indies, and after 1949 in the nation of Indonesia. [39] During this time, the Dutch began to develop the road network in Buton as well as building systems to provide fresh water to the city of Bau-Bau. [40] Buton's assimilation into Indonesia reached its culmination in 1960 with the disestablishment of the sultanate a few months after the death of the last sultan.

The Dutch partnership had a profound impact on how people from Buton view Westerners, and it is usually positive. The influence of the power of the Dutch in the Indies is strongly felt in Buton. This influence and how it was received by the Butonese may also have been one of the reasons that orthodox Islam never became as strong among these islands as it did in Makassar. [41] It has been said that there is documented history that a Dutch governor of Batavia (Jakarta) referred to Buton as "his son" and Buton referred to the governor as "its father." There are several stories in Buton's history about successful partnerships with the "people of white skin" and this can still be seen in stories and beliefs circulating throughout Buton today. To illustrate this, the daughter and granddaughter of La Karambau, the 20th sultan of Buton (and 23rd, he served twice), were presented to the Dutch Admiral Spellman

[39] Johan Willem (Pim) Schoorl, *Masyarakat, Sejarah, dan Budaya Buton* (Jakarta: Djambatan bekerjasama dengan Perwakilan KITLV Jakarta, 2003), 5.
[40] La Ode Rabani, *Kota-Kota Pantai Di Sulawesi Tenggara* (Yogyakarta: Penerbit Ombak, 2010), 82-83.
[41] Haliadi, *Buton Islam dan Islam Buton: Islamisasi, Kolonialisme, dan Sinkretisme Agama* (Yogyakarta: Yayasan untuk Indonesia, 2000), 291.

as a gift during his reign from 1751 to 1752. [42] It is assumed that these girls were educated and grew up in the Netherlands, and to this day that story is a source of pride for the Butonese, because it is evidence of the positive connection they had with the Dutch. The giving of one of your children is not something those in the West would consider a normal thing to do. The people of Buton come from a very different background, and at one time were leaders in the slave trade among the islands of Indonesia. Even the kindness of the Butonese sometimes reveals the hard nature of their past. Just like their civic symbol, the pineapple, their "sweetness" is cloaked with a very rough reality.

---

[42] Abdul Mulku Zahari, ed., *Sejarah dan Adat Fiy Darul Butuni* (*Buton*) I, II, III (Jakarta: Proyek Pengembangan Media Kebudayaan, Depdikbud, 1977).

II
Rough on the Outside

There are many things that have contributed to Buton's rough exterior. An anecdote from the period of Western exploration may provide insight into Buton drawn from a first-hand experience. The interaction was when a King of Butung (Buton) is mentioned as entertaining some sailors from the British East India Company. He is said to have been a curious fellow that offered them sweet meats to eat, and maintained a room in his house full of human skulls.[43] Around the 1930's a Dutch lady that spent much of her life in the Maluku islands to the east described the Butonese lumberjacks that worked for her as "a strange people" and she assumed that their "surly attitude was part of their native character."[44] Everyone has their own opinion, but almost all will agree that this is a place with mystery and it is certainly noteworthy. One British man I met has lived in Indonesia for over 20 years and spent a good deal of time sailing the seas. He said their general reputation is that "the Butonese cannot be trusted and if you are picking men for the crew of a ship, beware of those from Buton." Though many Butonese have a good reputation, he has heard this warning more than once, as the reputation of those from Buton is quite extensive throughout the archipelago. It is not as widespread as some of

---

[43] Giles Milton, *Nathaniel's Nutmeg* (New York: Penguin Books, 2000), 149-150.

[44] Ron Heynneman, *Ibu Maluku: The Story of Jeanne van Diejen* (Hartwell, Victoria: Sid Harta Publishers, 2002), 217.

the other Sulawesi peoples such as the Bugis and Torajanese, but those that have heard of them usually have had a lasting impression, good or bad. One of the primary things that influenced its reputation in the past was its notoriety as a provider of slaves. The trade of slaves was very important for Buton in the 17th and 18th century. Although it has played any number of minor roles, Buton has also been known as a survivor. Though it may not have been a major political and military power in the region, it did have an important role and managed to survive as a kingdom for hundreds of years. This would not have happened if they were a soft people. They worked rocky ground and they traveled on the unforgiving sea and managed to perpetuate over hundreds of years.

BOATS

Another notable aspect of Buton's history, was that its people were the main suppliers to Makassar of a variety of resources from the sea. To provide these resources they needed a large number of ships. Along with being farmers, the Butonese have always been known as sailors.[45] They sail ships with gross tonnage up to more than 50 tons. Most of the ships are not that large, but are used to carry large amounts of cargo throughout the islands. In the early 20th century there were about 300 ships throughout the sultanate. This number continued to grow, because in 1981 the small island of Wangi-Wangi, east of Buton, had 220 sailing ships, 150 still being used. But the larger sailing ships had lessened with the introduction of the engine, as only 37 ships were registered on that island with gross tonnage from 10-20 tons in 1975.[46] The decline in locally made wooden ships may be because of the dominance of larger metal and fiberglass ships as well as the high cost of fuel to run them. The large ships

---

[45] Michael Southon, *The navel of the perahu: meaning and values in the maritime trading economy of a Butonese village* (Canberra: Department of Anthropology, Australian National University, 1995).
[46] Schoorl, 6.

nowadays are usually constructed in other areas, but the wooden ships were not bought from neighboring islands or peoples, the Butonese made them with their own hands.

Of the many people groups in Eastern Indonesia, only five engage in inter-island boat trade (distinct from fishing and short-distance coasting); these are the Bugis, Makasar, Mandar, Butonese (also known as Binongkonese), and Madurese.[47] The Butonese have spread throughout Southeast Sulawesi, the Banggai archipelago, Maluku, East Nusatenggara, and Flores. The Bajo (sea gypsies) and Bugis settled in SE Sulawesi and are sometimes confused with them. The most well known of the large Indonesian wooden ships are the *pinisiq*, made famous by the Bugis in South Sulawesi. The heyday of the *pinisiq* was in the 1970s, when several thousand of these ships formed the biggest fleet of sailing traders in the world. They formed a major backbone of Indonesia's economy, but at about the same time the government's efforts in motorization brought about some major changes.

The Butonese vessels are predominantly the *lambo*, similar to the *pinisiq*. In the 1930's more and more of these indigenous ships (and others) adopted a new kind of rigging and hull-shapes as a result of European influence. For example, the *lambo* has a center rudder and stem and stem posts which are set in an angle onto the keel – in contrast to the traditional shape, where keel and stems form a continuous curve. Today there are still several hundred lambo vessels trading between the small islands of Maluku and the bigger ports in Java and Sulawesi.[48] The largest of these vessels are two-masted; they trade between Gresik (near Surabaya) and Maluku, between Surabaya and Flores, Surabaya and SE Sulawesi, and between SE Sulawesi and East Nusateng-

---

[47] H.W. Dick, "Prahu Shipping in Eastern Indonesia," *Bulletin of Indonesian Economic Studies* XI, no. 2 (July 1975): 73.
[48] Horst Liebner, "Traditional boats, Forum Makassar Straights: A website about maritime South Sulawesi," 2004. http://www.forumms.com/traditional_boats.htm (accessed on September 27, 2010).

gara (Solor, Alor, Wetar, Timor), as well as throughout the islands of Maluku.[49]

The east and west monsoons have always dictated the boat trading pattern. During the west monsoon, or rainy season, the winds blow from the NW through the Malacca and Makassar Straits and from almost due west across the Java Sea whipping up choppy seas. Towards the end of March they slacken, and become unpredictably variable. Then, about the end of April they hold steady from the southeast, blowing almost from due east across the Java Sea. The east monsoon or dry season brings light winds at first, which strengthen during August and September, die out by November, and vary for awhile and then, about the end of the month, set in again from the west. By the end of December most of the boats, except for the *pinisi* (the large boats made famous in Makassar), have returned to their village for shelter and to be refitted before setting out again at the end of the west monsoon. Traditionally, trade was carried out on a seasonal basis along an east-west axis. Nowadays only Butonese boats trading between Gresik and Maluku follow this monsoonal pattern. Some *pinisi* sail from their village in March to load teak logs for Makassar or Surabaya from SE Sulawesi, or they load mangrove wood for the paper mill in Makassar from Palopo.[50] The largest boats engaged in the copra trade are the two-masted Butonese *lambo* (similar to the *pinisi*) of about 200m³ which load mostly from the island of Sanana to Surabaya. That the Butonese tend towards classes of boats less than 50m³ and of almost 200m³ is an interesting implication that a carrying boat is not as profitable as a trading boat unless it is of almost 200m³.[51] Once again, the dominance of large metal ships today for carrying heavy cargo has led the Butonese to tend more towards the smaller ships.

---

[49] Dick, 74.
[50] Ibid., 84.
[51] Ibid., 100.

SLAVES

It is clear in the history of Buton that these ships were also used to transport slaves. Speelman noted that Sulu, Brunei, and Buton exported little else but slaves in the 17th century. He reported of Buton in 1613 that "this is all their trade, to take slaves and sell them, for those of Boutoune are thought to be the best warriors."[52] This feisty spirit was not looked on as a positive attribute by everyone, as an ordinance of the VOC on 18 May 1688 said, "Bugis, Balinese, Makasar, Butonese, Bimanese and other slaves from Celebes were declared to be 'of dangerous temperament.'" This may have been the reason that Buton was at one point limited in the number of slaves that they could provide to Java. By ordinance of 8 Feb 1701 the Sultan of Buton could only bring 50-60 young slaves to Batavia (Jakarta).[53]

The biggest contribution of slaves to Batavia (Jakarta) came from South Sulawesi. Of the almost 10,000 Indonesian slaves brought to Batavia in the two decades of 1661-82, Schulte Nordholt has calculated that 42% (4,110) came from South Sulawesi, 24% from Bali and 12% from Buton. Of the free Indonesian population of Batavia, most descended from freed slaves, from 1786-90 there were 1.4% from Buton. The slave trade pattern was generally from small divided states to large wealthier ones and from non-Muslim to Muslim societies. A number of states rose in prominence and flourished primarily on the trafficking of slaves, many of them seized by raiding expeditions against coastal peoples in the Central Philippines, Eastern Indonesia, New Guinea, Arekan or the Mekong Delta. Sulu, Buton, and Tidore were most well-known for this in the 17th century.[54]

---

[52] Anthony Reid, ed., *Slavery, Bondage and Dependency in Southeast Asia* (St. Lucia: University of Queensland Press, 1983), 170.
[53] Ibid., 258-259.
[54] Ibid., 29-31.

OTHER TRADE AND BUSINESS

There are also a variety of other resources that Buton provided to the archipelago. It was a recognized point of departure (rendezvous or point of reference) for trepang (sea cucumber) fleets. Buton was consistently the largest source of trepang for the Makassar market.[55] Makassar was the Indonesian center for the trepang trade.[56] The Makassar harbormaster's shipping list for 1717-18 indicates an established trade of trepang coming in from Buton for the Chinese.[57] Buton exported trepang, slaves, wax, and tortoise shell to Makassar throughout the 18th century, whereas the packet of goods imported to Buton showed a striking increase in complexity, covering a wide range of textiles, china, and metal goods.[58] In Bau-Bau today there is evidence of the china and ceramics that were imported hundreds of years ago.

There is evidence of this political and trade relationship between Buton and Makassar that still remains today. One of the bastions in the remnants of the Dutch Fort Rotterdam is named after Butung (Buton). There is also a part of the city of Makassar that is referred to as Kampung Buton. The Wajoq, the Bugis people that were tied very closely with the kings of Gowa, lived in Kampung Buton in Makassar. The Wajoq were leaders among the Bugis in matters of trade.[59] This is probably the reason why the well known Buton (Butung) market in Makassar is a center of trade, though there are not many Butonese that currently live there. This is a prime example of the way that the history of Buton is integrated into that of its neighbors in South Sulawesi.

---

[55] Heather Sutherland, "Trepang and Wangkang: The China Trade of Eighteenth-Century Makassar, c.1720s-1840s" in *Authority and Enterprise Among the Peoples of South Sulawesi*, eds. Roger Tol, Kees van Dijk and Greg Acciaioli (Leiden: KITLV Press, 2000), 85-86.

[56] Ibid., 73.

[57] Ibid., 82.

[58] Ibid., 92-93.

[59] Noorduyn, *Wajorese*, 107.

The Butonese also engage in business and in eastern Indonesia have a reputation for business acumen. There are people from Buton that have settled in the islands of Maluku and formed large communities that have been there for hundreds of years. Several of these communities can be found on and surrounding the island of Ambon. The Butonese were one of the prominent Muslim people groups that moved to this traditionally Christian area and started to tip the scales toward being an Islamic majority in the area.[60] Prior to the violence there in 2000, indication of trouble had already been evident since November 1998 when some Christians in a village near Ambon fought against their Muslim neighbours and on the walls of some buildings was written "expel BBM." BBM stood for Bugis Buton Makassar, which were the Muslim peoples from Sulawesi that dominated market and trade at Ambon.[61] The Butonese have had a strong influence on the island of Buru just west of Ambon. One of Buru's early kings claimed origin from Buton.[62] There is also a story about the line of the Moluccan kings that mentions Buton. The story begins with a man named Bikusigara, of the island of Bacan, who sailed around his island. At one point he saw some rattan shrubs near some rocky peaks, but his men did not see them. He went ashore, cut them, and so the story goes, they shed blood. Then in the same place he saw four serpent's eggs and a voice said he should take and keep them because men of great importance would be born from them. So he put them in a box and took care of them. Eventually three men and one woman were born from these eggs – the king of Bacan, the King of Papua, the

[60] John T. Sidel, *Riots, Pogroms, Jihad: Religious Violence in Indonesia* (Singapore: National University of Singapore Press, 2007), 170, 174, 176.
[61] Jan Sihar Aritonang and Karel Steenbrink, eds., *A History of Christianity in Indonesia* (Leiden: Brill, 2008), 224.
[62] Barbara Dix Grimes, "Mapping Buru: The Politics of Territory and Settlement on an Eastern Indonesian Island" in *Sharing the Earth, Dividing the Land*, ed. Thomas Reuter (Canberra: The Australian National University E Press, 2006), 143, 147.

King of Buton and Banggai and the wife of the king of Loloda.[63] These kingdoms would have been those with the most influence to the people of Bacan at the time. The account does conflict with the fact that the first ruler of Buton was a woman. However, it is evidence that Buton was seen as a kingdom with influence in the mythically defined "world of Maluku," of which the western part was regarded as belonging to Ternate and the eastern to Tidore.[64] Of the large number of Butonese that lived in Ambon and the surrounding areas, many returned to Buton after the violence there in 2000. Probably some 200,000 of the migrants from South Sulawesi and the island of Buton returned to their place of origin, or that of their parents.[65]

The Butonese like to go abroad for work, especially to the Malukus, so there is a season of migration to harvest cloves in the Malukus.[66] In the Banda Islands, the center of the spice trade, labor from the outside was needed and workers from Buton were generally preferred because they were hard workers. They came to the European estates to work voluntarily for a few months a year and earn some cash. Butonese seasonal laborers arrived in Banda packed in tiny boats. The journey to Banda could last a month and the passengers had to eat, drink and sleep standing up. They would earn 20 cents a day in the 1930's, would work for three months, save 10 to 25 guilders, then head back paying 3 guilders for the trip.[67] Those that choose to stay home usually farmed and those that went abroad usually eventually

---

[63] Hubert Th. Th. M. Jacobs, S.J., *A Treatise on the Moluccas* (c. 1544) (Probably the preliminary version of Antonio Galvao's lost Historia Das Molucas. Edited, annotated, and translated into English from the Portuguese manuscript in the Archivo General de Indias, Seville. Sources and Studies for the History of the Jesuits: Vol. III. Rome: Jesuit Historical Institute, 1970), 81.

[64] David Henley, "A superabundance of centers: Ternate and the contest for North Sulawesi," *Cakalele* 4 (1993): 54.

[65] Aritonang, 414.

[66] Schoorl, 6.

[67] Jeroen Touwen, *Extremes in the Archipelago: Trade and Economic Development in the Outer Islands of Indonesia 1900-1942* (Leiden: KITLV, 2001), 96.

returned home. Though the Butonese have always had a presence throughout the archipelago, this is often only temporary and they return to the land of their forefathers for some reason or another.

ASPHALT, OIL, AND MINERAL RESOURCES

Nowadays, the name "Buton" is synonymous with asphalt for everyone that has ever been through elementary school in Indonesia. The running joke on Buton is how the roads throughout the island are falling apart, even though the largest deposit of natural asphalt in Southeast Asia is on this island. In the past, asphalt in Buton was known as BUTAS (Buton Asphalt), and has been used to pave roads throughout Indonesia (Java, Bali, Sulawesi, Kalimantan, Ambon, and Sumatra). In 1969, the Bank of Indonesia invested in the Buton Asphalt Company (Perusahaan Aspal Negara Buton, or P.A.N. Buton), and the result of this was equipment that brought the production of asphalt from 150 tons/day in 1970 to 400-500 tons/day in a relatively short time. In 1971 production was planned to reach 120,000 tons a year. This asphalt company provided 800 jobs on the island of Buton. Back in the seventies and early eighties one could find large ships from China, Taiwan, and other surrounding countries in port outside of Pasarwajo (in a bay on the southeast part of the island), bringing some goods from outside of the country and providing jobs in the thriving mining industry north of Pasarwajo. In the early 1970's there was even a gondola like ski lift that would carry the asphalt from the primary mine up in Kabungka to Pasarwajo, and this lift would sometimes be found carrying people too. It has been estimated that there is 5 million tons of asphalt at Kabungka.[68] The demise of this booming industry is said to have come when Pertamina (the Indonesian national oil company and fuel provider) developed the ability to produce as-

[68] *Usaha Peningkatan Pemanfaatan/Penggunaan Aspal Buton* (Indonesia: Departemen Pekerdjaan Umum Dan Tenaga Listrik, 1971), 1-2.

phalt from their refineries. Natural asphalt is harder to process and usually needs to be mixed with refined asphalt anyway. So for many years the asphalt industry in Buton slowed way down and many people lost their jobs. The city of Pasarwajo used to be more developed than Bau-Bau, but has since fallen way behind as the asphalt industry has been plagued by corruption and to this day is not as successful as it used to be.

There are currently asphalt mines that can be found just east of Lawele (this mine is newer than Kabungka and is the largest deposit with 20 million tons of asphalt) as well as the one north of Pasarwajo (Kabungka). Both have nearby ports that they use to export the asphalt. The asphalt in these two mines is very different. The central element in asphalt is bitumen, and the asphalt from Lawele is around 25-30% bitumen while the asphalt from Kabungka is around 17-22% bitumen. It would seem that the higher the bitumen, the better, but the asphalt in Lawele poses another problem. It is too difficult to process at this point because it is soft and sticky. The natural asphalt needs to be brought to a certain temperature for it to be usable, but as the Lawele asphalt reaches this temperature it gets too sticky and clogs up the machines. The asphalt in Kabungka is rockier, and is easier to process, even though it yields less bitumen. So at this point the primary challenge for Buton asphalt is its capacity and efficiency in processing the natural asphalt. Until more investment is made in processing capacity, refined asphalt will continue to rule the day.

There are also smaller asphalt deposits in Waisiri and Wariti (1 million tons). In 1971 the goal of the government was to mine 200,000 tons of asphalt a year, which was never achieved. Even if it had, at 200,000 tons a year, it would still take 100 years to mine all the asphalt in these four deposits.[69] In early 1986 there was a survey done of several ports on the islands surrounding Timor (NTT) to gauge their capability for receiving asphalt from

---

[69] Ibid., 2.

Buton, which was at that time referred to as ASBUTON.[70] One of the problems with getting the asphalt to other islands to pave roads is the weight of asphalt, the amount of sealift required, as well as the heavy equipment required to pave the roads once it arrives. Though the jungle is still filled with asphalt, it is also being explored for other minerals, too. The Japanese exploration company (Japex) has the rights to explore southern Buton and has done this extensively since the year 2006 looking for oil and natural gas.[71] Formerly, a Conoco oil platform stood on the northern part of the island near Ereke (eh-REH-kay).[72] In addition to all of this, there is a manganese (used in the production of steel) mine just north of Pasarwajo. Although it may be rich in other resources, the reason that Buton is known by people throughout Indonesia is still usually because they are taught in elementary school that this is the place from which asphalt is mined.

---

[70] *Laporan Peninjauan Tim Direktorat Jenderal Perhubungan Laut dan Koordinator Angkutan Aspal Buton ke Nusa Tenggara Timur: 22 Januari to 5 Pebruari, 1986* (Jakarta: Southeast Asian Material Indonesia, Filmed by The Library of Congress Office, 1989).

[71] Japanese Petroleum Exploration Co., Ltd., "Buton Block," http://www.japex.co.jp/english/business/ overseas/india.html (accessed on April 3, 2010).

[72] Willy Ekariyono and Sugiarto, "Environmental Baseline and Impact Management of Jambu-1 Witaitonga Island – Southeast Sulawesi, Indonesia" (SPE Health, Safety and Environment in Oil and Gas Exploration and Production Conference, 25-27 January 1994, Jakarta, Indonesia: Society of Petroleum Engineers, Inc, 1994).

III

GETTING UNDER THE SKIN

The people from the islands of Buton may all just be "Buton-ese" to those from the outside, but their identity is much more complicated if you dig a little deeper. The varied people groups spoke different languages and were originally only loosely associated with each other before the kingdom was established. They led a fearful existence due to their vulnerability to pirates and other raiding parties from the sea.

There came a point eventually where it was determined that a kingdom needed to be created, probably for security. The concept of kingship seems to have come from Indian influence, and, as a result, kingdoms (or mandalas) were springing up throughout the archipelago as Indian influence spread.[73] This was probably the result of the spread of the renown of the great Sriwijaya kingdom of Sumatra and the Malay Peninsula, as well as the Majapahit kingdom of Java. It is very likely that the people who initially established the kingdom of Buton came from another land. Based on linguistic evidence it may be that the aristocracy originally came from central Sulawesi, and arrived with some sense of how to set up this type of government.[74] Most of the

---

[73] Paul Michel Munoz, *Early Kingdoms of the Indonesian Archipelago and the Malay Peninsula* (Didier Millet, 2007).

[74] Rene van den Berg, "Notes on the historical phonology and classification of Wolio," *Language and text in the Austronesian world: Studies in honour of Ülo Sirk* (LINCOM Studies in Austronesian Linguistics, 6), edited by Yury A. Lander and Alexander K. Ogloblin, 89-103. Muenchen: LINCOM.

locals in Buton believe that the men that came were from more distant kingdoms, most popularly Johor (Malay Peninsula) and China. Several stories circulate about how the kingdom that held together this complicated group of peoples from varying cultures and languages came to be.

ORIGIN OF THE KINGDOM

The oldest story is that of Sipanjonga who came from the kingdom of Johor, in a group of four men (*Mia Patamiana*) who founded the kingdom and established a village where the fortress now stands in Bau-Bau. They were the initial core for the kingdom of Wolio (Buton). Sipanjonga had a son named Betoambari, who was considered the ancestor of the *Siolimbona*, the nine ministers that chose the king. This group of people formed the second caste level in the social system of Buton. The two higher caste levels could not be easily separated and both had prominent roles in the kingdom. Those who came and brought these customs formed *Walaka*, and they were responsible for choosing the king. The second frequent story is an account of how the first monarch was chosen. She was a woman who came from a piece of bamboo, was sort of a goddesss, and was named Wakaakaa. Some say the story of her appearing from bamboo is only symbolic, and that she was actually a descendent of the founder of Islam, Muhammad, or Kublai Khan, and came to Buton on a ship. In any case, she married Sibatara, a son of the king of the Majapahit empire on Java. They were discovered by Betoambari, and eventually Wakaakaa was placed on the throne in the year 1332. The first level in the Butonese caste system, namely the descendants of the queen from the land of Buton, is the *Kaomu,* and all the kings were a part of this level.[75] The third version is that Dungkungcangia, the leader of a group of Kublai Khan's soldiers from Mongolia (or China), was separated from

---

[75] Prof. Dr. Achadiati Ikram, *Istiadat Tanah Negeri Butun: Edisi Teks dan Komentar* (Jakarta: Djambatan, 2005), 7.

the other soldiers when he was going back to Tiongkok after being attacked by Raden Wijaya in the 13th century.[76] He landed on Buton and helped found the kingdom of Buton. This is a viable account, as it is said that as Kublai Khan ran out of places to conquer on the land, he had to look to the sea to find new lands for conquest. The trading mission of his junks (Chinese sailing ships) brought back detailed information on places as far as the Spice Islands.[77] Though everyone believes there were already people on the island when these visitors arrived, there doesn't seem to be a very strong opinion about the details of where they came from. Other than these two royal levels in the caste, there were the *Papara* who were considered to have come later, but may have been in this level because they were not of the bloodline of these early leaders. They may have been the people that made up the original inhabitants of the islands. The slaves were the lowest level and were known as the *Batua*.

The four different levels of people in Buton, similar to castes, had a strong influence on the way people viewed each other and the role they played in the community and sultanate. One from the *Kaomu* could become the sultan, since they were part of the ruling class; the *Walaka* were also elite and their representatives chose the sultan; the *Papara*, the village residents, lived in autonomous communities; and the *Batua* were the slaves that worked for the *Kaomu* and *Walaka*. Polygamy existed primarily in the elite groups of the *Kaomu* and *Walaka*. The sultan especially had many wives. First, second, third, and fourth cousins were subject to certain regulations regarding marriage. In most villages it was forbidden to marry your first cousin, but the aristocracy was exempt from this. It was preferred to marry a second or third cousin to keep the possessions in the family. The slaves were freed in 1906 but it was some time until their lives were

[76] Susanto Zuhdi, "Berpikir Positif Orang Buton," in *Bunga Rampai Berpikir Positif Suku-Suku Bangsa* (Jakarta: Departemen Kebudayaan dan Pariwisata RI bekerja sama dengan Asosiasi Tradisi Lisan (ATL), 2005), 43-44.

[77] Jack Weatherford, *Genghis Khan and the Making of the Modern World* (New York: Three Rivers Press, 2004), 209-210.

made better. Since the time of Indonesian independence (1945-1949) the differentiation of these groups stopped socially and politically, but it informally continues in some sense, especially with marriage. Most Butonese have land rights passed down to them from ancestors; only the descendents of slaves, who were freed in 1906, are those that still may not own land.[78] In Buton, and throughout Indonesia today, where you come from is still an important element in how you are accepted by others.

Those who wanted to rule this hard land of Buton felt they needed to claim ties to more powerful distant kingdoms to solidify their rule. Several kingdoms throughout the Indonesian archipelago claimed ties with the Majapahit kingdom of Java. Despite this reputation of being a hard people, the first ruler of Buton was a woman, and the second monarch, Bulawambona, was also a woman. The son of Wakaakaa and the Majapahit prince are said to have later visited the east Javanese court and returned with royal gifts to inaugurate male rule of Buton.[79] Male rule began with Queen Bulawambona's son, Bataraguru. King Bataraguru is said to have visited the court of Majapahit, as well as his son, King Tuarade, who brought back four regalia, later known by the name *syara Jawa*.[80] The earliest recorded references to Buton were in the *Nagarakertagama*, which was written in the 14th century. Buton was mentioned with Makassar and Banggai as areas that had a connection with the Majapahit empire. In a Dutch East India Company document from 1613, the name Buton first appeared when a contract between the sultanate and the Company was agreed upon.[81]

The Kingdom of Buton's earliest years of self-recorded history come in the 16th century, and manuscripts can still be

[78] Schoorl, 7-9.
[79] Jean Gelman Taylor, *Indonesia: Peoples and Histories* (New Haven: Yale University Press, 2003), 102.
[80] J.W. Schoorl, "Belief in Reincarnation on Buton, S.E. Sulawesi, Indonesia" *KITLV Journal of the Humanities and Social Sciences of Southeast Asia and Oceania* 141, no. 1 (1985): 103.
[81] Ikram, 6.

found in the Wolio Museum in the fortress in the city of Bau-Bau. These manuscripts contain a wealth of knowledge not yet fully explored. The majority of them are about Islam, local law, and correspondence between governments. The manuscripts are written in Arabic, Indonesian, as well as Wolio, the local language, which is written primarily with the older script that resembles Arabic (called *Jawi*).[82] A detailed list of kings, and then sultans (after Islam entered), are public knowledge in Bau-Bau with various stories and beliefs surrounding almost all of these monarchs. It is interesting that the first six monarchs ruled for an average of about 35 years each, while the sultans that followed ruled for an average of 11 years each. This is reportedly because during the time of the sultanate the people were quicker to depose a sultan if some type of natural disaster occurred, because that was God declaring the sultan was no longer fit to lead. One sultan only ruled for three months. The historian and secretary for the last sultan was Zahari, who wrote about the history of the sultanate of Buton as well as on how Islam spread. His three volume history of Buton forms the bulk of the detailed information on the kings and sultans of Buton and their time in power.

ORGANIZATION OF THE KINGDOM

Under the sultanate there were four smaller divisions (*barata*) which had their own armies and a prime minister or counsel (*sarana*), but they had to pay tribute to the sultan and help if there was a conflict. The areas directly under the sultan and the *Sarana* Wolio (the ruling counsel in the sultanate), were organized into 72 villages (*kadie*), which had a little autonomy, in that they had their own *sarana*, which worked under supervision of a member of the *Sarana* Wolio. These *kadie* helped the sultan

[82]Hiroko Yamaguchi, "Naskah-naskah di Masyarakat Buton; Beberapa catatan tentang Keistimewaan dan Nilai Budaya," in *Menyibak Kabut di Keraton Buton* (Bau-Bau: Past, Present, and Future), ed. M. Yusran Darmawan (Bau-Bau: Respect, 2008), 97-104.

and *Sarana* Wolio by paying a tribute of money, food, and labor, in accordance with the written regulations. Though there are the current government divisions in Indonesia today (kabupaten, kecamatan ,kelurahan, kepala desa, etc.) there are some villages that still have traditional village minister (*sarana kadie*) functioning on the side, that work together with the modern village government. Some villages have no traditional leadership remaining at all.[83] Those that do have traditional leaders may have a *bonto*, which is a position that would have been appointed by the sultan in the past, and a *parabela*, which is a position held by someone elected locally by the village. At present, these two individuals fulfill similar roles.

The sultan was seen by his people as God's representative on earth who held responsibility for the welfare of the country. If disaster struck he could be forced to abdicate. At its peak, the sultanate had four vassal states (*barata*): Muna, Tiworo, Kulisusu, and Kaledupa. One story says that these vassal states were first ruled by a son of the original settlers.[84] Buton itself sought support from the VOC for its struggle for independence against the expanding kingdom of Makasar and the Ternate sultanate, of which it had been a vassal state in its former days. After the Makasar kingdom was defeated by the Dutch in 1669, Buton became part of the territory administered by the *Pax Neerlandica*, and experienced peace from outside invasion for many years. This provided some protection for Butonese traders, but the Dutch monopoly excluded them from the spice trade. In 1906, the sultanate was incorporated by the Dutch colonial government as a self-governing state. The last sultan, the 38th of the royal line, died in 1960, 15 years after Indonesia had declared independence.[85]

The neighboring island of Muna also had a kingdom closely tied to that of Buton. In the early 19th century, the involvement

---

[83] Schoorl, 10.
[84] Smith, 320.
[85] Muller, 212.

of Buton within the workings of the neighboring, smaller Kingdom of Muna was very weak, but Muna had made an important
contribution to Buton in the past.[86] A son of the king of Muna
married a daughter of the king of Buton, then inherited the kingdom of his father-in-law. He was known as Lakilaponto, Halu
Oleo (eight days) because he defeated the rebellion of La Bolon-
tio in eight days. Then after he died he was called Murhum, the
last king and the first sultan of Buton.[87] He is probably the most
famous of the rulers of Buton, though there are plenty of stories
about all of the others and their names pop up throughout the
town of Bau-Bau. Besides the kingdom and sultanate, there are
a few other things that have put Buton on the map and are now
items of interest.

The cloth money once used in Buton was the hand-woven
forerunner to the banknote.[88] The "great mosque" in the *keraton*
claims to be the oldest mosque in Eastern Indonesia (16th century). Inside is a sacred stone with two footprints, on which the
newly elected sultan was inaugurated. Each new sultan built his
own residence. Also near the mosque, in an enclosed area, is
the *yoni* (female genitalia) half of a *yoni-linggam* (male genitalia) stone altar, but the male part has been broken off and lost.
Holy water was taken from the *yoni-linggam* for the inauguration ceremony of the sultan, which was conducted at the *yoni*.
With the dissolution of the sultanate most of the court arts have
disappeared, but brass works, pottery, silver, and weaving are
still practiced.[89] The history of Buton is not only learned from
the positive things that the people there developed, but also from
the terrible things they have experienced. One of these is still
fresh on the older people's minds. Although there may have
been some internal conflict associated with the changing of sul-

[86] Schoorl, 10.
[87] Ikram, 8.
[88] Alb. C. Kruyt, "Lapjesgeld op Celebes [Cloth Money on Celebes]," translated by David Mead and edited by Rene van den Berg, June 2010, *Tijdschrift
voor Indische Taal-, Land- en Volkenkunde 73* (1933): 172-183.
[89] Muller, 213.

tans or high officials, it was not until the twentieth century, as
the sultanate was nearing its end, that a major period of rebellion
and violence returned to Buton.

FEAR AND REBELLION

This period of time in which Buton could not protect itself
is known to the locals as the *gerombolan*. The *gerombolan* followed Indonesia's initial declaration of independence from the
Dutch in 1945, but before the national government had solid
control over eastern Indonesia. Early on Irian Jaya (or West
Papua) was still in the hands of the Dutch and it was not until the
1960's that it was ceded to Indonesia. Even though Buton was
considered a part of Indonesia from the beginning, there was a
force of rebels, predominately in Makassar, that spread terror
throughout southern, southeastern and parts of central Sulawesi.
The people throughout the islands of Buton did not feel safe
while roving bands of rebels were storming through villages
looting and pillaging, taking advantage of a time of transition
when there were not enough forces around to protect the people.
In general, this rebellion was done under the banner of Islam
with the goal of making Indonesia an Islamic state.[90]

There are a variety of reasons this rebellion was conducted
based on Islam, the primary one being that this was probably
the only way it could win the support of the people of South
Sulawesi. The choice of Islam over Marxism was based on the
character of South Sulawesi society, the sources of their support,
as well as the nature of their rivals and enemies. The only organized socio-political force with roots of any depth in South Sulawesi was the Islamic organization Muhammadiyah. And the
aristocracy that was in place would have immediately refused to
support a communist revolution, but they may have thought they
could retain their position within an Islamic state. The leaders

---

[90] Cornelius Van Dijk, *Rebellion under the Banner of Islam: The Darul Islam
in Indonesia* (Leiden: KITLV, 1981).

of the rebellion could then use the egalitarian principles of Islam to indirectly attack feudalism. South Sulawesi was also fighting for their position in the newly formed government of Indonesia and up to this point those that received the more sought after posts in the government had a Western education, and came from Christian areas or were nominal Muslims from Java (*abangan*). Those of South Sulawesi, especially the smaller villages, had received a Muslim education. Once again Islam, which had provided an important mark of distinction between the colonized and the colonizers in the Dutch period, served to distinguish the people of South Sulawesi from those who they saw as their rivals and enemies, to some extent the Christian Minahassans and Ambonese, but more particularly the *abangan* Javanese.[91]

Since its independence in December 1948, Indonesia has seen several attempts to change the government by forcible means, but the rebellion that was the most significant in duration, number, and size of areas affected has, surprisingly, received the least attention from scholars. This is the *Darul Islam*[92] rebellion, which was a fight for the establishment of an Islamic State of Indonesia. There was a large outbreak in South Sulawesi, which in turn affected the islands of Buton in southeastern Sulawesi. It started in West Java, where the Islamic State of Indonesia was proclaimed on August 7, 1949, then subsequently spread to parts of Central Java, to South Kalimantan on Borneo, to South Sulawesi and to Aceh. *Darul Islam* activity was also reported in the Lesser Sunda Islands, the Malukus and Halmahera. In these regions, however, it took the form of a process of infiltration from South Sulawesi. It did not develop into a full-scale guerilla war, nor did it become as widespread as in the other regions. In most of these other areas the rebellious movement showed remarkable tenacity and spread over a fairly large area for quite

[91] Harvey, 253-260.

[92] This term refers to the concept that there are two realms in the world, the *Darul Islam* (Domain of Islam), areas dominated by Muslims and Islamic law, and the *Darul Harb* (Domain of War), areas not yet under the dominion of Islam.

some time. It was not until the early sixties that the Indonesian Army successfully suppressed the various uprisings, with Sulawesi being the last to be stamped out around 1965.[93]

The rebellion against the newly formed government of Indonesia in Sulawesi was led by Kahar Muzakkar. It affected large parts of south and southeastern Sulawesi for many years. As a young man Kahar Muzakkar came into conflict with the local *adat* chiefs (leaders of cultural law), how this came about is not fully known. Kahar Muzakkar was accused of sedition against the *adat* chiefs. He is even said to have "denounced the existing feudal system in South Sulawesi and advocated the abolishing of the aristocracy." So he was banned from the island, or to be more precise, ostracized for life. He participated in the struggle for independence from the very beginning, and was a leader in various Sulawesi youth guerrilla organizations centered in Java. On March 24, 1946, General Sudirman, the commander of the Republican Army of Indonesia, assigned him the task of preparing the formation of a Republican Army in Sulawesi. He was later put in charge of the coordination of the guerilla units in Kalimantan, Sulawesi, the Malukus and Nusa Tenggara.[94]

The formal recognition of independence by the Dutch had put an end to his commandership of these outlying areas. His actions eventually led those within the army to distrust him. He proposed to be the leader of a unit of former guerillas integrated into the Indonesian Army, but after this command did not materialize, he took his forces to the forest. A full-scale guerilla war eventually broke out between the Army and the guerilla forces commanded by Kahar Muzakkar.[95] On March 25, 1951, the long-awaited day of the *Persiapan Brigade Hasanuddin*'s official constitution as part of the Republican Army National Reserve Corps finally came as the government conceded to the guerillas. Kahar Muzakkar was officially installed as com-

---

[93] Van Dijk, 1.
[94] Ibid., 155-161.
[95] Ibid., 167-169.

mander of the National Reserve Corps of South Sulawesi, and he swore his allegiance to the Government and the State of the Indonesian Republic.[96] Even after this declaration of allegiance, some disagreements arose about how the guerillas would be integrated back into the Army, which led to their eventual return to the forest. Kahar Muzakkar was thought to be bargaining again for the guerilla troops being accepted wholesale into the Army and his own command of them. This adversely affected southeastern Sulawesi on mainland Sulawesi, Kolaka and the area to the north. The Indonesian government sought a peaceful solution, but Kahar Muzakkar became even more recalcitrant.

On January 20, 1952, he accepted the offer of command of the guerrilla force named the Islamic Army of Indonesia for Sulawesi. His main obstacle in starting an Islamic revolution was "the feudalists and the common people." About the Islamic population of South Sulawesi he observed that "it would take time to implant and cultivate the true Islamic spirit in them." This was surely the same situation among the islands of Buton, as can still be seen today. The leadership replied that Kahar Muzakkar should do his utmost to make the population "Islam-minded" and "Islamic State-minded," and further, to do anything else recommended by Islamic law in times of war.[97] Kahar Muzakkar was a long-standing enemy of the traditional rulers. The Republican guerillas likewise tried to eliminate the traditional rulers by force in different areas. Kahar Muzakkar tried to stamp out traditional practices in South Sulawesi by attacking its outward expressions, such as titles and marriages ceremonies. Further damage was done by seizing property and some possessions, to support the fighters and the "interests of the revolution."[98] Evidence of this campaign against cultural traditions is more widespread in South Sulawesi, while among the islands of Buton many of these traditions are still intact.

---

[96] Ibid., 179.
[97] Ibid., 183-188.
[98] Ibid., 191-193.

Kahar Muzakkar was a pious Muslim, and although occasionally Christians were victims of the raids, it appears that the people concerned were only killed if they resisted the rebels and refused to give them food and information. As a rule, civilians, Muslims and Christians alike, were treated well by him. The guerilla force was likely between ten and twelve thousand. At one point the Indonesian Army cleared parts of Southeast Sulawesi of civilians who had not lived and worked there long in order to isolate the guerillas. In one case Kahar Muzakkar took one of his commanders to task for the conduct of his men, who had betrayed the ideals of the struggle of the rebelling guerillas by stooping to rape and plunder.[99] The fear and lawlessness caused by this type of behavior is what is most remembered in Buton. Not only were people attacked on the land, but their boats were seized as well. During this time it was very dangerous to sail through the Strait of Selayar, which is always used when sailing between Makassar and Buton.[100] It may be that the islands were primarily being attacked by people taking advantage of the current lack of security caused by the rebellion, and were not directly tied to it. Whether this is true or not, this time of instability and fear was conducted at the same time as the *Darul Islam* rebellion.

The Army's only successful operations against the guerillas were those carried out along the coast. Mounting effective offensives in the interior were much more difficult. In September 1955, a combined operation was launched on the coast of Bone Bay, where hundreds of rebels were killed. Rebels fleeing from the Republican Army became easy prey for the combat planes of the Air Force as they tried to cross Bone Bay by canoe to retreat into the *Darul Islam* areas in southeastern Sulawesi. Two months later government troops landed at Wawo, in southeastern

---

[99] Ibid., 194-198.
[100] Abd. Rahman Hamid, *Spirit Bahari Orang Buton* (Makassar: Rayhan Intermedia, 2010), 193.

Sulawesi, to occupy one of the rebels' civil and military admin-
istrative centers.[101] Kahar Muzakkar continued his rebellion, and
when he defeated one of his rivals, Gerungan, in 1960, he and
his 150 followers, who were mostly Christian, were converted
to Islam. In the end of the 1950's Kahar Muzakkar was starting
to be overpowered by the Republican Army and at one point
had to fall back to the mountains north of Kolaka in Southeast
Sulawesi. The rebellion declined and the *Darul Islam* rebellion
virtually ended with his death on February 3, 1965. After that
the government remained on the alert against rebel remnants until as late as the end of the 1960's. During a visit by Suharto (Indonesia's second president) to southeastern Sulawesi in 1969 the
possibility of *Darul Islam* activities around Kolaka and Kendari
were still a security consideration, even though at that time they
no longer posed a real threat to the general security of the area.[102]
Kolaka was known as one of the favorite cities for the rebels to
gather. On the other hand, Kendari was one of the safest places
for the refugees because the Tolaki people surrounding the city
formed their own militia, *Pasukan Djihad Konawe* (Konawe
Jihad Troops, or PDK), to resist the rebels.[103] Though the majority of the large scale fighting associated with this movement
took place on mainland Sulawesi, others took advantage of this
time of rebellion. Raiding parties attacked people and villages
throughout the islands of southeastern Sulawesi fighting against
the cultural practices and local laws, as well as taking advantage
of and striking fear in the hearts of the people. The Islam that
was displayed by this rebellion is not the Islam that can be found
in Buton today.

---

[101] Van Dijk, 207.

[102] Ibid., 215-217.

[103] Esther Velthoen, "Mapping Sulawesi in the 1950s," in *Indonesia in transition: Work in progress*, Henk Schulte Nordholt and Gusti Asnan, eds., 103-
123 (Yogyakarta: Pustaka Pelajar, 2003).

MYSTICAL ISLAM OF BUTON

It is clear that there is a very dynamic relationship between Islam and the local culture of Buton.[104] According to researchers, the small percentage of Christians, Catholics, Hindus, and Buddhists that can be found on Buton originally came from other islands, and it is very likely that there are no people originally from Buton who have a religion other than Islam.[105] Though there is evidence that this has started to change in the modern era, the people very much identify with Islam and its role in one's life.

Islam was first introduced at the sultanate, where the elite were educated, and eventually spread to the villages, where knowledge about Islam was limited. It had spread through the archipelago, and Buton was going to fall in line like the others. This confession was not made by individuals embracing what they were convinced was the truth; rather, it was a decision of kings that the people generally accepted on the surface. Even the kings developed Islam into a style of their own, as can be seen by the variety of expressions of Islam throughout the archipelago. It is usually marked with a very mystical nature, spiced up with the local culture of the island on which it is found.

The sixth king of Buton, Murhum, was the first ruler to accept Islam (he was given the title of "sultan" by Sheik Abd al-Wahid). According to the traditions of Buton, Islam was brought to Buton by an Arab from Gujarat named Abdul Wahid. Abdul Wahid landed in Burangasi around the year 1527 after earlier stopping in Johor. His second visit was in 1542 (948 AH) according to Zahari, but Schoorl believes it was 1540.[106] This second visit was when Buton officially accepted Islam. Early

---

[104] M. Alifuddin, *Islam Buton: Interaksi Islam dengan Budaya Lokal* (Indonesia: Badan Litbang dan Diklat Departemen Agama RI, 2007), ix.

[105] Ibid., 321, footnote.

[106] Tawalinuddin Haris, "Benteng Keraton Buton," in *Monumen: karya persembahan untuk Prof. Dr. R. Soekmono*, eds. Edi Sedyawati and Ingrid H.E. Pojoh (Depok: Fakultas Sastra, Universitas Indonesia, 1990), 325-328.

in the process of the acceptance of Islam among these islands, mysticism or Sufism (also called *tasawuf*), played a very large role in the laws and practices of the faith in Buton. Even until the end of the 17th century *tasawuf* was pre-eminent when compared with Islam *fikih* (Muslim canonical jurisprudence). The manuscripts that remain of the sultanate of Buton are dominated by *tasawuf* teachings.[107] These *tasawuf* teachings come from Sufis (adherents to Sufi Islam) that were popular throughout the archipelago and were probably brought to Buton by visiting Sufi *ulama* (community of Islamic legal scholars).[108] There are several examples of syncretism between the Hindu-Buddhist culture of pre-Islamic Buton and the teachings of Islam because of the philosophy of *pata palena*, that "life is in the realm of ideas (thoughts)". This focus on things that cannot be seen and things spiritual has a major influence on the beliefs of the Butonese. One of the most notable of these beliefs is that of the *rohi polimba*, or "moving spirit," which can be described as reincarnation. In Komberi, East Buton, there are wooden graveside poles (*mayasa*) of those that believe in reincarnation. Elements of Butonese cultural beliefs and symbols are present in most all rituals and events on the island, even if these are Islamic in nature.[109]

Other examples of the unique flavor of Islam on Buton is that the call to prayer is heard more often in Bau-Bau than in the more remote areas, and people in the city generally seem to be more faithful to the month-long fast of Ramadan. Even so, in Bau-Bau those that are involved in manual labor are generally content to just do the first few days of the month-long fast of Ramadan then continue life as usual. It is said that, "3 days is the same as 30." Most Muslim holidays in Buton are celebrated by getting together and eating after a ritual called "*haro'a*." *Haro'a* in the beginning was believed to be an exchange of food be-

[107] DR. H. Abd. Rahim Yunus, *Ajaran Islam Yang Dominan Dalam Naskah Peninggalan Kesultanan Buton* (Ujungpandang: Pusat Penelitian Iain Alauddin, 1996/1997), 1-4.
[108] Ibid., 91.
[109] Haliadi, 298-299.

tween living family members and those that had already died. Now it is seen as a sign of thankfulness to God for his grace in providing food that we can enjoy.[110] Nowadays people also say that *haro'a* is just a way to commemorate those heroes of the past that have died without receiving their *haro'a* at their funeral, or just a way to celebrate the culture of Buton. Some may not know the original meaning of the ritual in relation to their ancestors, but I believe most people are simply trying to make it sound more modern, even though they still believe it is marked with a real connection with their ancestors.

Islam is overwhelmingly the major religion among the islands of Indonesia, but it is not the Islam you usually think of in the Middle East. It is Sunni Islam, but also has a very mystical or Sufi feel to it. Within Indonesia, mystical Islam, or Sufism, developed in the 17th Century in Aceh (north Sumatra), the point from which it influenced Buton. Sufism is more copasetic with the Hinduism that was present before Islam. One example of this Hindu influence is the reincarnation teaching already mentioned. Though mystical, this Islam did have regulations that were to be strictly adhered to. There used to be a *Sarana Agama* (religious minister) or *Sarana Hukumu* (legal minister) who conducted all religious activities in the sultanate with a connection to Islam. This person was located at the Great Mosque in the fortress. He oversaw the Islam which was mixed with the traditional law. One example of a local regulation is the role of the 4 to 12 *moji* (*modin*, *muazin*) or *bisa* who were individuals tasked with performing special rituals to protect the sultanate from natural disasters and outside attacks. They would then give guidance to the villages as a result of these rituals.[111] The influence of Sufism is not only strong in Buton, but also holds a prominent place in the rest of the Muslim world.

---

[110] Alifuddin, 348-349.
[111] Schoorl, 11-12.

SUFISM AND SYNCRETISM

A Pakistani diplomat, Husain Haqqani, has estimated that half of the world's Muslims show Sufi tendencies. It is certainly a fact that Sufism can be found everywhere in the Muslim world, even in Wahhabi-dominated Saudi Arabia.[112] A Sufi-oriented movement, Nahdatul Ulama (NU), can be found throughout Indonesia and has 40 million members, larger than the population of most Muslim countries.[113] Moderate Islam, or Islamic pluralism, of which Sufism is the most significant example, is prevalent throughout the islands of the former sultanate of Buton. Its tenants include extreme humility in the presence of divine love, dedication to spiritual harmony in contemplation of the divine, and understanding of other and earlier devotional habits. While Sufis trace the origin of their beliefs to the Quran and the Hadith, Sufism in history reflects the encounter of Islam with the metaphysical wisdom found in other religions. The Sufis aim at purification of the self, or *tasawuf*. This was anticipated in the Quran and the Hadith, or oral sayings of the Prophet Muhammad, and developed in Islamic metaphysics, called *marifah* in Arabic. Through this refinement of the personality, the individual is prepared to approach the Creator.[114] Sufism has often been dismissed as "folk Islam," but in some regions of the Muslim world, Sufis are more often than not extremely cultivated in their reading and worldview.[115] The more remote you get, the more people are quite good at making all religions "folk," especially Islam and Catholicism. The same can be found in Buton, although the center of the former sultanate in Bau-Bau probably exhibited more of the generally accepted Sufi tendencies.[116]

---

[112] Stephen Schwartz, *The Other Islam: Sufism and the Road to Global Harmony* (Doubleday: New York, 2008), 17.

[113] Ibid., 234.

[114] Ibid., 13-15.

[115] Ibid., 7.

[116] Abd. Rahim Yunus, *Posisi Tasawuf dalam Sistem Kekuasaan di Kesultanan Buton pada Abad ke-19* (Jakarta: INIS).

In order to guard against the accusation that the Islam in Buton is syncretistic and watered down, there are several stories and locally written books that claim Buton is the source of true Islam. A locally written book referred to as the *Buku Tembaga* claims that Muhammad and his followers (in Mecca) heard loud booms that marked the emergence of two island groups, Buton and Muna. Muhammad then sent two of his relatives as ambassadors to these two islands in order to pass on to them the teachings and prophecies of Islam. "Mecca is the head, Medina is the body, as it was the place that the followers and teachings of Muhammad gathered, Buton is the stomach, where the innards are, and where the heart is. Buton will be a repository for the secrets and teachings of Muhammad. Muna is like the feet."[117] Many local people believe that Buton holds the secrets of true Islam, which is supported by the belief that the name "Buton" came from the Arabic word for stomach (*butuni*). There are also books locally circulating in Buton that explain the origin of life and Muslim teachings in a very mystical way. People often receive these as fact and as deep secrets. They use the shape and form of Arabic words to explain the parts of man, and usually show how the shape of the island of Buton is like a human, with the stomach centered on Mt. Siontapina.[118] To go to the core of Buton, one must go to this mountain.

Some of what we know of Buton is a collection of the sparse information that can be found about the island in books, but the rest of this story is more about what the people claim about themselves. Many people today claim that there is much more to the story of Buton than what is read in these books. Foremost is its mystical power, which struck fear into the surrounding islands. Supposedly the righteousness of the people of Buton gave them the power to speak and cause people to instantly die. They also understood the secret knowledge required to make day-long journeys in a few hours, and go from one island to another in a

---

[117] Unknown, *Assajaru Huliqa Daarul Ba'tainy Wa Daarul Munajat*, 1.
[118] Unknown, *Pengenalan Diri Pada Maha Pencipta*, 10.

single step. They were aware of words that should not be uttered when navigating difficult sea passages, so that tragedy would not befall them (including sea monster attacks). The problem is, people today are not as righteous, and therefore don't have the same powers. But make no mistake, the people of these islands still believe that the land of Buton and the people within it still hold a special role in the world. There are some that still take their cultural heritage very seriously. These beliefs about their ancestors are not just manifested in their discussions, but also in the rituals that they carry out. Some of these rituals open doors for the people of Buton to talk with those who have been dead for hundreds of years. They meet on Mt. Siontapina.

IV
A Glimpse into the Past

Deep in the jungles of Buton every year, eight villages gather to meet with their deceased ancestors of the past and receive guidance about the year to come. This is not only for leaders, but for everyone: men, women, and children. The presence of the ancestors is not something that is hidden away in the back of a dark room; they walk around among the people and speak with them. After several meetings you can even develop somewhat of a friendship. They possess the bodies of your friends, but they speak with you as though you rarely meet. Please join me as I recount what I experienced on my October 2008 trek to the top of Mt. Siontapina and week-long stay with an elder from Wasuamba, and you will have a glimpse into the past of Buton.

The events and ceremonies carried out annually on Mt. Siontapina have probably been around for hundreds of years, even before Islam. It is said that there used to be one village hundreds of years ago that could be found on the top of Mt. Siontapina (which means "nine layers"), which has a commanding view of the surrounding area. It is the tallest peak around, with few obstructions. This village was called Wasambua. It eventually split into nine villages, which formed the initial core of most of the current villages around the foot of the mountain today. The villages on the side of the mountain where the sun rises (*Matanaio*) are primarily represented by Labuandiri. The villages on the side of the mountain where the sun sets (*Sukanaio*) are pri-

marily represented by Wasuamba, but also include the villages
of Lawele, Rukua, and Tira-tira. Within the former sultanate,
these outlying villages on Buton were organized into individual
kadies. Some of these *kadies* were grouped into where the sun
rises, while others were grouped as places where the sun set
(east and west).[119] These terms are still used among these villages today.

ARRIVAL

Every year at a time determined by the local leaders (usually
between August and October), all of these villages hike up to the
top of Mt. Siontapina for a series of rituals and events that are
truly a glimpse into the past. This series of events and rituals
at the top of Mt. Siontapina take place over a period of about
a week. The hike to the top is guided by ancient regulations
and traditions that are preserved by the local leaders. There are
usually around 500 people who make this journey, though this
number did surge to over a thousand in 1999 when there was a
scare (from a radio broadcast) that a tsunami was going to come
and wipe out the coastal villages. Several government leaders
have tried to stop this event from happening in the past, but it is
said that those that have tried have ended up being the victims
of terrible accidents.

The hike to the top of the mountain from the village of Wasuamba takes about six hours of walking plus breaks. The hike
can easily double to twelve hours if it has been raining frequently, but most of the time the rituals are held during the dry season.
As a general rule, if families are walking up the mountain, they
probably take anywhere from 3-6 hours of break time, including
lunch, when walking. But this journey is usually not completed
in one day. For the men who transport food and other items to
the top for the week-long festivities they may go up and down

---

[119] Pim Schoorl, "Power and Trade in Buton," in *State and Trade in the Indonesian Archipelago*, ed. G.J. Schutte (Leiden: KITLV, 1995).

in one day, but for those that are going to the *keramat*, or the sacred ground at the top of the mountain, they usually spend two nights on the trail to the top. On the Labuandiri side they usually spend 3 or 4 nights on the trail to the top, stopping at the places that their ancestors used to stop when they went up the mountain. It is said that going on this journey too hurriedly and with a disregard for the ways of their ancestors can be dangerous. On one of these journeys up the mountain, a lady gave birth halfway through their four day journey and she just kept hiking up to the top with her newborn and spent the following week in the jungle. Sometimes strange things may be seen in the jungle that are often considered a "testing" of the people by their ancestors.

Wasuamba always arrives at the top first. This may symbolize their village's role as the woman that then receives the male representative, Labuandiri. This is supported by the fact that female names in Buton traditional begin with the prefix "Wa-" while males names begin with "La-." At the top, there are also little wood stilt-houses that have been built for this occasion, but they are not inhabited until everyone has arrived at the top according to their pre-determined order. Most people sleep under them at first for some type of protection in case it rains, but many sleep up near the outstanding overlook to the hills and ocean on the eastern side of the mountain. When everyone arrives, it is then okay to start sleeping and hanging out in the houses. Before that, no one enters them, except the men who are doing annual maintenance to prepare them for the week ahead. There is a certain way that the men are to be formally received for the week when they arrive at the *keramat*.

Everyone must wear a *sarong* (a piece of cloth worn like a skirt) at the top and all the men must wear a *songko* (a black, brimless hat) on their head, and the local cultural leaders wear a headscarf tied a certain way (*kompongarui*). Upon arrival the children are usually the ones who carry all the belongings to the spot where you will be sleeping, while the adults undergo a special reception. There is a man from Wasuamba in charge of

receiving you. If it is your first time you will stand on a certain
rock and he will say some type of prayer for you. Then you will
walk up to the grave of the King of the Jungle, *Oputa Yikoo*, or
La Karambau, who was the 20th (1751-52) and 23rd (1760-63)
sultan of Buton (he served twice), and famous for his rebellion
against the Dutch which culminated in an attack on a Dutch ship
in the port of Bau-Bau. After this rebellion he fled to Mt. Siontapina.[120] It is said he then married a woman from Wasuamba in
the area around Mt. Siontapina, and made it part of his mission
to preserve their culture. You will enter his fenced in grave site
and sit around a rock that is just barely visible. With all hands
touching it, a prayer will be said, and then you touch your face
and heart. Afterward you walk to a rock near the foot of an
ancient banyan tree and formally greet those with the task to
receive. You have then officially entered the *keramat*.

If you hiked up with the early arrivals from Wasuamba, you
still have a couple of days of sleeping beneath the little stilt huts
before everyone arrives and occupies the huts. For the days before everyone arrives some of the stronger men are hiking up and
down the mountain leaving loads of various items at the border
before entering the sacred ground. Then others who have officially arrived will take the items to where they are staying. Then the
men get to work that have been appointed to repair the huts and
make them ready for occupation. After everyone from Wasuamba
arrives, then the people from Labuandiri arrive. Wasuamba symbolizes the role of a woman in receiving the people of Labuandiri
for the event that is going to be birthed in the days to follow.

BEGINNING

Once everyone has arrived people move to the huts and begin living there. There are not enough huts, so many continue to

[120] M. Yusran Darmawan, ed., *Naskah Buton, Naskah Dunia* (Bau-Bau: Respect, 2009), 9.

sleep below them or out under the stars if the weather is good. I actually found it a little cooler under the hut. The women continue to cook outside on some rocks, and make a trip down to the water source a couple of times to wash. There are also men who go up and down the mountain to bring water, since there is no water source at the top. There is a nearby creek, but, depending on the time of year, there may not be much water in it, and that water gets dirty fast with about 500 people up there. To take a shower or bath you head to the water source, and can even go to a nice big waterfall about an hour's walk away. You can wear shoes once you get off the peak of the mountain, but I kept mine off for the whole week just so I could say that I did. I felt like Tonto. To go to the bathroom, you just head out into the jungle, usually along one of the paths that everyone uses. The biggest medical fear I had was that all that walking around barefoot would lead to a few cuts on the bottom of my foot, then I would step in a pile of "you know what" and get a pretty good infection. Amazingly it never happened.

The afternoon after we entered the huts, the cultural leaders started to gather beneath the ancient banyan tree. There is a certain place that they sit and discuss the events of the week. They spend most of their time there from this point on, even late into the night. There is a man who takes care of their food being delivered. After he has ensured that each family is ready to bring the food, he loudly calls out "*sangke*" which means "lift" and everyone brings the food out for their man. This gathering of men is the center of activity over the next few days. As far as I understand it, all decisions are made by these men. They are close to the two trunks of the banyan tree, between which is an area that symbolizes the birth canal which is curled around a rock that symbolizes a womb. The men may be waiting for an idea to be born from this sacred place and believe they are receiving some type of guidance from this important location on the top of the mountain.

The music and dancing started that first night we were in the huts. I woke up around midnight to see some silhouettes dancing in the light powered by a generator. There was an eerie song being sung in the Muna language to the slow and steady bang of a gong. When dancing, the women usually have some type of scarf across the back of their shoulders as they have their arms extended to the side and spin around back and forth slowly and steadily. There are usually two women and they stand next to each other about 5 feet apart and try to move in unison. They first approach the group of men seated beneath the tree, take a slight bow, then begin dancing. Once the women are in place, then usually two men approach, take their bow, then start dancing. The men's dancing is much more spontaneous and takes more skill to develop well. It is clear who has done it before and who has not. They dance circles around the ladies with one foot behind the other, scooting it very quickly on the ground while either snapping or doing a Hindu-looking gyration of the hands. This goes on every night and gets a lot of participation and excitement from the crowd. There are also times that a woman takes her scarf and lays it on the shoulder of a male as a sign that she is going to dance and wants the man to return the scarf to her, and join in the dance, too.

The first night just had the gong playing gently, but the following nights had accompanying cymbal type instruments being banged loudly and rhythmically. Indonesians are very comfortable with sleeping in the middle of loud music and lights. I think the fact they usually sleep together in one room, and generally have no privacy, has led to this being the normal way of life for them. Even out in this beautiful natural place, the instruments are blaring and the generator is cranking through the night. I found myself praying that the generator would die and the power would go out. Sweet dreams!

The second night in the huts was the first night for the loud music. This was the first night that everyone got out and started dancing. There are those that have no idea what they are doing, there are those that have been doing it a long time, then there are always a few brave kids around who love jumping in any chance they get to showcase their developing skills. After the dancing had been going on awhile, an older man started dancing and just couldn't stop. Everyone was getting really hyper and cheering, and this went on for about ten minutes. The man was shaking a good bit and just kept on dancing. I was then told that he was possessed and that pretty soon, some possessed women were about to join the fray. All of a sudden the women appeared. They came down the hill with scarves draped over their heads and jumped in with all the dancing. Things were starting to get pretty crazy. Then they were led over to the house closest to the tree, their feet were washed, they had a smoke, and the meet and greet time began.

This is the first example of the way that this whole thing is run. It is said that certain spirits of ancestors return every year to give permission and direction for these ceremonies to take place. This was the first one. This was Wa Ode Kulinsusu who had returned in one of the ladies (I think it is the same lady every year), with all of her attendants. She was the one that had to appear and give permission for these three days to begin. So all the leaders and various other people go in to talk to her, and if they have wants or desires in their lives, they ask her. She is supposed to have the power to grant them. The elaborate handshake or greeting (grasping hands, muttering something or staring, then touching face and heart once, then grasping hands again) is done with each of the ladies, and some of them hand you a handkerchief when shaking their hands for you to press up to your face then hand back to her. But these are not the only possessed ones who appeared.

The way that you can tell there are other men who are possessed is if they are wearing sunglasses and dressed quite nicely. When standing still they usually also have a little shake to them. There is one dressed in red, one that wears a little green, one that is all white, and various others a few days later. Each of them represents something, and each is supposed to be an ancestor from Buton's past. These are men whom I have been talking with throughout the last few days, but they act as if they are meeting me for the first time when possessed. If I am to be accepted, they must accept me. It has been said that the one in the red had encouraged Westerners to come. The one in the green declared that he was ancestor of Buton when I met him. It was hard for me to tell if this was for real or just an act, but regardless, everyone believes it is real, so in many aspects it makes it feel real, almost surreal. The older men say that there is a secret way to tell whether those possessed are just acting or not by touching their skin in a certain way. Apparently all of these were certified to be real. Because the people who have these roles of being possessed eventually die, there are others who are specifically chosen to take their place. So once again, those that were possessed gave permission for the festivities to begin, and the night eventually settled into the eerie singing of the old men.

CLEANING

The first big day is the day of cleaning. You are to wear blue or green. The top of the mountain must be prepared for what is to come. People usually throw their trash down wherever they are, and on this mountain is no exception, but there is a special day when it is cleaned up. First of all a couple of men go to the womb rock, say a prayer, then start filling bottles with the water that has gathered in the rock over the past year. This water is supposed to promote healing and have other magical powers. They say that it never runs out, but it looked to me like it ran after everyone had their bottle filled. I'm sure there will be more next year. Then there are two processions of about ten people that head to the perimeter of the *keramat*. Each procession includes two girls wearing gold, flamboyant Hindu-looking headdresses, as they walk to certain rock formations that symbolize reproductive body parts. There the black, muddy water that has gathered in them over the past year is cleaned out. Then the two processions end up meeting together at the last spot, the place where Wa Ode Kulinsusu used to bathe. Someone else made mention that the water that is in this rock is the water of death used to put on bodies before they are buried, but some also believe it to be water of life like in the womb rock. While these processions are underway everyone back at the main campsite is sweeping all the leaves up with sticks and making it as clean as possible (though all the trash and leaves are dumped right outside the camp). The ground is no longer covered with leaves, but the dirt and roots that have been walked over for years are exposed.

NEW BIRTH

The second big day is that of new birth. The color is white. There is a ceremony over a certain rock where about 15 of the leaders gather around closely and construct a stand, then place a little metal box wrapped in white cloth, some rice, and a few other things on top of it after saying some prayers. The top of this stand that has been constructed (it took about an hour) is then carried over to a spot behind the banyan tree and placed on top of another stand as an offering. Then the four Hindu-looking girls appear again and have a seat on one side of the womb rock. The older ladies who coach them in everything take some of the rice from the offering and force it in their mouths, even though they do not open their mouths to receive it. They look forward apathetically and allow the rice to be forced into their mouths gently. Then they stand up, one on each of the four corners of the rock, and do the typical dance where they slowly spin back and forth with a scarf in their hands. They then proceed through the two main trunks of the tree (symbolizing the birth canal) to the spot in front of the leaders. They do their dance again, followed by their older coaches taking a turn at the dancing. The significance of four girls and four corners is supposed to deal with the four sides to mankind: the front, the back, the left, and the right. Then men join in with their dance and everyone starts yelling excitedly.

This seems to be a celebration of the first life on the planet, or maybe just the miracle of birth. Along with this new life comes challenges that are then acted out by a series of events. The first is a series of three different men, the *monsieys*, who each in turn take a wooden sword, kneel and pray at the foot of the banyan tree, and then emerge to fight the forces of evil in the world. He then moves with purpose to the top of the hill and begins acting like he is fighting a large group of excited younger guys who are jostling around him. He is doing battle, symbolizing the challenge of fighting for that which is right. This is repeated by two other men, who at the end of their performance end up in front of the leaders, where they bow and surrender their weapons.

The next is a series of three different styles of ceremonial fighting. The first involves two men fighting each other with large wooden swords. Then next are two men that have *keris* knives (with the wavy blades) and fight each other while they grunt and dance around, which is called *mengaruh*. The last is two men who do *pincat silat*, where they manipulate and gyrate their hands in such a way that they look like they are harnessing some type of power that they are going to use against the other person. There is also slapping and making contact with the hands forcefully by the two involved. Volunteers that are brave enough to take part or feel the urge to step in front of everyone make these events happen.

The last activity of the day is comprised of two men carrying a white chicken over to the womb rock and taking turns throwing it gently up onto the rock and watching what it does. There is a third man who always retrieves the chicken for another throw after a few seconds. This goes on for about 45 minutes, and based on the chicken's reactions, indicators are given of how the harvest will be in the coming year. There is a very complicated way of interpreting the chicken's movements that only a few people know. It is kind of like Groundhog's Day in America, but a little more complicated.

SPINNING THE UMBRELLA

The third day is the spinning of the umbrella. This is the culmination of all that has happened over the last couple of days. In keeping with the theme of birth and new life, the two that appear could be symbolizing the local version of Adam and Eve. The king of the jungle (one of the former sultans), and the queen, Wa Ode Kulinsusu, return, and this isn't some Disneyland performance; this is like the real king and queen sitting in your presence. These people are said to have been possessed, and with them are all of their attendants. Watching the queen go up the hill in all her gold regalia, walking smoothly with her hands moving like a Balinese dancer, with an old royal umbrella spinning above her head is pretty awesome. She is moving her hands and dancing when she moves like the Hindu gods and goddesses in all the paintings. The king is in the traditional Butonese dress and moves about solemnly as if he bears the weight of the kingdom and is pondering much. It is said that he holds a secret no one knows, but everyone is trying to find out. And make no mistake, everyone believes this is 100% real, which makes it all the more amazing and leaves you wondering, what if it is?

There has been a sort of royal bench prepared for the procession, and one of the ladies sits behind the queen for the sole purpose of propping her up like a chair. The younger Hindu-looking girls dab any sweat that forms on the queen's face as she continually looks downward with her eyes almost shut. Then one of the possessed men gives a speech about how we are all from the same mother and same father, all of us throughout the world, and at this point on the mountain we come together again and are one. This man may symbolize the mouth. The man in red may symbolize blood. My friend thinks the possessed attendants each symbolize their own characteristic or feature of humanity. After the speech, everyone starts to shake hands with all of those that are possessed. After the leaders shake the hands of the king and queen, this otherworldly event then takes the form of most other Indonesian activities that involve a line. Chaos. Everyone is elbowing their way to shake everyone's hands. You may have little conversations with the men, and I found that the ancestor I met a couple of days before recognized me and it was like I made a new friend, with the same guy, twice. After things settled back down, everyone went back to hanging out, but there was always a group of people around the king discussing various things. There were people asking him for things, and he would ask them their reason for coming to this mountain. I think people were also trying to find out the great secret he keeps hidden.

CONCLUSION

That evening there was the traditional time of "reading and praying," which primarily consists of eating together from individual platters of food provided by each of the families, so that the journey down the mountain is safe. The next day everyone was getting ready to head home. The Wasuamba crew is generally much more ready to hit the road than that of Labuandiri. The people of Labuandiri like to take their time. Some leave first thing in the morning, but they are really supposed to wait until the incense is burned in late morning before they can leave. The older men head back up to the grave of the king and some money exchanges hands (not sure where that comes from). Then they say a few prayers and start the journey home. Then it's off to the races going down the mountain.

This time on Mt. Siontapina was one of the most interesting experiences of my life, and probably the closest thing to original Butonese culture that you are going to get. The people involved are proud of their cultural heritage and always point back to the creation of mankind. They believe this is where it was started, and being on the mountain during this time provides plenty of time for thought and reflection. The ancient banyan tree with snakes living in it is enough to remind one about the Garden of Eden. Add to that all the ceremony and speeches about there being one mother and father of us all, and the world begins to get much smaller, even though I am 10,000 miles from where I was born and raised. Life is so much simpler on this mountain, and people are reminded of where they came from. Many of the cultural events I saw carried out in Bau-Bau seemed somewhat out of place in the city, but when I think back to Mt. Siontapina they start to make sense. The events on Siontapina show us where the Butonese come from and where some of them would like to return. It shows us the Butonese vision of the world, where it came from, and where it is heading.

Siontapina means "nine layers" and is thought to refer to the nine nations that are said to have come from this area. At the top of this mountain is the grave of the Sultan Himayatuddin Muhammad Saidi, who is better known as La Karambau (his given name), or the "King of the Jungle." He was the only sultan to serve twice, as the 20th and 23rd sultan. He is said to have established his government on this mountain in rebellion to the presence of the Dutch East India Company.[121] On Mt. Siontapina business is still conducted with the same philosophy and values that guided the sultanate of Buton during its 600 years of existence. The Murtabat Tujuh was the constitution that guided the activities of the sultanate, and elements of it can be seen carried out during these rituals on Mt. Siontapina.[122] The body that instituted and removed the sultan as well as helped keep everyone in accordance with the constitution was called the Siolimbona. The rituals carried out on Siontapina provide a living example of the sacral body of traditional law that provided the essence and soul of the Siolimbona. The rituals that still occur

---

[121] Harisun, "Kedudukan Nilai Kearifan Lokal di Indonesia Kaitannya dengan Hukum Adat Buton di Siotapina," (Skripsi, Universitas Dayanu Ikhsanuddin, Bau-Bau, 2009), 30-31.
[122] Ibid., 9.

on Mt. Siontapina guard that which has been passed down by the ancestors.[123] This focus on the guidance of the ancestors, what they did and believed pervades Buton and is seen most clearly in these mountain rituals. But this is not just some isolated gathering. The Wolio fortress and Siontapina are tied together and cannot be separated.[124]

---

[123] Ibid., 33.
[124] "Popaua Dan Gambaran Keraton Siotapina," SKU *Berita Keraton*, Edition 60 (2001): 5.

V
CLOSER TO THE CENTER

Peeling back the rough exterior, we now turn to the task of finding some of the sweetness that the pineapple symbol promises. "Sweetness" may be a strong word, but there is definitely a desire on the part of the people of Buton to make sure outsiders feel safe when among them, regardless of their origins. The peaceful diversity of the people of this land is witness to that. The diversity also contributes to the mystery surrounding these islands. The numerous languages of the island, the question of origin and where the first people landed, and how they have governed themselves are mysteries of the people and their history. What natural resources lie beneath the mineral rich island of Buton surrounded primarily by islands of coral (except Kabaena) as well as the variety of natural wonders and places of interest on land and under the sea are other mysteries currently being explored. What the people believe and how this impacts the way they see and govern themselves is something that gives insight into their lives today as well as telling us more about the past.

TRADITIONAL LAW

It is well known that the Butonese are their own people, who choose their own way. Though tradition is strong, their beliefs and practices can be fluid. They have been known to follow the currents of thought and life as they perceive them, while also maintaining strong connection to their culture. I read an article that declares Buton was the most democratic kingdom in the archipelago and one of the few early examples of democracy among the islands.[125] The position of king/sultan was not just passed on to the next in the bloodline, it was a result of the decision of the Siolimbona, nine elders from the Walaka caste. It is said that the rulers of Buton were not corrupt and feared God because they could be removed from power at any moment by the people. If a great tragedy happened, or any other evidence that God was not blessing this ruler, he could be deposed. One sultan only served about two weeks before being removed from power, and at least one was executed. The people of Buton are used to living in a somewhat fluid environment. Especially out in the more remote villages of Buton, one can see the room for spontaneity that resides in the way they conduct their traditional ceremonies. It is as a people that are not yet totally settled on the truth, but are still looking for it and trying to receive guidance from their ancestors through the cultural ceremonies that they conduct today. In Java the ceremonies and belief system are generally set in accordance with doctrine that comes down from Muslim authorities and is enforced by those in authority within the mosque and the local government. In Buton, Islam is ingrained in the people, but it has not replaced the way that they make decisions as a community.

There are also several villages that continue to practice the ceremonies and beliefs that have been passed down by their ancestors since before Islam arrived. They continue to meet and carry out their rituals regardless of the previous heavy-handed tactics to stop them by government authorities. They are convinced that they are doing the right thing and that they should live in accordance with what their forefathers have told them. In some cases their ancestors have made prophecies and given

[125] Melayu Online, "Kerajaan Paling Demokratis Di Nusantara," Opinion article,http://melayuonline.com/ind/opinion/read/59/kerajaan-paling-demokratis-di-nusantara (accessed on April 3, 2010).

guidance about the future: the kind of people they are to work and associate with, where they are to live, where and when they are to meet, etc. Their traditional system of law is known as *adat*, and it guides the way that they gather together to seek clarification on these prophecies, as well as conduct ceremonies, problem-solve, and make decisions.

Adat in most cases is not written down, but is usually knowledge passed down through the old men, who form a type of council to discuss and work through problems and set norms for life. Within these groups of older, culturally astute men (*tokoh adat*), there are those who hold specific titles, many of which have been around since the Butonese kingdom of old. The offices of *parabela* and/or *bonto* indicate leaders of *adat* who are given the needed flexibility and ability to react to developing situations along with the other *tokoh adat*. This includes identifying and responding accordingly to any situation that may in some way fulfill a prophecy made by their ancestors. Each ceremony is conducted under the auspices of one or both of these figures. They determine many things based on intangible factors, such as, who is allowed to participate or when it starts and ends. They are entrusted to have the eyes to see when prophecies are beginning to be fulfilled and how to conduct rituals as new and previously unknown factors appear. They are to mystically sense what is going on in the situation and make the right decisions.

In the city of Bau-Bau this is seen less and less as things become more modern and people are more plugged into the general prevailing culture throughout Indonesia. These ceremonies are also stifled somewhat as Islam sets in place its system of worship, belief, and celebration. For example, in Java there is less of this taking place because Islam has a stronger hold and as the Javanese are usually those in power throughout the country, the prevailing thought is that they feel a burden to keep everyone else in line. As a result, since the independence of Indonesia there have been Javanese sent throughout the islands working in government positions and especially early on were there to replace influential local leaders who had been "promoted away" to Jakarta.[126] The people of Buton in general have not yet toed the party line and in some of the villages they seem to still resent the influence that Java tries to impose on them regarding religion and how they should live.

PLACE OF PEACE

Buton does take pride in being a place of peace and has throughout its history been a place where people have fled for safety, such as from the recent violence that took place in Ambon in the first few years of this century. Many Butonese have lived in and around the city of Ambon, in the nearby Maluku islands, going back hundreds of years. The Maluku islands are the closest neighbors to the east of Buton. The trip to Ambon now takes about 24 hours by ship from southern Buton, but I spoke to one man who said that before they had engines the trip used to take seven days if the wind was really blowing strongly; if not, it could be 20 days. Regardless of the time it took to get there, people have always traveled in between these two islands. From 1998 to 2002 in Ambon, groups of radicals from the outside came in and started killing people along religious lines, which led to thousands of people dying and hundreds of churches and mosques being destroyed. Throughout Buton today, there are people who fled Ambon during that fighting. Most had families originally from Buton that had settled in Ambon. When they got wind that the trouble was coming, many returned to the land of their ancestors. It is said that some of the radical militant leaders of the persecution in Ambon then came to Buton and met with the man who would be considered the sultan, if it was still an official sultanate today. (Despite the fact that there is no longer a sultanate of Buton, the lineage of the sultan is still maintained informally.) These militant leaders wanted to

---

[126] Heynneman.

ask the 'sultan' for permission to continue pursuing and killing Christians on Buton. Permission was not granted, giving credence to the understanding that Buton has always been a place of refuge for those that are in danger.

Buton's decision to provide refuge to the Bugis Prince Arung Palakka was not only because it seemed reasonable at the time, but in part because the prophecies of their forefathers indicated such a thing should take place. The leadership of Buton had made the decision to side with the Dutch and the Bugis as they fought against Sultan Hasanuddin and the Sultanate of Gowa in Makassar. Siding with the Dutch was seen as a betrayal of fellow Indonesians by many in Makassar (they especially thought of the Bugis in this way), but even now one gets the sense that when the leadership of Buton makes decisions, the people feel at peace with them, despite outside pressure. While most people would look at the situation and say that those originally from these islands should stick together, I have heard from some of the old men that they are more concerned with the relationships stemming from the one mother and father of all humanity in the beginning, and from this standpoint they are just as much akin to the Dutch from the West. So to spurn the connection that Buton has with the Dutch people of the West would be just as serious as opposing Gowa. There are many stories that speak of a special relationship between the people of Buton and the people of white skin from the West, one such story holds that all the people on earth found their origin on Buton and will one day return. This includes people of all skin colors, but I hear people of white skin mentioned most often. So Buton makes its own decisions, and these are not usually determined by accepted opinions of what is politically correct; it is a result of their own type of reasoning and a perceived faithfulness to the guidance that has been passed down and entrusted to them over the generations.

PLACE OF DIVERSITY

In spite of the amazing amount of variety in language, there are several unifying factors throughout the islands of Southeast Sulawesi.[127] Most of these probably come from the influence of the sultanate. Southeast Sulawesi is composed of a segment of mainland Sulawesi (on the southeastern peninsula), along with several surrounding islands. The part of mainland Sulawesi in the province does not seem to have been involved much in the history of Buton until it was made the capital of the newly formed province in the 1970's. Buton has always been an island kingdom. Though currently the islands of Buton fall within the province of Southeast Sulawesi, momentum is building for Buton and many of the surrounding islands to compose their own province, Greater Buton. If this happened, Greater Buton would separate from their current province of Southeast Sulawesi. Its capital would be on the island of the same name, in the city of Bau-Bau. At this point the capital of the province is the city of Kendari on mainland Sulawesi. Regencies are the largest political divisions below the province. A regency is led by a *bupati* (regent), who controls most of the land on the islands of Buton. The exception is the city of Bau-Bau, which in 2003 became a municipality with its own government and mayor (on the same level of authority as a *bupati*). The two dominant islands, and each the seat of the two larger island regencies in the region, are Buton and Muna. They both have had kingdoms in their history. Buton was always more powerful, and continues to be more influential today, though Muna has its own history and much to call its own.[128] Muna is also the central land of the largest single people group in the region, the Muna people, whose language is expressed in different dialects on the islands of Kadatua, Siom-

---

[127] See map "Bahasa-Bahasa Sulawesi Tenggara" (Southeast Sulawesi Languages).

[128] J. Couvreur, *Sejarah dan Kebudayaan Kerajaan Muna*, trans. Rene van den Berg (Kupang: Artha Wacana Press, 2001).

pu, Telaga, and several smaller neighboring islands along with considerable segments of Buton.

Buton (or Butung) is the name of the largest island in Southeast Sulawesi as well as the name of the former kingdom and sultanate that had the most power in the region. The reach of the former kingdom of Buton was quite extensive. The local people still see themselves as Butonese because of the influence this kingdom had, and the city of Bau-Bau is still considered the heart of this area as well as the center of trade and culture. Within the city of Bau-Bau, those who live within the walls of the old fortress, or *keraton*, are seen as guardians of the culture of this sultanate, though there are several guardians of Buton's ancient culture throughout the island. Of the sultanates still in existence when Indonesia first declared its independence on August 17, 1945, only one still remains (in Jogjakarta). The Buton sultanate was the last to fall. Though it is no longer officially a sultanate it is said that there is still a group of people that continue to carefully pass on the position of sultan as if there was still a sultanate. Those with the last name "Manarfa" were most recently considered the family which would be ruling if the sultanate were still in existence, but the man who held this position passed away in 2009. Since the position of sultan was never automatically passed down in accordance with bloodline, the decision was made by the group of nine Walaka caste individuals, the Siolimbona. It seems that since Sultan Mohammad Aydrus there has been a bloodline connection between the sultans, but prior to that it was more democratic. I was told over a year after Mr. Manarfa's death that who would be the next "sultan" still had not been agreed upon.

Farther to the east are the Tukangbesi (Metal Worker) or Wakatobi islands, with "Wakatobi" being an acronym for the four primary islands in this chain: Wangi-Wangi, Kaledupa, Tomia, and Binongko. These islands are home to the second largest National Marine Park in Indonesia and have been made famous to Westerners through the British Operation Wallacea as well as the exclusive Wakatobi Divers Resort. The term "Tukangbesi language cluster" has been used by some to categorize the variety of island language groups that can be found on the islands of Southeast Sulawesi, but in actuality, Tukangbesi refers only to these easternmost islands in the regency now referred to as Wakatobi.

There are a couple of other outlying islands around Buton that each have their own individual character, though are usually tied in some way with people on larger nearby land masses. The island of Batuatas is the southernmost island in the province. There the people speak Cia-Cia and are closely related to the people on southern Buton. The mountainous island of Kabaena dominates the distant western skyline from Bau-Bau on clear days, and is closely tied to the Moronene people on nearby mainland Sulawesi, close to the city of Kasipute in the regency of Bombana. Wawonii Island is off the northern tip of Buton and east southeast of the city of Kendari. Their language is closely related to that of the Kulisusu people in northern Buton. Along with several other smaller islands throughout the province, especially along the western side of Muna and surrounding the Wakatobi islands, Buton offers endless possibilities for exploration. There are also many Bajo people whose villages can even be found built on top of submerged sandbars in the middle of the ocean, miles away from land.

Two of the most well known exports among these islands are teak and asphalt. Teak has made Muna famous, and asphalt is identified with Buton, as mentioned earlier. Both of these resources are rife with corruption and the local people do not really see the benefit of their local resources. This corruption is usually attributed to the *bupati*, who have authority over the jungles and villages of these islands. Many of the regency and city boundaries roughly follow where different major people and language groups are found, and can usually provide a starting point for locating the different people groups.

The several distinct people groups referred to above could be broken down into even smaller groups because their dialects may contain such great differences that communication is difficult at best. There are also several small villages and areas that have their own unique language.[129] The people of Buton have been living and working among several languages their whole lives. I have met men with little formal education out in remote villages that can speak seven languages. Most people have a working knowledge of three or four languages. If you ask the locals they will tell you that there are hundreds of languages in Buton, and though they may be right if counting every little variation in dialect as a different language, using larger groupings based on major language groups is more helpful to conceive of the major groupings of people here (those with a population of 30,000 and above). The major people groups seen as indigenous to these islands are the Wolio, Muna, Cia-Cia, Wakatobi, Kulisusu, Kabaena (Moronene), Wawonii, and Bajo (in other parts of Indonesia and Southeast Asia, also known as Bajau or Sama). Though distinct in language and certain areas of history, there is much that they share in common. There is some readily apparent overlap in language; for example the word "*uumbe*" means "yes" and is the same in many of the languages throughout the islands. The titles of "La Ode" for men and "Wa Ode" for women signifies that they came from the aristocracy or are in some way connected to the former royal family of Bau-Bau. This is especially prominent in Bau-Bau and Buton, but can also be seen throughout some of the other islands where some type of royal family connection was established such as Muna, Kadatua, and the Wakatobi islands. The prefix "Wa" at the beginning of a woman's name is simply an identifier that the person is female, as with "La" for males. Another thing in common is that all of these islands have fortresses that were built long ago to protect their people from raiding parties from the sea.

---

[129] See the number of languages identified on the "Bahasa-Bahasa Sulawesi Tenggara" map.

The following chapters have been written after having conversations with people from every walk of life throughout all of these islands, and some of it is from my observations. It has usually been confirmed by two or more witnesses, or by the old men in the villages or people groups. I mention the old men because usually when historical or origin questions are asked, the middle-aged and younger people say those are things "that have been kept a secret by the older people." In most cases I think this means that these younger people have never thought about these questions, and since there are usually no real, written historical records (except some Wolio), the older people are the only ones who remember the way things were. Most of the older people have a tougher time with the Indonesian language (preferring their local language), and they are usually limited to speaking, rarely being literate. This scarcity of written resources is the reason for the oft-repeated phrase "it is said" in this publication. So many of the stories and historical information in this book cannot be verified to be true, but it is included because it definitely affects the consciousness and worldview of the people of this region as they generally believe these stories to be true.

VI
PEOPLE AND HISTORY

Just as *Siontapina* provided the soul of the *Siolimbona*, the lives and beliefs of the peoples of Buton provide the soul to the political history of the sultanate. The origin stories of mankind on the islands of Buton vary depending on the people group asked, and many are convinced the world started right here in Buton. One of the most vivid examples of early life on these islands can be found on the island of Muna, at the caves of Liang Kabori and Metanduno, south of the city of Raha. These paintings may be hundreds of years old, but there is no exact date available. There is also another cave nearby that has a painting of a man flying a kite that may be more recent, and one man believes that if it is proved to be ancient it could serve as the first evidence of kite-flying in the world.[130] Among the Butonese there are old manuscripts that were maintained by the sultanate. The only other Sulawesi kingdom that still has royal records are those of the Bugis in South Sulawesi. The Bugis also have an epic tale that has been preserved (*La Galigo*), while the Butonese manuscripts deal more with the business of the sultanate. Other than this, the evidence that remains of this period is in the stories that have been passed down from generation to generation.

---

[130] Ben Ruhe, "Time Will Give More Answers: Muna Cave Painting Is Hard to Date," *Drachen Foundation Journal* (Fall 2003): 15-17. And Wolfgang Biek, "Just how old is this kite cave painting?" *Drachen Foundation Journal* 10 (Fall 2002): 18.

In the period of pre-history it is guessed that people made their way from central China across land bridges to the various islands of Indonesia.[131] There are probably a number of theories about how this island was initially populated, but if you ask some of the old men out in the villages the real question is how the first people in the world that arose out of Buton populated the rest of the world. Not all, but some, hold to the belief that the origin of man was on the island of Buton.

The people of Buton are very different than those of Java. They are a hard people, skilled seafarers, and are accustomed to going abroad for several years in search of money. If all goes well, they then hope to return with enough capital to start their own business or even live somewhat of a life of leisure. In Malaysia the Butonese can often be found working construction, and the first time I ever passed through Malaysia I saw a newspaper article in Kuala Lumpur about a man from Buton that was recently arrested as an illegal immigrant after being found hiding under a mattress. I have also had quite a few people tell me of the time they "visited" Singapore and Australia, and how they ended up getting punished when it was discovered they were there illegally. In Singapore they were caned and sent home. In Australia the discovery was usually instant, as they would still be far from the shores of the country in a wooden boat and get arrested for illegal fishing. Apparently there is some type of underwater terrain feature at the border, and on the Australian side the fishing immediately gets a lot better. One man I met was even trying to sneak a boat full of about 150 Afghan refugees into Australia from Indonesia. In most of the cases they would be discovered, their boat would be burned, then they would get thrown in a "detention center" where they were taken care of very well considering their usual standards. They even received

[131] S.W. Ballinger, Theodore G. Schurr, Antonio Torroni, Y.Y. Gan, J.A. Hodge, K. Hassan, K.H. Chen, and Douglas C. Wallace, "Southeast Asian Mitochondrial DNA Analysis Reveals Genetic Continuity of Ancient Mongoloid Migrations," *Genetics Society of America* 130 (January 1992): 139-152.

a small salary. Eventually they were given a free plane ticket home. It ends up being a great adventure and story to tell.

I talked to one young man on the island of Binongko (the most remote of the Wakatobi islands) who had spent a year and a half in Singapore. He put on a lifejacket that was stuffed with cigarette packs, and swam with a friend from the nearby Indonesian island of Batam and came ashore on Singapore near the airport. He then began selling clove cigarettes that were delivered to him regularly by being brought over illegally, hidden under piles of sand on tugboats. He said that they could buy a pack of cigarettes in Batam for $1.00 and sell them in Singapore for $2.50. After a year or two of this, he ended up doing pretty well, and he is no doubt pretty secure financially when compared with his neighbors. He eventually got arrested, caned and sent back to Buton.

After the Butonese work abroad, they eventually find their way home to spend the money they have earned and settle down and grown corn and cassava to have a little more money coming in. This time abroad means a family life where the father is rarely at home. A marriage will take place; the wife will become pregnant, and then could easily not see the father for a couple of years, except for an occasional visit. There are other cases where the wife has a couple of kids and the husband is a couple of hours away at some other city working, and he just returns home once or twice a month. They think of marriage in a very different way from those of us from the West. The normalcy of not having a father at home is also prevalent in other areas of Indonesia. More often than not, it seems that fathers are rarely involved in the upbringing of their children. Part of this seems to be economic factors, and it also seems to have just become the status quo, so people do not expect anything different. This is a generalization, but it is very prevalent. Of course there are also many families that have both parents at home, as well as a large number of the extended family living under the same roof.

The tendency of many to go abroad for work and the affect on their families is similar for all of these people groups. Apart from this, there are many other aspects to life and work that are more specific to the individual people groups. You will still see some activities and stories that overlap, but you should get a sense of the differences between the people. These are unique peoples who have been intertwined by the sultanate that once ruled them.

A. **Wolio** – These people are proud to be identified with the center of Butonese culture and authority. Living within the walls of the fortress in Bau-Bau are some who are seen as the guardians of Butonese culture. The Wolio have always been identified with the sultanate and kingdom of Buton, and even words from the Wolio language (the sultanate trade language) are used throughout the islands in the area. Their influence is extensive because they were the ones who brought the people from the islands together to form a kingdom. While the center of Wolio culture is in the fortress these people are also found throughout the city of Bau-Bau and the surrounding area. There is a Wolio community in the village of Tolandona nearby on the island of Muna, one on the island of Little Telaga off the southern side of Kabaena, one in the city of Dongkala on Kabaena, as well as one on Makasar island which is in the bay across from the port of Bau-Bau. Wolio who live outside of the walls of the fortress do not think those within the walls are really special, but those within them do have a certain sense of pride. When people live in Bau-Bau they usually learn some Wolio to get around a little easier, but Indonesian is readily spoken in the city. It is usually just in the outlying village areas and islands where older people only use their local language. The Wolio are at the center of things for the people of Buton, but are not the most populous people group. There are around 90,000 Wolio, and it is possible that the 2,000 people of Kamaru in east-central Buton could be included in these numbers since their language is very similar to Wolio.

The story goes that the Wolio and the original founders of the city of Bau-Bau, which became the seat of the sultanate, actually came from Johor, in what is now Malaysia. It may be that this is true, but it could also be that they came from somewhere else and said they were attached to Johor because of the prestige associated with this sultanate. Johor would have been well known in South Sulawesi and areas surrounding it because of the long and influential history the Bugis have in this sultanate, which they actually ruled for many years.[132] One linguist that has extensively researched the languages of Muna and Buton believes that it is possible they originated from languages such as Pamona and Kaili in Central Sulawesi because of similarities to the Wolio language.[133] The first four Wolio men that ever existed are referred to as the *miapatamiana*. The stories of the origin of the Wolio are closely tied to the creation of the kingdom of Buton, though there are some other resources specific to the Wolio.

There is a museum of Wolio culture that can be found up behind the fortress. There are still many manuscripts and source documents available in the museum that are taken care of by one man that used to work with the prolific writer of Butonese history, Abdul Zahari. The task of guarding the history of Buton has been passed down through his family, and his father was the primary force behind the local written sources of the history of Buton in the last century. At this point it seems as if things in the museum are well taken care of, but in the past there were probably many documents that were lost or handed out haphazardly. I have a friend who was here with the United Nations (UN) about 20 years ago, and when she visited Bau-Bau, someone tried to give her some of the ancient manuscripts to take home for a souvenir. Thankfully she refused and told them that they should guard them carefully, as this is the record of their history.

[132] Winstedt.
[133] Berg, "Wolio."

An island near Bau-Bau is named after Makassar, and there are a few stories that attempt to give an explanation of this. The most probable is tied to the famous Bugis leader, Arung Palakka from the Kingdom of Bone, and the time he spent in refuge in Bau-Bau. Apparently after some type of battle around Bau-Bau some of the soldiers from Makassar or Arung Palakka were given land and permission to live on the island of Makassar, hence the name. Not only did this make the island famous, but also the fact that La Cila (also Laelangi, a sultan of Buton) was exiled there because people were jealous of his womanizing abilities. Several young men idolize the sexual prowess of this sultan and tell stories of how he drove the women crazy, had several wives or mistresses, and when he was exiled to Makasar island (and eventually executed), he dropped a book with all his secrets of romance into the water after sealing it in a watertight container. It is said that in the water between Bau-Bau and Makasar island, this book still remains though any who dive searching for it may die because of a curse.

A piece of political history that is significant for the city of Bau-Bau was in 1965, during the time that Suharto became president after a *coup d'etat* and thousands of people identified as communists were executed. Many Butonese see this year as the end of Butonese control over local government and the final demise of Buton within the local context. The crackdown on communists that started in 1965 was particularly traumatic in Buton. It was seen as an instrument wielded by the Bugis and Makasar people to discredit and imprison Butonese, especially since the number of communists on Buton was negligible.[134] Supposedly someone in Makassar reported that Buton was full of communists, and it is even reported that a ship was directed by the PKI (*Partai Komunis Indonesia*, Indonesian Communist Party) to drop off 500 weapons to aid in the communist revolution in Buton. Because of this, on March 24, 1969, the Indonesian mili-

---

[134] Velthoen, "Mapping."

tary arrested hundreds of suspected communists, including government leaders and Butonese soldiers, and even the Regent of Buton (located in Bau-Bau at that time). These prisoners were tortured, and during this ordeal the Regent of Buton died. He was replaced by someone from outside appointed by Makassar. This was a tragic event in the history of Buton, especially since it seems that there was no evidence those arrested were actually communists intending to revolt.[135]

B. **Cia-Cia** – Since Bau-Bau has become an official municipality, the capital for the regency of Buton has moved to the city of Pasarwajo, which is seen by some as the center of the culture that dominates the more rural areas of southern Buton, Cia-Cia (CHEE-ah, CHEE-ah). Literally "Cia" means "nothing," so "Cia-Cia" means "a bunch of nothing." This was jokingly told to me by a friend of mine that is Cia-Cia, but I have found that there is actually quite a lot that can be discovered among these people. This same friend also asked me why he so frequently saw "CIA" written in the subtitles of movies from America. He thought it might have something to do with his people, but laughed when he found out it was an acronym for the Central Intelligence Agency. The Cia-Cia can also be found out on the island of Batuatas, which is the southernmost island in the province, and the people on the eastern side of the island of Binongko (southernmost major island in Wakatobi) also speak Cia-Cia. The Cia-Cia on Binongko are descendents of soldiers sent there in the 1700s by the sultan of Wolio to quell an uprising on the island.[136] They have many distinct aspects to their culture and are proud of their heritage. The place where the ship carrying the first monarch WaKaaKaa is supposed to have landed is in the Cia-Cia village of Wabula. There is a legend that she came

---

[135] Irianto Ibrahim, *Buton, Ibu dan Sekantong Luka* (Yogyakarta: Framepublishing, 2010), 11-12.
[136] Mark Donohue, *A Grammar of Tukang Besi* (New York: Mouton de Gruyter, 1999), 2.

from bamboo, but many believe this is just a symbol and that she actually arrived on a ship from another country. Some say she is from Arabia and a direct descendent of Muhammad that founded Islam. In the village of Lapandewa (which means "men brave enough to maintain their culture") there is a gravesite that is believed to be the resting place of the first Cia-Cia couple, a sort of Adam and Eve for the Cia-Cia. This village seems to be a good place to start when trying to understand the Cia-Cia.

Lapandewa still has the remains of an old wall around the central part of the village, where the central meeting place, a special rock, and the graves of the first Cia-Cia are also found. Though most of the *adat* is passed down verbally to certain people they also seem to have some type of respect for written materials and they are certainly proud of their language. They had a book that recorded the visits and the message of all the foreigners who have come while they search for the one that will fulfill their prophecies. It has been said by their ancestors that they are not to leave their land because someone with white skin is going to come and reveal something precious to them. According to *adat*, they are not allowed to sell their land (only pass it down through the family) and they are not allowed to move. They also have an old document in Wolio, from the sultanate. It has been copied down repeatedly. It refers to a visit of Europeans to Buton hundreds of years ago that may form the origin of this connection with the people of white skin. From this story and others, it has been deduced that within Buton there is a relationship between parts of the island that are similar to that between a mother and father, while those from the West are seen as a son in that same family. The extent of this relationship is not always clear, but those from the West are usually welcomed with open arms.

Traditionally it seems the Cia-Cia lived inland, away from the coast. Nowadays in the southern part of Buton, there are only a few villages that remain away from the coast. I have heard it said from several sources that in the 1970's the government, backed by the military, came into several of these villages and forced them to move to the coast. This may have been to make these people become more accessible to the outside world, and to help them see how access to the sea is a great source of fish and other means of livelihood. It could also have been part of the government's plan to separate these people from the land of their heritage, so they would not be tied so closely to their past and to tradition. It did not work with Lapandewa. Because of what they had been told by their ancestors about the importance of their land, they would not leave the land that had promised to bring blessing to them in the future. So the military came, but the people would not move. They said things like, "We are going to die anyway; it might as well be today!" In Binongko, the remotest major island of Wakatobi, the government similarly forced all the villages to move from the center of the island to the coast. Now all the villages on that island are located on the coast.

As a result of their proximity to the sea, the Cia-Cia are skilled fishermen. The primary fishing techniques they use are portable trap fishing and angling. When sharks are caught, usually only the fins are retained, and the carcass is thrown back in the sea (called 'shark finning'). There is also collecting (including shell fishing), poisoning, netting, rod and line fishing, trolling, and spearing. The fishermen of the village Wawoangi also engage in kite fishing. A detailed study of the fishing activities of the Cia-Cia in the South Buton village of Bahari was conducted over a two year period, between 1999 and 2002.[137]

This desire of the government to separate the people from their traditional law and traditional beliefs has continued in various forms throughout Buton. Alongside the Cia-Cia, there is

---

[137] Daniel Vermonden, "Reproduction and Development of Expertise Within Communities of Practice: A Case Study of Fishing Activities in South Buton (Southeast Sulawesi, Indonesia)" in *Landscape, Process and Power: Reevaluating Traditional Environmental Knowledge*, ed. Serena Heckler, Vol. 10 in Series entitled "Studies in Environmental Anthropology and Ethnobiology" (New York: Berghahn Books, 2009), 209-210.

also the rich jungle of Lambusango national forest in the central, wide part of the island that is home to several related peoples. The language of these people is similar to that of Muna, but the traditions are more closely identified with the island of Buton, of which the Cia-Cia make up a large contingent. The tallest mountain in this central area is Mt. Siontapina, with events surrounding it explained in a previous chapter, but mentioned here because of similarities between their beliefs and those of the Cia-Cia. They have been ordered at various times in their history not to meet together on Mt. Siontapina, like they have met every year for hundreds of years. In the 1980's in the land of central Buton, especially among the Cia-Cia, there was a Head of one of the districts (a Bugis man) who was especially infamous. He would visit villages to put fear in the people and often demand one of the local young ladies sleep with him for the night. He was a very dangerous man if you did not comply with his wishes. He also sought to squash out many of the traditions of the past. During his time in power, many people fled Buton in order to escape his wrath.

I suspect the same root of tradition and way of life runs through many of the villages in central and southern Buton, so that if they needed to identify themselves with a larger ethnic group of people both of the groups would use the word "Buton." A distinct and powerful form of greeting is often practiced between these people, though it is not filled with words. When seeing someone again after a long time or when meeting for the first time, you clasp hands together, put a solemn look on your face, and stare into the other person's eyes for about 15 seconds as if you are looking into their soul. It is enough to make one uncomfortable and early on I found myself breaking into a smile spontaneously, but there is a feeling of respect that you are meeting face to face with another that was made in the image of God and you are reminded that "the light of the body is the eye."[138] You spend a few minutes reacquainting yourself with the other

---

[138] Holy Bible, King James Version, Matthew 6:22-23.

person, and "you say it best when you say nothing at all."[139] Getting close to someone and taking a deep sniff of them is also a way to show you are glad to see them after a long time apart. The ladies especially love to do this.

Towards the southwest corner of the island of Buton there is a sub-district with the name Majapahit. This is in the Batauga district that is primarily Cia-Cia, and there are two different explanations I have heard as to why it has this name. The version I heard first hand was that a ship of soldiers from the Majapahit empire, including the famed military leader Gajah Madah, came to Buton in search of secret treasure. They went into a cave, the outside of the cave collapsed, and they were buried alive. A harsher version of the story does support the idea of Buton being a place of refuge, but the eventual outcome in this situation is tragic. It is said there was a group of Javanese on Buton who had left the Majapahit empire after its Islamization, because they wanted to remain Hindu. Buton was considered friendly territory. But under the first sultan of Buton, Murhum, they were also forced to convert to Islam. They are said to have refused, preferring voluntary death, and marched their way into a mass grave they had dug themselves in order to die. The Butonese living in that area were told that the group had departed after the silencing of the gong.[140]

C. **Kulisusu** – The people in this newly formed northern regency of the island of Buton (2007, formerly in the regency of Muna) are known as the Kulisusu. They have their own language and own history, and in many ways are tied with those outside Buton as much as those within. Legends report that the first Kulisusu entered this region travelling overland, not by sea. The seat of their culture is found in the city of Ereke, which is separated from the southern part of the island and Bau-Bau by

---

[139] Paul Overstreet and Don Schlitz, "When You Say Nothing At All" (Universal: MCA Music Publishing, 1988).
[140] Schoorl, "Reincarnation," 104.

the worst roads on the island. They were certainly well-established in this area by the seventeenth century, having constructed stone ramparts to protect themselves from marauding pirates; these stone walls are still standing in some places today.[141] Their language is more similar to that of the people on the island of Wawonii and to the Tolaki language that is found on mainland Sulawesi near the city of Kendari.[142] They also have a historical connection with the Sultanate of Ternate in the Malukus. The name "kulisusu" refers to a type of shell (like a giant clam), specifically one that can be found within the walls of the old fortress (*keraton*) in Ereke (the largest city in North Buton). It is said that until you step on this large shell you have not yet set foot on the land of Kulisusu. The other half is purportedly on the island of Ternate. During the warring that took place between Ternate and Buton, the sultan of Buton eventually took control of North Buton, and the influence can still clearly be seen today. As people of Buton, they do have some connections with the people that live in central Buton, and it has even been said that they may have been the first people that populated the Wakatobi island of Wangi-Wangi hundreds of years ago (not sure about this). There are about 29,000 Kulisusu and a few community development organizations are currently working among them in order to train them in current farming and foresting techniques.

Among the Kulisusu it is hard to tell if more people consider Kendari or Bau-Bau the closest city with which they identify. Regarding language it seems that the direction of Kendari is the closer fit, but as those that reside on the island of Buton there is some pull to the seat of the former Sultanate in Bau-Bau. The way that they dress at weddings seems very similar to Buton, and the name "Kulinsusu" is mentioned frequently in southern Buton. The fact that they used to be a part of the Muna district

---

[141] David E. Mead, *The Bungku-Tolaki Languages of South-Eastern Sulawesi, Indonesia* (Canberra: Pacific Linguistics, Research School of Pacific and Asian Studies, The Australian National University, series D, vol. 91, 1999), 44.

[142] Ibid., 1.

also pulls many of them to the city of Raha on Muna for their needs. They are fairly centrally located between these three pivotal cities in the life of Southeast Sulawesi. Most people use boats at least part of the way to each of these cities, and the roads in this regency are some of the worst in Buton (with promised improvement in 2010).

They seem to be more comfortable on the rivers and in the mountains in North Buton as there are still several villages up in the mountains that use rivers to get to the sea. In general the Kulisusu people are considered fishermen, but there are also those that grow cassava, corn, cashews, and chocolate. The place that is considered the heart of the Kulisusu culture is in their *keraton* (fortress and former seat of government) in Ereke, but the village of Bone on the west side of the peninsula just south of Ereke is probably the place where the Kulisusu language is spoken the purest, and most of the people are fishermen. It is far enough outside of the city of Ereke that all the outside influences of the different people groups have not affected them as much.

D. **Muna** – Muna is the second largest island in the province. Old cave paintings offer evidence of early life on Muna, as mentioned previously. These paintings primarily depict animals, but also show the kite flying for which Muna is famous. Kite flying is a vibrant part of the history of Muna and there is even an annual Muna cultural event that celebrates this, usually each July in Raha. People still make kites the old way out of leaves and fly them in a competition. In the past there have been several international visitors to this event. This is also an opportunity to showcase the tradition of horse fighting that was made famous in the nearby village of Lowu, where the horses don't kill each other but engage in a pretty violent confrontation. This is another old tradition on Muna, and I'm not sure if it is done anywhere else in the world. It is apparently possible to have one of these horse fights organized for individuals if they are willing to pay enough, but it would be a matter of finding the right person to make it happen. The preparations for the event would then probably take at least a full day. There is also a horse fight every year in conjunction with one of the summer festivals.

The first village that arose on Muna is thought to be at Kota Muna, in the central-eastern side of the island. It is said that in the early days most of the people on the island lived inland in the area now referred to as the district of Tongkuno.[143] Now this is one of the least populated areas on the island. In this area the "rock that flowers" can be found. The word "muna," which in the local language is "wuna," actually means "flower." So this rock is probably the place that the island and people got their name. Early on it is believed that they also lived closer to the coast, but eventually moved inland because they were so vulnerable to Butonese raids in search of people who could be sold as slaves.[144]

The history of how these first cities and this kingdom was established is not totally clear, because the stories on power in the region usually focus on the kingdom of Buton. A history has been written on the island, though.[145] Muna is different from the other islands in the region in that the Muna people are much more sensitive about Buton being in a position above them. They are content with Buton being referred to as the older brother, but not as the father. The other islands concede that Buton is clearly more dominant and are more comfortable with this. Muna has had a more prominent role in the history of Buton than the other islands. Buton and Muna have always been connected, and this is readily seen in the way that the two former kingdoms related to each other. It is an interesting fact that the most famous sultan of Buton, Murhum, was a son of Muna. Similar to the Wolio tra-

---

[143] Rene van den Berg, *Grammar of the Muna Language* (Dordrecht/Providence: Foris Publications, 1989), 2.

[144] J.I. (Hans) Bakker, "Resettlement of Bajo 'Sea Nomads': Rapid Rural Appraisal of an IRD-IAD Project in Sulawesi, Indonesia," in IRDR, vol. 1., ed. J.I. (Hans) Bakker (Guelph: Guelph-Wgeningen IRD), 129-166.

[145] Couvreur.

dition, it is also claimed that the first king of Muna was related to royalty from a Javanese kingdom.

The first king of Muna was Baizul Zaman (or Benonenunto), and he was supposedly one of the sons of a Majapahit king in Java. His name means that he "came from the bamboo" because where he came from and how he rose to prominence is somewhat mysterious. His children were known as the Sugis, and several of them were kings of Muna. Sugimunano had three children, two boys and one girl, and the girl, Potowoto (Wa Ode Pogo), is currently buried on the island of Kadatua. Her most prominent boy, Murhum, or Lolotongo, was the first Sultan of Buton and the last king of Buton (because he was the first king to accept Islam). He was sent to Buton from Muna in order to receive training in being a king, fighting, etc. from the kingdom seated in Bau-Bau. He also went abroad to an island off the coast of Australia, and then later to the island of Banggai, in order to show the kingdom's presence in this island that may have been included in the Butonese empire at one point (it is currently part of Central Sulawesi). He took part in the killing of the famous pirate Labulotia, and brought his head back to Bau-Bau as proof of his death. The skull is said to still be in Bau-Bau. This was around the time that Islam entered into the Kingdom of Buton, in the year 1540. On Muna, Islam was brought by Said Raba. The king on Muna when Islam entered was La Ode Abdul Rahman (otherwise known as Sangia Togo). There are also interesting facts about Muna's history that can be found in the better documented history of the Butonese, or Wolio people, including stories of the best known king of Buton, Murhum, who was actually the son of one of the kings of Muna, Sugimunano.

There are also connections with the Kingdom of Luwuq on the north side of the Bay of Bone in South Sulawesi that are part of Buton and Muna's history. One of the sons of the King of Luwuq is said to have come with his crew on a ship and settled

on Muna and supposedly founded the first village there. He became one of the early leaders, but was never a king. There was
also a princess from Luwuq that came to Muna and married one
of the first leaders on the island. Luwuq was one of the earliest
Bugis kingdoms and the remains of this mysterious kingdom
can be found in a valley near the coast on the Bay of Bone.[146]

It is also interesting to note that Muna was the site of a Japanese POW camp during WWII. From October 1944 to April
1945 Anthony Cowling (RAF) was in a Japanese POW camp on
the island of Muna (near Raha) with hundreds of other prisoners.
Hundreds died and his time in this prison even saw an escape
attempt when a boat he was being transported on was sunk in
the waters around Muna by two Allied P-38 Lockheed Light-
nings. With nothing but an inhospitable coastline to swim to he
was soon captured again and returned to Muna. He was eventually freed. He and some fellow former inmates made a reunion
trip to Muna a few years ago.[147] Other than this book, the only
other reference I have heard to the time that the Japanese were
here was from some of the older men. They spoke of how they
started to learn Japanese in their schools and at night they had
to have strict light discipline to prevent the area from being the
target of Allied bombing.

Muna today is a very interesting place, and the Muna people form the largest people group among the people of Buton
with around 300,000 people. The current political boundary of
the regency of Muna includes the northern half of the island of
Muna, some surrounding islands, and with a large section on
the northwest part of Buton. Those within the Muna regency
feel pride in being Munanese and identify with the city of Raha,

---

[146] David Bulbeck and Ian Caldwell, *Land of Iron: The historical archaeology
of Luwu and the Cenrana valley* (Results of the Origin of Complex Society
in South Sulawesi Project (OXIS), Centre for South-East Asian Studies, University of Hull; School of Archaeology and Anthropology, Australian National University, 2000).
[147] Anthony Cowling, *My Life with the Samurai: How I Survived Japanese
Death Camps* (Vancouver: Premium Printing, 2001), 160-179.

particularly those in the north, and would never initially concede that they are tied to Buton, though everyone knows they used to be under the power of Buton. The southern Muna people often identify themselves with the people of Buton, probably because Bau-Bau is closer than Raha and they are under the authority of the regency of Buton.

In southern Muna, there are a couple of fortresses, one near the peak of Mt. Kaigula, which is the highest point that can be seen on Muna from Bau-Bau. The second fortress that can be found in southern Muna is above the village of Lakudo. There are some in this village that claim it was the first village on the island, and that the remains of the fortress are the remains of the first village. Buton and Muna are often referred to as husband and wife or big brother and little sister, and the people of northern Muna claim that Muna is the male and Buton is the female. In southern Muna it seems in general they consider Muna as the female and Buton as the male, just as the people of the island of Buton.

It does not take long to see how Muna has had influence throughout these islands. The people of Muna also seem to be open to change at certain points in their history as there are two villages that accepted Catholicism many years ago, as well as one village where many became Christians (Protestants), though they subsequently moved and created a new village on the west coast of Buton and eventually moved to Ambon.

The Muna language has found its way to the inner jungles of Buton and to many of the surrounding smaller islands. The people of central Buton that use a dialect of Muna are culturally very closely related with the other peoples of Buton such as the Cia-Cia. It is apparent that the geographical location and culture of these Muna speakers in central Buton is a stronger influence on them than the language they use. They do not show any more of a connection to the island of Muna than the other peoples of Buton, such as the Cia-Cia and Wolio. Their Muna dialect is different enough from other dialects of Muna that comprehension by other dialects is difficult. The two major dialects of Muna found in central Buton can be referred to by the representative names of Kapontori (central-west Buton) and Wasuamba (central-east Buton). All of these peoples are related in terms of their stories and culture, but they each have unique differences.

The Wasuamba Muna speaking villages in the central eastern part of the island annually take part in an event that is probably the best remaining picture of pure Butonese culture, which was described earlier.

E. **Wakatobi** – The Tukang Besi (Wakatobi) people do not claim to be native to their area. The origin myths from Wanci (pronounced WAN-chee) relate that the ancestors of the modern Tukang Besi population arrived from across the ocean from the area of *Palakarang* to the south-west coast of Wanci. On arrival they found the island to be inhabited by the people who built the stoneworks that can still be seen on the summit of Tindoi. The stories tell that there was originally a village of these pre-Tukang Besi people on the top of Tindoi, but all that remains are the ruins of stone walls; the area is now the site of a primary rainforest (the only one still on the island).[148]

Those people that are actually Tukang Besi are also confused by the presence of another people, the Bajo, who can be found throughout the islands of Wakatobi, on Kaledupa (Mantigola, Sepela, and LaHoa), Tomia (LaManggau) and Wanci (Mola, founded in the main in 1957 by refugees from Mantigola, though there was a small settlement in Mola Utara before 1957). The count of the total population of Tukang Besi speakers will probably never be made accurately, with many communities in eastern Indonesia being listed in local censuses as Bajo, Bugis, or simply as an undifferentiated "Buton." When asked about their ethnic origins, most of those people will say that they are from Sulawesi, and if pressed specify Buton. An outright admission of coming from the Tukang Besi islands is not easy to ex-

---

[148] Donohue, 5.

tract, this location being thought to be too insignificant to merit any mention.[149]

The people of Wakatobi have their own identity and own history distinct from that of Buton, though they do admit they have always been under the sway of Buton's authority. There is more mystery surrounding these islands because they are so remote, though most of the people have probably visited Bau-Bau at least once in their lives. I have heard it said that the original people of Wangi-Wangi (the northernmost island in Wakatobi) are descended from the Kulisusu people in northern Buton. In general Wakatobi has had a reputation of being a somewhat lawless area in the past, but is improving since becoming its own regency. This status brings with it more government money, buildings, jobs, and policemen. Creating more government throughout more remote areas is the national government's way of aiding their development.

The population is about 35,000 on Wanci, 20,000 on Kaledupa, 15,000 on Tomia, and 20,000 on Binongko. This is exclusively the Tukang Besi speakers, with the Bajo numbering 4,000 in Wanci and 1,500 in Kaledupa, and the Cia-Cia at about 3,000 on Binongko. The addition of the Tukang Besi communities that are scattered throughout Indonesia is likely to double this total (in Fakfak, Papua, alone there are approximately 10,000 speakers, for instance). Most of the gardening work on Wanci is done by men, all except the final harvesting and transportation home of the cassava that is ready for eating, which is carried out by women with a male guard. Some inland gardens, far from other villages in the north and north-east, are also the domain of women, but this is considered exceptional by most Wanci people. Women are also responsible for harvesting the tidal flats, searching in the shallow water, or more commonly on the flats when the tide has receded (which can create an area up to a kilometer wide along some parts of the coast), digging up crabs, mollusks and starfish, which are eaten. Men conduct

---

[149] Ibid., 2.

the fishing and trading that involves traversing the deep water beyond the coral drop-off that marks the end of the shallows, but do not engage in any productive work in the tidal flats. Culturally, it can be said that the Tukang Besi people fall within the cultural dominion of Baubau and the Sultanate of Wolio, having had their local ruler (the Meantu'u of Lia, on Wanci) appointed by a Sultan 400 years ago, and generally giving obedience to and having pride in the sultan, though noticeably less so than the mainland peoples on Buton. Many of the traditional stories are identical to those told by Wolio speakers, as well as those in other areas further west in the Wolio cultural area, such as on the island of Muna.[150]

The northernmost island of Wangi-Wangi (capital is Wanci, pronounced "Wahn-chi") is especially famous for taking advantage of its remote location and having some rough characters. In the past it was said that you could find just about any illegal merchandise you wanted in Wanci. Ships would go to mainland China, Taiwan, and Singapore and somehow get their hands on merchandise, then bring it back to Wanci without going through any type of customs fees or taxes. It would be illegally imported. It was said that you could just walk down the street in certain parts of town and stop in houses for various types of shopping: one house would have Harley Davidson motorcycles, the next would have nice TVs, the next would have designer clothes, and so on. This is hard to find nowadays, though most of the second hand clothes that are sold in Bau-Bau come through Wanci, and there are several houses with shoes and clothing that may have a few nice surprises for sale.

I heard another story about the people from Wanci from a British man who has lived in Bali for about 30 years and spends his time as a boat captain and travels around building ships. The story may be true because there is a long standing connection between some of the people of Wakatobi and the people of the

---

[150] Ibid., 3.

faraway island of Rote. [151] The story goes that there is a group of men that take a good sized ship from Wanci to Surabaya (east Java) every year to load it up with plastic furniture, plastic containers, and anything else made of plastic, then they head down to the island of Rote, which is the southernmost island in Indonesia and the closest one to Australia. There they set up their little plastic trading operation in Rote and accept no money for the plastic; they barter for as many barrels of palm sugar as their ship can carry. After the plastic is all gone and the palm sugar is ready to go, they head back to Wanci and start making *arak*, which is the Indonesian version of moonshine (yes, these are card-carrying Muslims). After they have turned all the barrels into moonshine, they load up the ship again and head to Makassar to sell it all. They take the money from the sale, and head back to Wanci again to have a few months of vacation, then begin the cycle all over again. They do the same thing every year. This must be quite a life.

The Wanci islanders are the most oriented towards trade, with fleets of up to 40 vessels regularly smuggling second hand clothes and karaoke stereos from Singapore to most of Indonesia, as well as more mundane trade in plastics and agricultural tools. They have the greatest number of people living in cities away from home, typically staying for up to a year away from the islands, working in odd jobs and helping family in business ventures, before returning to their villages for half a year to help with harvesting and ceremonies.[152]

The island of Kaledupa is a little more mountainous and has a whole lot more Bajo people living around it. I have also heard a generalization about the people from Kaledupa, that they respect men more if they have killed someone or have some history of violence. This reminds me of the gangster rap culture in America, though on the surface these people are just as friendly

[151] Natasha Stacey, *Boats to Burn: Bajo Fishing Activity in the Australian Fishing Zone* (Canberra: Australian National University E Press, 2007), 58.
[152] Donohue, 4.

as all the other Indonesians. According to an old lady in the oldest Bajo village in Wakatobi, Mantigola, her ancestors were starting to establish a village on Kaledupa but had to move because there were too many evil spirits on the land. So that led to the establishment of this little village on the sea. I have also been told that the original people on Kaledupa were actually from Maluku, so they have much darker skin. If this is true it has been diluted through intermarriage because most Kaledupans do not look much different than others in Wakatobi. There are also a few thousand people that live on the island of South Lintea (on the south side of Kaledupa) as well as one village on the island of Hoga (to the east of Kaledupa). Hoga is also the island where the British Wallacea Trust operates, so there are hundreds of European college students who come out every summer to study.[153] There is also a little resort on the island for backpackers or for those who just want to get away and don't need all the luxuries of larger resorts.[154] Far to the east is the sparsely populated island of Runduma, also in the district of Kaledupa.

On Kaledupa, there is also an emphasis on education, as the island has a tradition, since its conquest by Tidore in the 1600s, of sending sons to centers of learning, and even more important there is a tradition of well-educated teachers returning to Kaledupa. The Kaledupa people are not particularly known for their seafaring abilities, riding when necessary with cousins from Wanci or on motor-powered vessels, and are well known for their lack of business acumen. Kaledupa is the one island in the group without shops prior to 1991, when a market area was built by the government to promote commerce on the island.[155] The men of Kaledupa, like those on all the islands of Wakatobi, often go abroad in search of work. This has given the women of

---

[153] Operation Wallacea Trust, "Wakatobi," http://www.opwall.com/ (accessed on April 3, 2010).

[154] Hoga Resort, http://www.tukangbesidiving.com/ (accessed on April 3, 2010).

[155] Donohue, 4.

these islands an extra load of responsibility while the husbands are away.[156]

Tomia has a reputation as one of the cleaner and better managed islands in the chain. I have heard from a few people that there is generally a strong desire on the part of the people to learn, and that the libraries are well used. The people on this island have also had more exposure to Westerners because of the presence of Wakatobi Divers, a luxurious resort on the nearby island of Onemobaa (pronounced Oh-nay-mo-bah-ah). The resort is blocked off from the rest of the island where many locals live. The grave of the man that brought Islam to the island is a tourist spot, along with a former fortress at the highest point, as well as other fortress ruins east of Waha (on the north side of the island). These people are said to be descended from Sumatrans.

Tomia is regarded as the most culturally intact of the islands, with the least impact from other cultures and regions. Tomia speech is thought of as being the most refined of the dialects, and Tomia is considered to have the finest dancers and musicians. Tomia has the lowest population, due to a very low number of outsiders moving in and poor conditions on the island itself. Not known for their trade, there are but a few natives of Tomia in the Maluku region, scattered around Ambon, Banda and a few other islands.[157]

Binongko is an interesting place, and a great spot to hear a wide variety of interesting stories about the island. When talking to the old men that like to tell stories, you definitely feel the mysticism that is still prevalent on this island. It is a fun place to visit, as long as you do not need to have nice accommodations. It is the most remote of the major Wakatobi islands, and no daily boats go there, but one leaves three times a week from Tomia and once or twice a week from Bau-Bau. It is also famous for being surrounded by big, rough waves throughout the year. It

---

[156] Sumiman Udu, *Perempuan Dalam Kabanti: Tinjauan Sosiofeminis* (Yogyakarta: Penerbit Diandra, 2009), 150.
[157] Donohue, 4.

is interesting that the eastern half of the island speaks the same language as the Cia-Cia. The eastern half of Binongko seems to be inhabited with people who came from Buton as the Sultan was spreading the influence of his sultanate throughout these islands. There are some remnants of a fortress and some cannon in the city of Wali on the eastern side of the island, where it is said, some of the Sultan's family came to live after his marriage to a woman from Binongko. There are also some cannon at a mosque in the city of Popalia (on the Wakatobi speaking side). This is another island impacted by the 1970's government program forcing villages to move to the coast and out of the jungle. All of the island of Binongko complied with this, so all of the villages are on the coasts, which seems to be for the best because it is said that the land is not very fertile. This same program also affected villages of the Cia-Cia in the southern end of Buton. I have heard that the original people of Binongko are descended from Arabs.

Binongko has a smaller population than Tomia, but has probably the highest number of emigrants to other regions of any of the islands. The Tukang Besi communities with permanent residents on islands in eastern Indonesia tend to be descended from Binongko traders, and the island of Kapota west of Wanci is largely populated by Binongko people. The island of Binongko is very poor, infertile, with little fresh water, and none close to the villages, which are all located on the coast. Binongko is also situated in an area poor for fish (the best area being just east of Kaledupa), therefore many people have taken to crafts to earn their livings, the source of the name Tukang Besi (blacksmith in Malay).[158]

The name Binongko has turned up in random places in history, which is odd for such a small and remote island. In the Malukus prior to World War II there were ships from Makassar, heading to Ternate, that would stop in Namlea to deliver goods, mail, money, news, and business associates. When these ships

---

[158] Ibid.

pulled into port it was instant excitement and everyone would put on their nicest clothes to look their best. One Dutch writer described the scene at the port where "every Chinese has put on a jacket, the Arabs wear their finest embroidered fez, the Ambonese parade around in stiffly pressed trousers, and the Binongkos in brightly checkered sarongs."[159] It seems as if Binongko could even have been used to describe people from all over Buton in instances like these. This is quite a lot of influence for one of the most remote islands in the sultanate.

F. **Kabaena** – The island of Kabaena is part of one of the mainland regencies, Bombana, but has its own distinct language and history. The language of Kabaena is in the same family (but a different dialect) as that of the Moronene people who live on mainland Sulawesi near the cities of Kasipute (formerly Rombia) and Poleang and the surrounding areas. These mainland Sulawesi places of Rombia and Poleang may have been the only part of mainland Sulawesi under the sway of the former sultanate of Buton. Kabaena definitely used to be part of the sultanate, so the people have a close tie with the former sultanate. The word "Kabaena" contains the root "bae," which means "rice" in the Wolio language of the sultanate, so the name of the island is a Wolio term meaning "the ones with rice." Nowadays there is a stronger tie to their neighbors directly to the north on mainland Sulawesi. Not only do they share the same language as the Moronene to the north, the capital of their regency is found in Kasipute, so they naturally see it as a center of activity that impacts their lives. Kabaena is related to the other islands of the province in that it shares the characteristics of island life and history, but the native people actually have more similarities with the people of mainland Sulawesi. The Moronene in general also feel a very close kinship to the Mekongga that are centered in the city of Kolaka, and live around the same mountainous area. These two people groups are very similar in language to the Tolaki people

---

[159] Vuyk, 29.

that dominate most of the mainland in this area. That means then that they are in the same language family as the island of Wawonii, the Kulisusu of North Buton, and even the Bungku people of central Sulawesi. Even so, there are a good number of Wolio living on Kabaena, especially on the eastern port city of Dongkala. Buton knew the importance of having Kabaena as an outpost to spot threats from the West (like Gowa), and no doubt made sure there was some Wolio representation on the island.

One story that came from the oldest village head on Kabaena said that the origin of the name "Moronene" came from the union of the first man to come to this land, who was a Moro person from the Philippines, with the first woman, who was from Mongolia where some of the women were supposed to be referred to as "Nene" in their language. The result…Moronene. Most of the peoples throughout these islands, and probably throughout the world, usually trace their lineage back to some powerful or influential kingdom to give them more status.

The mountains of Kabaena surely hold a great many secrets and have not been thoroughly explored. Johannes Elbert's Sunda Expedition in 1909 was the first to explore Kabaena Island, even though Kabaena itself, remarkable for its nearly mile-high peaks, had been known to Western explorers since the late sixteenth century.[160] On one such mountain ridgeline, overlooking Dongkala, there are the bamboo remnants of an old village that are all wrapped together with vines and covered with foliage. A little farther up the ridge is an old fortress that was supposed to offer protection from raiding parties from the old sultanate of Ternate and Gowa. This defensive fortress can be located after walking four hours from the village of Ulungkura, but there was also supposed to be a fortress that the people lived within that has not been found yet. There are also several stone walls of fortresses just above the highest village on the island, Tongkeno (also called Enano). It is said that there are five of these little fortresses surrounding Tongkeno, and if there was the threat of a

---

[160] Mead, 3.

raid in their village, the people would flee to one of these strongholds. At least one of them is supposed to still have cannon in it. The people would have probably defended themselves individually with spears and machetes, as well as possibly just throwing rocks.

It is said that when the people on Kabaena speak their language it is as if they are singing. The women on Kabaena are also generally considered to be more beautiful than the surrounding islands. They are famous for having lighter colored skin, which is generally found very attractive throughout Asia. The dialect of Moronene that is spoken on Kabaena is referred to as Tokotua, which is how the people of Kabaena refer to themselves in their local language. The "To-" prefix at the beginning of some of the people groups is supposed to mean "people" so this could actually be understood to mean "the people of Kotua." It may also be that the root "tua," which means "old," is a reference to the Tokotua being the oldest people, or original people of this people group.

There is still enough jungle on this island that wild honey is plentiful. Some locals explained to me that there are two main types of bee's nests on the island. The first is the giant honey bee, whose nest hangs in a tree. In Indonesia, these honey bees are the most aggressive in defending their nest. The bees are then usually smoked out, the honey is taken, and then hopefully the bees return to make enough honey for next year. Sometimes the bees completely cover this nest on the outside so that you can't see how big it is until the bees have been smoked away. The second type can be found in holes and in caves, and it is said the best way to get these nests is to just stick your hand in there and grab it. You are going to get stung, but apparently the sting of these cave bees is less serious than that of the others. Several of the men have stories of how they were stung all over their body by bees as they were trying to get some honey.

The island is also famous for its palm sugar, and men can be found in the jungle stirring big cauldrons of it, then filling little containers made out of old coconut shells that have been cut in two. They put bamboo tubes in these palm trees to gather the sap, and then they go collect them and pour them together into the cauldron and cook it until all the water is boiled off. Then just the sugar remains and it is wrapped up into the skin of corn husks. This is then used to make the little sweet bundles of coconut and palm sugar for which the island is famous. These are often sold to people passing through Bau-Bau as souvenirs.

Kabaena is also home to quite a few Bajo communities on the west and north and Kabaena is bordered on the south by the islands of Big and Little Telaga that are home to Muna and Wolio speaking people. The Buginese are also prevalent on the west side of the island. There are also some Balinese and Javanese transmigration communities on the northern side of the island near Pising. There is a song about Kabaena that most kids throughout Buton learn when they are young. It talks about how even the big waves look flat when viewed from atop the mountains of Kabaena (especially the tallest, including and surrounding Mt. Sabampolulu). This is an island that still has many stories circulating about spirits and curses and other supernatural things that can be found in its mountains and caves.

G. **Wawonii** – This island was said to originally have been uninhabited, so everyone has come from other areas. Some say the first to come were from the Moronene or Tolaki people from mainland Sulawesi to the west. They probably originally came to the island because they were running from some type of marauding bands of thieves or warring kingdoms. These first communities lived in the mountains, were still somewhat nomadic, and the name of the original village was supposed to be Waworete. Its remains are supposed to still be on top of one of the mountains. It is also said that the surface area of the island used to be a lot smaller, but over time the waters have receded and now more than just the central highlands are above the ocean waters. According to legend, the Wawonii people have twice vacated Wawonii Island and lived on the mainland during times of sickness and war.[161]

After a number of years of inhabitation, the Wawonii kingdom was established. While it is said to have been an independent kingdom, it was usually under the power of either Buton or Ternate. The primary city during this period was called Ladianta. The word "*ladi*" is supposed to mean "keris knife" in Wolio (Buton) while "*anta*" is supposed to mean "grill" in Bungku of Central Sulawesi. Because of this early evidence of the outside language presence, both places claim that they were the first ones to the island. The language of Wawonii is most similar to Bungku (Central Sulawesi) and Kulisusu (northeastern Buton Island). According to the linguist David Mead, one could even say that Wawonii lies in the middle of a language/dialect chain with Bungku on one end and Kulisusu on the other. Once again, this demonstrates that people from many different places came and influenced Wawonii.

There is also supposed to be a fortress in the jungle nearby the village of Wawongkeuwatu. It is also supposed to have been from the period of the kingdom, and may be somewhat hard to find. Wawonii was probably a sort of outpost of the Kingdom of Buton as it was on the northern side of the kingdom's influence where it bordered the kingdom of Ternate to the north. This is also similar to the city of Ereke in the northern part of the island of Buton, which spent part of its time under Ternate and part of its time under Buton. Ternate probably had the earliest influence, and as Buton gained power, they took control of this nearby island.

I was also told that the Japanese saw it as a strategic outpost because they were supposed to have built a fortress on the east coast during their World War II occupation. The local people also believe that the Japanese had a great number of weapons that they buried somewhere on the island. One man said the Japanese also supposedly took some artifacts from Wawonii that

---

[161] Ibid., 47.

helped explain the history of the island when they left. None of these weapons and artifacts have been recovered.

The local Wawonii people today have pride in their island, but the history is not clear. While Buton and Ternate did usually have some type of authority over the island for hundreds of years, it seems evident that the actual inhabitants of the island probably came from mainland Sulawesi. The language of Wawonii is similar to that of Tolaki on the mainland, and they share a special food called sago paste. Sago is a type of palm tree, and inside the tree is a soft pith which is chipped out; water is run through the chips to extract the starch, which is collected at the end of a trough with a sieve. The collected starch is then drained and dried, becoming sago flour. Later, at home, the flour is turned into a viscous, clear, jelly-like substance by dousing the starch with boiling water and stirring. This food is jokingly said to have a consistency like glue (with some truth to it). This is hard to find on the island of Buton and Muna, but is prevalent on mainland Sulawesi among the Tolaki. When I visited Wawonii and asked about it, they already had a big bowl of it in the house and were happy to eat it together for dinner. They were surprised I asked about it, because it is usually not in high demand. It is rarely sold in restaurants, and is usually only found in local homes. It is served in a little bit of a fish soup, and the crazy thing about eating it is that it is not supposed to be chewed (which is almost impossible anyway). This food is immediately swallowed when put in your mouth, so it is important to have bite-sized pieces so you don't choke when it is sliding down your throat. It is served from a bowl with two sticks that are twirled together to get a ball of it like you would a bowl of taffy. This food is starting to be a thing of the past because after a plateful of this we went ahead and had some rice to eat with our fish and vegetables. I also had sago paste with some Tolaki people on mainland Sulawesi and it was served with an assortment of fish and vegetables all cooked a certain way, and mixed together with the sago paste. This style of eating it was very good. On the other islands of Buton, the staple food was made from cassava for most of the twentieth century, but in most households rice has now taken over.

There are also a large number of Bajo on the island, especially in the city of Langgara, which is the connecting port with Kendari. Bajo can also be seen on the island of Saponda and on the coast of mainland Sulawesi, which are both clearly visible on the ferry ride to Wawonii. The language on Wawonii is closely related to that of the Kulisusu on north Buton, the peoples on nearby mainland Sulawesi, and even on the island of Kabaena.[162]

H. **Bajo** – These people are always identified with the sea and it is intertwined into every aspect of their culture. They are often referred to as the Bajau or Sama people throughout Malaysia and the Philippines, and the language of the Bajo in Southeast Sulawesi is definitely in the same language family, but it is clearly a different dialect and would be difficult at best for Bajau from other countries to understand. The Bajo language throughout Indonesia is very similar. There are also some Bajo in South Sulawesi, around the island of Banggai in Central Sulawesi, and on the west side of the province of Gorontalo, but the majority of the Bajo in Sulawesi can be found in Southeast Sulawesi. Within Southeast Sulawesi they are not isolated in one or two locations, but are spread out in villages along the coasts of the province.[163]

The Bajo live in houses that are built over the water. Some of them live just off of the coast or even connected to the coast, while some off the northwest coast of Muna can live as far as a kilometer from dry land. These villages have been built on the sea with houses on stilts that are on top of a foundation of rocks from the sea that have been piled up. They are one of the more unique groups of people in the area. There have been attempts

---

[162] Ibid., 1.
[163] David Mead and Myung-young Lee, *Mapping Indonesian Bajau Communities in Sulawesi* (SIL International, 2007).

to resettle the Bajo on land so they have closer ties with the surrounding communities and better access to schools.[164]

Though the Bajo could be viewed as one of the people that
have come to Southeast Sulawesi like those in the transmigration chapter, I think they have more roots here than the others.
They definitely form communities, and are usually only seen
separated from each other as a result of marriage to one of the
land dwelling people groups of Buton. When speaking with the
old men (and women) about the history of the Bajo in Southeast
Sulawesi, each village I visited and questioned pointed to a "La
Ode" or "Wa Ode" (descendants of the sultan) that was married
to or was the one responsible for founding the Bajo villages. As
the Bajo are generally somewhat marginalized wherever they
dwell, they usually try to identify themselves with some type
of local source of power and legitimacy in the area. It could be
that this tie with the sultanate's family is true, but how they got
linked in with the family of the Butonese sultanate is confusing.
The old men also frequently point to their ultimate origin being
from Johor, Malaysia, as descendants of the powerful sultanate
that used to rule there. Out in the Wakatobi islands everyone
says that the first Bajo community was in Mantigola on the west
side of Kaledupa, while on Buton they usually point to Pasarwajo. One of the old men in a Bajo community southeast of
Pasarwajo said they are also sometimes referred to as the Wajo,
because other stories claim that they originated from the Bugis
people of Wajoq in South Sulawesi.

There are two prominent places in Buton that have the name
Wajo, and the stories of how they came to have those names
are interesting. Wajo is the name of a sub-district in the city
of Bau-Bau, just below the hill of the fortress. Several people
believe that the ocean used to cover most of the present-day city
of Bau-Bau and bump up against the hill on which the fortress
is currently built. Along the same lines of this theory, one Bajo
old man that I spoke to (who had a La Ode father) said that there

---

[164] Bakker, 134.

used to be a Bajo community that lived in this area of Wajo, and their houses were built on the sea. This area is currently solely covered by land and is a few kilometers from the ocean.

The other story of Wajo concerns the area of Pasarwajo. *Pasar* means "market" in Indonesian and there apparently used to be a market or trade that was conducted between the hill dwellers of southeast Buton (probably Cia-Cia) and the sea-dwelling Bajo. The Bajo would bring their fish onto the land and put them in a specific place and take a fair amount of land crops in trade. The hill dwellers would bring some of their crops and take some of the fish the Bajo brought. The people did not meet; it was just on the honor system to take a fair amount for what you brought. This eventually evolved into a normal market, and the city of Pasarwajo was eventually born. So regardless of what the story is of where the Bajo came from, they are very intertwined in the history of the people of Buton, and appear to identify strongly with the sultanate of the past.

There are also many Bajo that can be found on the southeast peninsula of mainland Sulawesi. A trip among these Bajo is recorded by a British man that was trying to find a connection between the Bajo people throughout Southeast Asia. The author was searching for Bajo that still live on boats and spend some time around *Teluk Dalam* (Deep Bay), a few hours north of Kendari. The Bajo in this area are very similar in language and history to those throughout the islands of Southeast Sulawesi.[165]

[165] Sebastian Hope, *Outcasts of the Islands: The Sea Gypsies of South East Asia* (London: HarperCollins, 2001), 204-238.

VII
BELIEFS AND LEGENDS

One of the five tenants (*Pancasila*) that the nation of Indonesia is built on is "Belief in One God." As a country that is so spread out with thousands of islands, getting everyone on the same page for just about anything is a challenge. There were many (and still are) tribes and villages in the more remote parts of Kalimantan and West Papua that still held to their animist roots, so had trouble reporting in which monotheistic religion they believed. An allowance was made for people to report their religion as "other" and not one of the larger world religions. So there has been some tolerance for those adhering to local tribal beliefs. It is also interesting that Buddhism and Hinduism, the religions that dominated the ancient kingdoms of the archipelago, have been officially recognized as religions in accordance with the monotheistic criteria. Buddhism in the strict sense does not really believe in a personal God, and Hinduism believes in thousands of gods. So this "One God" seems like it can also include "One Ultimate Power," such as the ultimate power source that forms the center of Hinduism and Buddhism. This can also be seen in animism, though prayer and offerings are usually made to ancestors through special rock formations or places of past significance. This feeling of oneness or the presence of non-personal powers can still be seen throughout the islands, though there is often a veneer and daily practice of one of the major monotheistic religions of the world, Islam or Christianity (no significant Jewish presence in Indonesia).

Islam dominates the region officially, though it is apparent that there is a Hindu/Buddhist and Animist foundation for many of the traditions they still practice. But make no mistake about it, the daily call to prayer can still be heard throughout the islands, and people still know that they are supposed to pray at the mosque at certain times throughout the day, celebrate certain holidays, refrain from pork, and generally follow what they have been taught about Islam in the mosque. Though not as prevalent, among the islands of Buton there are some Christian communities, most notably some Catholic villages on the island of Muna. There is also one Protestant community originally from Muna that now lives in Ambon and on Buton. There are many more churches than this in and around the cities of Bau-Bau and Raha but their members are primarily composed of people not native to Buton and they primarily minister to people living in the area from Christian cultures outside of Southeast Sulawesi (Toraja, Minahasa, Ambon, Chinese, Flores, Kupang, etc.). Many of the people in these churches have been born and raised in Buton, and may have been here for generations, but for the most part the only people from indigenous people groups that attend these churches have been converted through marriage.

The Protestant Church actually entered mainland Southeast Sulawesi via the island of Buton. As a result of the explanding colonial rule the number of predominantly Protestant civil servants and military personnel grew rapidly, especially after 1906 when the pacification of Southeast Sulawesi was intensified. Until the outbreak of World War II in Southeast Sulawesi there existed four congregations of the Protestant Church, in Kendari and Kolaka on the mainland, in Bau-Bau on Buton (1940: 150 members), and in Raha on Muna. These congregations were too small to have their own minister, though each of them was visited once or twice a year by a minister from Makassar, except Raha which was too difficult to reach. Usually a member of the local church council would lead Sunday services as well as take charge of the other congregational duties. On the eve of the Japanese invasion in 1942 the total number of members in the Protestant church, on the mainland and in the islands, was about 700. The vast majority of these were civil servants or employees of companies who originated from culturally Christian islands of Indonesia.[166]

The indigenous people of Buton are usually very mystical about their beliefs. There are quite a few similar stories about belief that tend to surface regardless of what island you happen to be on in greater Buton. A couple of the things that keep coming up throughout these islands are the beliefs that ships ran aground in the past and became rock hills that can still be seen today, that all the histories of the different villages and peoples is tied in some way with the family or power of the past Butonese sultanate, and that in the ocean or water there are giant anchors, gold items, and large squid or ocean creatures. There are also stories, or beliefs, about the future that have some type of origin in the past, whether that be prophecy or just stories that have been passed down from generation to generation. One of these is a positive relationship with people of "white skin" and that people of all nations will one day gather on Buton.

This affinity and willingness to work with Westerners on the part of Buton can even be seen today in the stories and beliefs among some of the villages in the heart and southern parts of Buton. They have been told by their forefathers that there is a connection with the people of "white skin" and that this relationship is tied with some type of blessing in the future. It is also said that the nations of the world will gather in Buton in the future for some reason that is not altogether clear right now. Part of this stems from the belief that some hold that Buton is considered to be the center of the world. This view may have been altered by some that want to be good Muslims, such as the hole in the earth in the center of the keraton where it is believed that one can hear the call to prayer in Mecca if you listen close enough. Though it seems the culture and old stories of Buton give people their identity and pride here, Islam has definitely had a major influence.

As with most places in Indonesia, Muslim traders on ships first brought Islam to the island. The first place it was supposed to have landed is Burangasi, in southern Buton in the district of Sampolawa.[167] The process of Islamization in Buton was slow, and a large part of the Islam was mystical, not formal and legal, and some even continued to believe in reincarnation in Buton. So in the 1960's there were only a few mosques among the islands because of feudalism. The elite were closer to Islam than the lower people.[168] Islam has spread out through the villages today, but one does get the sense that those in the larger city of Bau-Bau are more concerned with it than those in the villages. While 99% of the peoples of Buton identify themselves as Muslims on their government identification card, there is some interesting history about how some of these people became Christians in the past.

The only churches of native Butonese people were started on Muna. In 1925 the nominal Catholic governor of Makassar refused permission to Catholic missionaries to live in Muna, because he believed that any attempt to convert those in the sultanate would cause serious problems. This was in spite of the advice to the governor, from A.J.L. Couvreur, the Assistant Resident of Buton (Dutch representative), that "the spread of Christianity should be done carefully, as one of the means most effective to free areas like this from being closed. While at the same time Islam, with its tight conservatism, is forming a stumbling block for the progressive development of the residents." Couvreur also observed that the highest class of *Laode* (in Bu-

---

[167] Abdul Mulku Zahari, *Islam di Buton: Sejarah & Perkembangannya* (Unpublished manuscript, Wolio Museum, Bau-Bau, 1982), 51.

[168] Karel Steenbrink, *The Spectacular Growth of a Self-Confident Minority 1903-1942,* vol. 2 in series "Catholics in Indonesia 1808-1942: A Documented History" (KITLV Press, 2006), 472.

ton), mostly Bugis that came to Buton, had power over half the residents that were still *kafir* (not Islam), which were called *Papara*, and were slaves at that time. Under the influence of *Laode* many *Papara* went to Islam. The prefect Walter Panis from Manado wrote that Father Kapell had already talked with the Sultan of Buton about missionaries coming, and the sultan said "religion is like goods for sale which can be traded freely in the market." Panis criticized the Assistant Resident of Buton which stirred up local leaders to protest against missionaries coming. Panis also got the impression that Couvreur personally also gave more sympathy to Islam than the Catholic Mission.[169] In spite of these mixed opinions of whether Catholicism would be good for Buton, Catholic churches were started, the details of which are in the Muna section that follows.

The only indigenous Protestant church that is currently on the islands of Buton was started after a Christian & Missionary Alliance (CMA) missionary to Makassar, Robert Alexander Jaffray, trained some Torajanese men to go to Muna. They started a church in Unchume (Oon-CHEW-may), which is on the east coast of Muna right across from the Butonese village of Palabusa, near where the Strait of Buton becomes the narrowest. The story goes that the first that believed were among the local children, who in turn went and told their parents. This led to a great number of people becoming believers. This was in the 1930's and after a number of people accepted Christ they were concerned about how they would be received by their Muslim neighbors (beliefs, eating pork, etc.) so they decided to move to a portion of land that was offered to them across the strait on the island of Buton, known as Batu Sori. This isolated little village was hit by a sort of tsunami caused after a large rock face dropped in the ocean from neighboring Muna. This wave destroyed the village, though thankfully no one was hurt because they had moved inland after a similar wave scare the previous day. They were offered some options by the government about

---

[169] Ibid., 473.

where to move, and they spontaneously decided to move to the city of Ambon in the Malukus, where this community still lives today in a hilly part of the city near the airport, with the same name of Batu Sori. The CMA associated churches are known as "Kemah Injil" (Gospel Tabernacle) in Indonesia and this church that started in Muna and moved to Batu Sori was the first on Buton. There was eventually another church farther east on Buton near the asphalt mine of Kabongka, but the only one that is still left today is one north of Pasarwajo in Tembe. It was started in the 1970's and has a little Christian community that lives around it. There is also a small group of believers with a few families that came from the original Batu Sori area but that now live around Liabuku, north of Bau-Bau.

The other churches on Buton and Muna are the Protestant Church of Southeast Sulawesi (German influence, many Torajanese), the Protestant Church of Western Indonesia (originally formed to support Minahasa and Torajanese Christians living abroad), Pentecostal Church of Indonesia (from America and primarily Chinese), along with Bethany Church and Bethel Church (started by the Church of God in America, and eventually split into two denominations, primarily Chinese), along with Word of God Christian Church (primarily Minahasa from Manado, North Sulawesi). There may also be followers of Isa Al Masih that worship together with other believers in their homes in a way consistent with the cultural Muslim context in which they were raised and that is all around them. They are Christian in that their belief system is in accordance with the teachings of the Bible about Christ and that the reference to Islam is only in regard to cultural characteristics such as dress, Arabic expressions, etc.

Of the numerous traditional customs and outworkings of belief already being practiced when Islam entered Buton, some continued under a veneer of Islam, while others ceased. There is a sense of apathy towards Islam in some of the more remote regions of Buton, as they value more the older traditions of their ancestors. These older beliefs about powerful rocks or places of prayer or offerings are usually topics reserved for the "old men" to speak about. Even "saying something wrong" can bring some type of wrath on people, so people do not speak freely of these mystic and mysterious things, resulting in secrecy. I have heard stories of how of people "spoke wrongly" when on ships in the past that ended up with the ship being sunk by a giant sea creature. So when speaking of some things I guess it is important to guard your tongue.

Some of the customs that ceased because they were in contradiction to Islam include the belief that a person's spirit was reincarnated when they died and that it did not go to another realm, but stayed on the earth. This belief in reincarnation is still held by some.[170] Supposedly when a person died all of the person's belongings used to be thrown in the ocean to cleanse something. In the past, little statues or idols were sometimes worshipped or used as objects of worship. Setting food out in front of your house to appease or feed the spirits was another practice that could be found formerly in Buton. It is not clear whether a stronger application of Islamic principles forced these practices to cease, or whether they were not very important to the people. It is also possible that they are still believed and practiced today, but in less visible ways.

It is also believed throughout Buton (and Indonesia, even Asia) that certain things bring virility and fertility when they are eaten. Among these include anoa (wild, small cow-like horned animals in Sulawesi), wild honey, and duck eggs. Everyone is looking for some type of secret drug, medicine, or herb that will make them stronger, more fertile, or be desired by those of the opposite sex. When I have been hiking in the jungle with locals they usually ask if I take some medicine to be able to walk faster. The answer to good fitness is basically exercising and eating right, but there isn't much of a culture of exercising here and food choices are usual made on the basis of sustaining the

---

[170] Schoorl, "Reincarnation," 103-134.

family and tasting sweet to the kids; "health food" is not really available here. So people are usually looking for some type of secret potion to give them power and strength.

I have even heard that there are also special prayers that can be prayed, as well as praying to certain saints or ancestors to solve all types of problems and fulfill all types of desires. The way that people point out special places of prayer or worship that the old men used in the past shows that this was around before Islam, but now in many places these places of prayer are tied with Islam. There have also been several people that have told me about special Islamic prayers which can forgive sin, and special saints (like Joseph the son of Jacob) to whom one can pray in order to be desired by the opposite sex (usually young men or kids pray this one). On Java the powerful, or holy grave sites are of the nine men that are said to have initially brought Islam to Indonesia, but on Buton the holy grave sites are those of the important local ancestors. What is said during these times of prayer seems to be secret and mysterious, too.

A. **Wolio** – Islam can most readily be seen in Bau-Bau, but it is mixed with several local beliefs. The most prevalent is the presence of *haro'a* at almost all of the Islamic holiday celebrations. *Haro'a* seems to have been a ceremony used to call up ancestors from the dead and obtain guidance from them. I have recently been told that it is a commemoration of heroes that have died and did not receive the proper ceremony at their death or burial. So this *haro'a* may also be a ceremony that prepared someone for death or made things right with the ancestors. The ceremony involves having a man read prayers from the Al Quran or other Islamic related source in Arabic, so that no one can really understand. In front of the man there is a brass stand holding food that is covered (these are seen in all ceremonies where eating is involved). There is also a little tray brought out that usually has some type of box covered in a white piece of cloth as well as a very small little brass container. At the end of the ceremony incense is always burned, and the man who led the ceremony is usually paid discreetly. This is the clearest example of local beliefs being mixed with Islam. This can also be called *baca doa* which means to "read prayers" and refers to the time spent reading or reciting from the Al Quran.

There are also several other examples of how people do not hold to the strict teachings of Islam. Many people claim that during the month of Ramadan fasting for three days is the same as 30 days, so they opt for the shorter. How is someone supposed to work and get anything done if they are fasting for 30 days? Although this very un-Islamic teaching is often practiced, most people would probably condemn it, if you pressed them.

There are many stories of magic, secret books, etc. surrounding this city in the water. Near the primary recreational beach near Bau-Bau, Nirvana beach, there are quite a few families that live, fish, and harvest seaweed. One of the older men that lives there believes that there is a village of people, that resemble humans, that live under the ocean. This story is similar to that of an Atlantis that has not been discovered yet, but is believed to exist by some. There is also a cave of brackish water near Nirvana beach in which ancient ceramic pottery can be found. After diving in this cave several times I was peppered with questions about whether I saw furniture or other signs of human life beneath the water. They also asked if I saw a large, golden shrimp. This belief in underwater communities of people is found in cultures throughout the world.[171]

Something I have heard a few times is about the righteousness and the power of the old men and ancestors of the past. It is said that the people of Buton used to be feared because they could cause a person to die with their words. The reason that they had such powers was because of their righteousness and purity. There was also a story going around that in order to stop the

[171] F. Morvan, *Legends of the Sea* (New York: Crescent Books, 1980), 113-116.

Lapindo mud flow[172] in East Java, there was a traditional leader in the area that said if there were thirty human heads brought from the outer islands they could be thrown in the hole to stop the mud flow. The fact that these sacrifices had to be people from the outer islands upholds some type of sense that people in Buton or the more remote places are more pure or holy and would be accepted as sacrifices. I usually don't hear anyone talking about their righteousness, but there is a sense that the people of Buton are somewhat unspoiled, especially those in the past. Like the idea of the "noble savage," that remote people throughout the world would continue to live their pure, organic, and eco-friendly existence if we would just leave them alone. We all know this isn't really true, because all people have short-comings and problems.

Among the people of Buton there are several customs that have continued, maybe because they were not seen as a threat to the fundamental beliefs of Islam. One of these is the feeding of a pregnant woman during the seventh month of her pregnancy. Also the cutting of a child's hair for the first time, which is now included with the Islamic practice of Aqiqah. Also when a child takes his first steps he is immediately turned to face the east so he won't be bothered by the spirits. Circumcision was also practiced and later given Islamic characteristics. The practice of women being isolated in their house from 1 to 7 days with other women to learn the secrets of being a good wife is also practiced (*Posuo*). Young children also take part in a ceremony (*dole-dole*) where a food offering is put together and the children are swung back and forth over it. After this they are wrapped in banana leaves and rocked back and forth. You may also be invited to parties (*syukuran*) just out of thankfulness to God for a person's recent purchase of a house or motorcycle. Wedding parties also happen quite frequently and are interesting cultural events. The bride and groom are always dressed in gold and

---

[172] Adianto P. Simamora, "Four years on, victims of Lapindo mudflow still in limbo," The Jakarta Post, May 30, 2010.

flashy outfits that look to have some type of Hindu or Indian origin. The traditional rules and customs regarding weddings are full of meaning and are still practiced today.[173] Even with all this local flavor, it seems that the Wolio consider themselves as guardians of Islam in the area to a certain extent because of their former authority in the sultanate.

B. **Cia-Cia** – The traditional beliefs of the Cia-Cia are generally among the strongest of the peoples in the area. It may be because many of them still live in more rural areas, but it could also be that the old men or forefathers among this people put an extra emphasis on the traditional law (*adat*) and prophecies. These people actively look for fulfillment of prophecies and stories of their past leaders. Their communities are vibrant with improvisation and local leadership giving direction in the way that decisions are made and things are done. In some villages there are stories passed down by their spiritual leaders about people that will come and bring important news that will change everything. They seem to be a little more comfortable than other peoples with the fact that their traditions came from a Hindu/Buddhist/Animist background (before Islam entered Indonesia), but they still identify themselves as Muslims officially.

Some Cia-Cia believe that their language is the language of heaven, that it is the language that God speaks. Even if it is true that God can speak Cia-Cia, it is debatable whether this is His language of choice. There is a real ethnocentric feel from some people when speaking about the Cia-Cia, though they are not too proud to be friendly and are always excited about working with others (especially Westerners).

The village of Lapandewa is known for its diligent adherence to the customary laws and traditions of its forefathers, and the name of their village reflects this. "Lapandewa" means "men

---

[173] Abdul Mulku Zahari, ed., *Adat dan Upacara Perkawinan Wolio* (Jakarta: Departemen Pendidikan dan Kebudayaan, Proyek Penerbitan Buku Sastra Indonesia dan Daerah, 1981).

that are brave enough to protect their culture." Some of the traditions and stories of Lapandewa are shared in many ways with the villages of Wasuamba and Labuandiri in the central jungles. While these two villages have a different language than Cia-Cia (closer to Muna), their location inland and adherence to the old teachings brings them together. There is definitely a general commonality among the peoples on the island of Buton, especially the Muna speakers in central Buton, the Cia-Cia, and the Wolio that have not been too modernized by living in the most modern city among the Butonese, Bau-Bau.

In the village of Lapandewa, which is similar to other villages throughout Buton, there are a couple of places that are considered sacred where offerings are still presented. These offerings are usually tied with the desire to receive an abundant and successful harvest. The centerpiece of these offerings and prayers is the *ombo*, which is a rock that is narrow and about four feet tall. It was a place where ancestors prayed, so now the people still pray there, or at least an older man that is a representative of the people prays there during the harvest festivals. He says a prayer that no one can really hear or understand, but he is trusted to say the right thing. The other sacred places in the center of the village are the graves of what are believed to be the first people that founded Lapandewa. It looks like an old rock formation that has taken a form that could possibly be two graves, and it is said to hold the remains of the man Labukuturendi and his wife Wahankami (who was the child of Lankaili-ili). Labukuturendi is supposed to have come from the area of Pasarwajo and met Wahankami, who was the daughter of a well-known man in the area, Lankaili-ili. Whether this is accurate or not, these names still live on and the place considered to be their graves is still visited and food and coconuts are still placed on it. The other sacred place in the village is the largest tree still standing, and people go there to place offerings tied with the harvest.

If it is around one of the harvest times (there are three a year) one can also see or take part in a *maa'taa* or *maa'cia* which is a type of feast where everyone has a large, covered, brass or rattan stand of food in front of them to eat and includes other rituals such as walking around the tent a few times carrying certain items and saying a few special words. These eating events can also include sessions of *picat silat* or *mengaruh* where two men dressed in traditional garb use their knives, along with grunting and dancing movements, and lunge at each other as if to stab the opponent. Most of the time no one gets hurt and these events are a representation of how these communities resisted invasion in the past.

As in Java, there is the belief that at some point in time, and even now, there are certain people that can do these special types of dances or martial arts in a way that can truly manifest displays of invisible power. There are stories here and throughout Indonesia of how there are some people that cannot be stabbed or harmed by knives. Though they are stabbed, or even swallow knife and sword blades, there is no blood.

C. **Kulisusu** – These people almost all profess Islam, too, but they seem to lean more in line with the Cia-Cia when it comes to their daily lives and how Islam weighs up against the beliefs and practices of their ancestors. In Ereke, there were some mosques present and some being built, but I do not think I ever heard a call to prayer blaring loudly. There was not a real strong presence of people going to pray, and I was told that many of the older beliefs were still strong and practiced, especially out in the villages. There are definitely strong ties among all the people of Buton, but with those in Ereke they also seem to have strong ties with their neighbors up north, such as Kendari, Wawonii, and even Ternate.

In the hard to reach district of West Kulisusu in North Buton there are many transmigration communities of Javanese, Balinese, and even those from the islands east of Bali and Lombok. In these areas there are many Hindus and Christians. So the background of these people is varied and may have some impact

on the beliefs of the local people. The same situation with transmigration communities can be found in central Buton around
Lasalimu, but throughout that area there are still several villages
that hold as strongly to their traditional beliefs as anywhere else
on the island. Probably among the mountains of North Buton
there is some Islam present, but the traditional beliefs hold the
greatest power. Throughout the land of the Kulisusu the *haro'a*
ceremony is also conducted on Islamic occasions just as they do
in Bau-Bau among the Wolio.

According to David Mead, the Kulisusu people celebrate
haroa'ano, a ceremonial meal associated with Muslim holy/
festival days. In addition, there are household feasts called *pe-
kocupaano sangia* (with stem *kocupa*, which are rice cooked in
packets plaited from coconut leaves, Indonesian *ketupat*) usually held in February. Not only are rice packets set out on trays
(which later the people eat), but also four rice packets are hung
from the rafters during the entire meal, along with four fronds
of immature coconut leaves (Indonesian *gaba-gaba*). This event
also consists of prayers, pouring out water, and pouring out coconut water.

D. **Muna** – The religion of Muna is primarily Islam, but
there are Hindu and Animistic roots similar to the other islands
in the region, along with previous efforts by Europeans to plant
Christian communities, primarily Catholic, on the island. Apart
from the major religions that are present, the local beliefs of
these people are similar to those in the surrounding islands. Another thing to note is that the people that speak each of the various dialects of this language live on a variety of different islands
and therefore have many connections with the traditions of the
islands they live on, whether it be Buton, Muna, or any of the
other smaller islands that they inhabit.

On the island of Muna there are several places that are considered sacred, just as on the other islands. *Bakialu munaente*

is supposed to be some type of tourist site or sacred place.[174] In Wakumoro, which is near the center of the island of Buton, there is a place that is believed to be where the past kings used to bathe. There is also a cultural event that takes place there every year.

At certain places on Muna offerings of food (topped by a white flag to attract spirits' attention) are made regularly. Every year in mid- to late January, during the lull in the rainy season when the planting of the corn takes place, a week-long ritual happens, called *tolak bela*, which means "warding off disaster." The village head, consulting with people, decides the exact date every year. It helps avert disasters like epidemics and boats overturning and proposes to ensure an abundant harvest. With the boys on one side, and girls on the other, they recite formulaic quatrains spur of the moment (*pantun*) to show off their wit. Then there are kick-fights between the young men. At harvest time, in late August and early September, many places on Muna hold festivals. There are dances where guests must participate, after being pulled out of the crowd by a pair of lovely ladies. Food is cooked overnight on hot stones in a covered pit. Bamboo tubes filled with cassava paste and red sugar are a local specialty. The harvest festival is held at or close to the time of the full moon, and lasts from one to three days.[175]

Another cultural event unique to Muna is horse fighting. Horsefighting is easiest to arrange at Latugo village, which is about 24k (15 mi) from the city of Raha. It will take a day for them to get the horses and set up the arrangements. A wide field is used where two groups of mares are shown to each stallion to "put them in the mood." Then with ropes around their necks the two stallions are introduced to each other. They rear up and fight for supremacy of the passive mares with the crowd cheering them on. Eventually one runs off to the jeers of the audience. Another challenger is brought in. They do bite and kick but

[174] Couvreur.
[175] Muller, "Buton," 216.

damage is usually not serious. If it gets too rough the horses are pulled apart. These fights were once performed to celebrate the return of victorious war parties with human head trophies. They were also done at festivals among the aristocracy, like weddings, first hair cuts, 40 days after birth, etc. There is also usually a lady jockey that rides on pillows as well as men demonstrating deer hunting with a machete.[176] Just as in Buton there were many traditional rituals and ceremonies conducted in the past, some of which remain, and some of which have disappeared. You will notice many similarities to the practices in Buton among the Muna.[177]

One of the differences between the two is that there are Catholic communities on Muna that have been there a long time. The direct reason for an initial request for missionaries from the Catholics was that there were 20-40 pearl divers from the Philippines along with lumberjacks from Flores that were living in Raha. A lumberjack from Flores, David Salmon Pella, played a pivotal role in starting the Catholic community on Muna. He may have been originally from the island of Rote, then moved and was educated in Flores. Mr. Pella was a foreman for the locals working for the lumber company *Vejahoma*. He would occasionally get Catholics together at his house. In 1912 a priest was invited to baptize his son, Salomon Pella, which was the first name in the Raha baptism book. There were also other children and adults baptized on this visit. *Vejahoma* shifted to the government forestry department in the late 1920's, and Mr. Pella received a wide area of land in Raha as a result of the transition. He arranged for the old company buildings to be sold to the Catholics, which became a parish and church for the coming of the first permanent missionaries in April 1930. Mr. Pella later died in Raha in 1960. [178]

Catholics then opened four schools in villages in 1930 but

[176] Ibid., 217.
[177] Couvreur.
[178] Steenbrink, 474.

Islam in Muna proved strong. On February 15, 1932, the head of Rumbia (Moronene area on the Sulawesi mainland), Simon Badaru, was baptized with 20 families of his clan. This was the first group of more or less 'local' Catholics on Muna. Another small group that accepted Catholicism in the mid-1930's were a non-Muslim indigenous clan in the region of South Muna, Wale-Ale and Lolibu.[179] After the group from Rumbia was baptized, Mr. Badaru was called to talk to the Sultan of Buton about this apostasy and he made an oath that this would not affect his obedience to the sultanate. Because the Butonese were generally also faithful to non-Islamic practices it could be compared to *abangan* in Java, which really does not follow formal Islam. These Moronene were in Lamanu, 15 km from the new post in Lasihau, central Muna. Catholicism moved very slowly. Other than the Moronene people, those from the Philippines, Flores, and the Chinese in Raha made up the majority of the Catholics. In the early years, very few members of the Catholic community were ethnically Muna people.[180]

A breakthrough did come on Muna after a miraculous event in October 1940. In the beginning of that month one of the local leaders, La Dee, was severly wounded by a water buffalo. His son stayed at that time in the parish house in Raha. When this boy heard the news he came to Wale-Ale together with a doctor and the priest. They brought La Dee to the Raha hospital where a nun nursed him and asked him whether he wanted to be baptized. Under the condition that he would be buried in Wale-Ale, this man was baptized as Lambertus La Dee on October 15, 1940. A few days later he died and was buried with a Catholic ritual in Wale-Ale. For the pagan population it was a curious but impressive ceremony. During this burial ceremony a water buffalo emerged from the bushes. While all the people ran away, the water buffalo came to a standstill in front of the grave and bowed his head. After that he disappeared. The conversion of

[179] Aritonang, 485.
[180] Steenbrink, 475.

132 THE MYSTERIES OF THE ISLANDS OF BUTON

La Dee and the events at the burial motivated some of the inhabitants of Wale-Ale to become Catholic. Between July 1, 1941 and the beginning of the Japanese occupation in April 1942, 120 people were baptized in Wale-Ale.[181]

One famous member of the Muna Catholic community was Gerardus La Mbaki, born in 1922, from Lolibu. He was educated in Wale-Ale. Though he was from an orthodox Muslim family, he was pulled to Catholicism. After primary school he became a candidate for the priesthood in Raha. During the Japanese occupation in 1942 he became the organizer for the Catholics with David Pella. In 1939 there were 413 Catholics (32 from Europe and China, 215 from Toraja). Then in 1990 the numbers reached 8,000.[182] Catholics were successful in spreading Catholicism on the island of Muna in two villages especially, Lakapera and Lolibu, which are still known as Catholic communities today. In 1953 La Mbaki moved to Lolibu, and started a Catholic community which already had 1,695 members in 1965. In the early 1960's the young Belgian missionary M. Mingneau started an agricultural project in Lakapera where the marshland was drained and each family was given 2 hectares of land to grow cashews, which was very successful. In Muna the Catholics counted some 4,000 members in 2001.[183] At one point an organization was established in Makassar called "Celebes Missie Steunfords," which gave financial support to missionaries in Muna.[184] The story of the Catholics on Muna is included because very few know of this story. Most live according to Islam and their local customs because it is the most visible and prevalent way to live among these islands.

The villages that hike to Mt. Siontapina and meet with their ancestors every year speak one of the dialects of Muna. This is an example of the far reach of the Muna language, though in

[181] Aritonang, 486.
[182] Steenbrink, 476.
[183] Aritonang, 486.
[184] Steenbrink, 463.

many cases the Muna speakers form unique communities on the different islands that have their own traditions and beliefs. It is clear that the annual meeting on Mt. Siontapina revolves around animistic practices that still play a very important role in the lives of the people involved.

E. **Wakatobi** – This is the most untouched district in the province, religiously speaking, and I guess in every other way, too. There are no known churches throughout these islands nor Hindus or Buddhists. Even in the official data and statistic book of the district it says that there are no churches or temples, only mosques. There are several Non-Governmental Organizations (NGO's) that are working or have been working with the coral reefs and eco-tourism. The people are Muslim if you ask them their religion, but especially on the lesser developed islands there is probably more of a leaning to beliefs passed down by their ancestors. One exception is the city of Wanci, which does have a strong Islamic tradition, maybe because it was the out-post of the former sultanate of Buton among these islands and felt the same responsibility as Bau-Bau in keeping people in line with the religion of the sultanate. Even with this reputation of adherence to Islam, there is still much that is believed that does not fall in line with traditional Islamic belief.

The Tukang Besi are nearly 100% Muslim and practice their faith fervently, while incorporating many elements of the pre-Islamic beliefs that are common in the area. These animistic be-liefs take the form of offerings to male and female spirit shrines in certain locations, and the widespread use of shamanism to guarantee success in agriculture or fishing. A detailed spirit world is accepted as existing in the same space as the normally accessible world, but is inivisible and immaterial to most people; only those with the rare ability to see the other world are capable of manipulating it and its denizens. Many unusual landscape features, such as protruding rocks or unusual trees are thought to be inhabited by spirits that dwell there either voluntarily or through having been bound there against their will by another spirit or person. In the event of a storm in which such a tree collapses, the spirit is released, and can pose quite a problem to a nearby settlement or garden. Skilled shamans (*mia pande*, clever person in Tukang Besi) can interact with this world to combat the effects of spirits, and some become entwined with the beings of that world to the extent of marrying a spirit there, or retrieving weapons and wealth from some of the other world's cities.[185]

The top of Mt. Tindoi, near Wanci, is a sacred place full of spiritual significance for those that know and visit it on the island. You are not supposed to wear the color red when visiting this place, because the spirits do not like it. As you near the top you will pass a few graves. These graves are supposed to be those of the first man, woman, and child that ever came to this island. This is where they are supposed to be buried, but it may just be a place to commemorate them. At the top there is also a place that has been identified as a footprint of one of the ancestors. The print of the other foot is on the nearby island of Kampote (about 8 kilometers away). It is said that these footprints were made in one step. These stories of ancestors possessing superhuman abilities can be found in Buton also. Many believe that there was special knowledge that allowed the people of the old days to shave miles and hours off of their journeys. They could cover vast distances and teleport themselves with this special magic or knowledge.

This place at the top of Mt. Tindoi is also considered sacred to those that are preparing to make the Hajj to Mecca. Before taking this journey, the pilgrims will often spend a night or two up here praying (possibly to ancestors) and preparing themselves so they will have a safe journey. It is a neat place, one that I would recommend trying to find. There are nutmeg, clove and cashew trees along the path and it is one of the few places on the island where one can have a relatively cool walk in the

---

[185] Donohue, 5.

jungle. Visiting a sacred site of the island is also an interesting experience.

Of special note in Wakatobi are the people of Binongko. They are believed to have special powers, like the ability to pull glowing iron from the hearth without tongs, and to beat metal into machetes with their hands if necessary.[186] There is said to be a hole on the island that will grab your shadow and pull you in. There are also stories of the history of Binongko and of how there was a man that was seven forearms wide. Two people could sit on each of his shoulders. Also there was a man that was over three meters tall in the same family line. The current head of one of the communities in Popalia says he is descended from them, and he is a fairly big man, especially for an Indonesian. Two men that we met were introduced as being over 100 years old, but they were still out and about and looked healthy and one of them even chipper as he talked about when the Japanese were there during World War II. It is also said there is a *sarong* that can be seen from time to time in the jungle. The weaving of this *sarong* was started at the same time that the island of Binongko began and it is still being woven today. Sometimes it is meters long and other times it can fit in your hand. The one weaving it cannot be seen. So are the stories from Binongko. By just visiting Binongko and spending time with the local storytellers you can see that mysticism and beliefs in the powers at work around them are still very strong.

F. **Kabaena** – Kabaena is another place where great stories are told of the past and present. When trying to climb the mountains you will surely be warned of what colors you can and cannot wear (do not wear red) and advised to expect to see things that are abnormal. If you violate the ways you are supposed to act, there could be dangerous consequences such as a brushfire on the top of the mountain. It has happened before.

---

[186] Ibid., 4.

There is a local legend surrounding the mountain of Sabampolulu and the peak directly to its east, Kamonsope. There was
a water spring that could be found amidst the two mountains, but
it was actually the property of the one that guarded Mt. Kamonsope. This guardian was a woman, but she was very powerful
and stubborn. The guardian of neighboring Mt. Sabampolulu
was a man, and he continually asked for water from this spring,
but was continually refused by the woman. He eventually got
so frustrated at this woman that he tried to shoot her, but he tried
twice and did not hit her. She then shot him and he was immediately wounded. He nearly destroyed the top of the mountain,
which is why it looks like the shape of the chipped blade of an
adze that has hit something hard. The word "Saba" means "fall-
en off" referring to the chipped part of the mountain missing and
"Mpolulu" means "adze." So the name of the mountain refers to
the shape made by the v-shaped crevice at the top of it.[187]

The village secretary (and the one that guides everyone on
their hikes), whom I spoke to about climbing the tallest mountain on the island, Mt. Sabampolulu, said that he prefers children
come along on the hike. Children are said to possess the ability to see things that adults cannot. Maybe it is because they
are purer of mind and spirit, because they usually obtain some
blessing from what they see on the mountain. One time a child
went along on the hike and found a big jewel that no one else
saw. Other times they see spirits that no one else sees. Even
adults are said to hear and see strange things on the mountain.
Sometimes vehicles are heard passing at the top of it as well as
the appearance of random spirits. Goats are said to magically
appear, and if you catch one and do not let it go you probably
won't be able to find your way back down the mountain. It is
also said that in the past when pirates were raiding the highest
village on the island, Tongkeno, there were some men that fled
to the mountain with their gold and hid it somewhere on the

[187] La Ode Sidu, *Cerita Rakyat Dari Sulawesi Tenggara* (Jakarta: PT Gramedia Widiasarana, 1995), 6-8.

mountain. It has still not been discovered and is just up there waiting for someone pure of heart to find it.

There is something about mountains that causes people to think mystically and tell stories of the mysteries they hold. There are still large parts of this island that have rarely been explored because many of the people have a fear of spirits that are in the mountains and would rather stay in their village. In the highest village of Tongkeno I assumed that most of the people of the village would have a pretty good idea of the different mountains and how far each would be, but this is not the case. Most of them have no idea, because they have not been there. For the most part Indonesians don't explore for the fun of it, but they will often answer your questions as if they know the answer when in truth they have no idea. Those that have a good deal of experience hiking in the jungle have a healthy respect for what may be seen, but are not deterred by it. Those that rarely make the hike often request Islamic prayers of safety from some of the local old men before venturing into the mountains that are believed to be a gateway into a world of spirits and unexplained phenomenon. It was often repeated to me that "what you see you see," so just know that you have seen it and you do not need to say anything else about it.

No known indigenous churches are on the island, but each community usually has a mosque. This is interesting because the Moronene on the mainland do actually have an indigenous church, which is Dutch Reformed and similar to that of the Tolaki. There are also supposed to be some transmigration communities in the northern city of Pising that will have some Balinese Hindu as well as possibly some Christians among the Javanese and Moronene. The island itself is primarily made up of Muslims but is also one of the rare gems of an island that is remote and rich enough to still be full of stories about powers at work in the mountains and things you should and should not do when climbing them. The respect you are supposed to give and prayers you are supposed to offer when in sacred places have often been Islamicized as can be heard in the language of the prayers.

G. **Wawonii** – This island has its fair share of mystical beliefs known only to the old people. One story about the early days of Wawonii is that the top of the highest mountain was the only visible part, and over time as coral grew around this island, and the waters receded, the island became what it is today. There is supposedly a place in the jungle, near a mysterious field of tall grass, where the original village once stood that has mangrove trees growing around it. Because mangrove trees usually grow just near the coast, in some people's minds this supports the theory that the island used to be much smaller, but these trees are one of the places that are mystically difficult to find if you are really looking for them. If you go into the jungle trying to find them, you won't. If you go out walking in the jungle open to whatever is revealed to you, you may see the place. There is also supposed to be some type of tall post on top of one of the mountains that is a marker of the site of the center of the former kingdom on this island. This post is supposed to not rot.

Waworete was the name of this mysterious first village on the island. There is one man that lives in North Wawonii that has walked around the island for days looking for antiques, and he happened upon the site of the former village. He is a teacher in a city in East Wawonii, and knows the most about the history of the island. There are also reportedly water buffaloes that roam in the forest, and are very hard to find. One of these animals is supposed to be white, which is very rare and expensive (especially among the Toraja in South Sulawesi who sacrifice them at funerals).

Around the Tamburano waterfall there is a story about a boy and a girl that did not receive permission to marry from their parents. As a result they both committed suicide. I heard once that the boy and girl jumped together from the upper falls, and the other time I heard that the boy jumped from the upper and the girl jumped from the lower. Everyone agreed that they both committed suicide. People at the falls also say that there used to be a golden water buffalo that could be found in the area, but it cannot be found today. Supposedly if you have any type of gold with you the mist of the waterfall will find you, and make you wet, no matter how far away you are. The water spray will follow the gold.

.H. **Bajo** – The Bajo consider themselves Muslims, but have long been considered outsiders to the surrounding community and are even looked down upon because of their way of life. They have many stories and traditions tied with the sea and their dependence on it. The Bajo of Sulawesi link their mythic origins first to Luwuq, then to Gowa, and finally to Bone, reflecting, in the eastern Indonesian world, a parallel succession of political legitimacy.[188] The history of the Bajo is closely tied with that of the Bugis, and there is an ancient story that tells how a Buginese king's daughter was lost at sea and there was a group of people that were sent to find her. They were told that if they did not find her they were not to return. Since she was never found these people were doomed to eternally wander the sea. This is one of the origin stories of the Bajo in Sulawesi.[189] And just as people groups throughout Indonesia still give offerings to the Queen or King of the sea, the sea has an even larger part to play in the culture of this people that have always lived on the sea.

After talking to some of the leaders of a Bajo village off the Wakatobi island of Kaledupa, they said that they call the god of the sea *Mojango Dewa*. This god should be prayed to in a certain way, reciting mantras that only a few of the older people know. This older guy should recite the mantra for you before you go on a long journey. But if a storm happens to suddenly appear when you are out at sea you can go ahead and try to recite

[188] Clifford Sather, *The Bajau Laut: Adaptation, History, and Fate in a maritime fishing society of South-Eastern Sabah* (KL: Oxford University Press, 1997), 17.
[189] Hope.

a mantra or call out to the god yourself. It never hurts to try and get a little help any way you can get it.

Another interesting note has to do with the placenta after a woman has given birth. Throughout these islands (and maybe throughout Indonesia), the placenta is referred to as "the older sibling" when someone gives birth. Most of the other people groups put the placenta in a can or coconut husk and bury it, sometimes under a tree or bush so that the demons can't find it. The Bajo throw it in the sea, where it then lives, so that everyone believes they have a sibling in the sea. Sometimes they toss food in the sea to feed it, and do other things to show that they care for their "sibling." In some villages we heard that the Bajo people believe that they should protect the reef and the environment because it is the home of their "sibling." I think this sounded a lot like a belief reinterpreted by a conservationist in order to convince the Bajo to keep the environment in mind.

Many Bajo confirmed that in the past (and I'm sure in some places it still continues) if they catch a turtle they keep it in a cage under their house until it is time to thrown a party for their son when he reaches adolescence or is married. Then the turtle is eaten, to the horror of those trying to protect these animals of the sea.

VIII
STRUGGLING AND STRIVING, WAITING AND WATCHING

Life in Buton will continue to be a struggle for the families found throughout the islands, just as it is throughout Indonesia. No matter where you are or who you talk to, the thing that usually drives people each day is trying to make a living. For many this is taking care of the little plots of ground they own, and growing corn and cassava. For others it means going away for years at a time and looking for work on other islands and in other countries, later to return and live in relative luxury from the money they have made abroad.

There are many stories of what these people have experienced abroad, and as you travel through the villages the people are usually willing to tell them to you. To other ethnic groups and countries all of these people groups are generally known as Butonese, regardless of their specific people group among these islands. One exception is the Bajo people, as various forms of sea gypsies are prevalent among the islands of Southeast Asia and have their own identity. The Butonese are known as a hard people, and rightly so. They are usually involved in manual labor and can survive on very little in terms of comfort and material possessions.

As the Butonese come and go from other islands and other lands, more and more modern ways of thinking and working will surely work their way into these islands, as they have already been doing. The people want to make a living and understand that it usually takes steady work to make it happen. But work is not usually done as a means of fulfillment, but as a means to make money. This is probably generally true throughout the world, but especially in Indonesia if people in the villages come into a large amount of money somehow they will probably stop working until they spend it all. The people that I have met are usually pretty quick in spending the money they receive.

The politicians and leaders responsible for the development of these islands often seem to think of their job as a financial windfall, and not necessarily a way to help those they represent, though there are exceptions. There are government leaders throughout these islands, especially in Bau-Bau, Raha, and Wanci that are doing all they can to make this the next tourist destination. They see what has been accomplished in Bali, and think that Buton can one day be in the same position. They know that Buton is a beautiful place with much to discover. Several people have told me that the treasures of Buton (usually referring to oil, minerals, and other natural resources) will only be fully discovered when honest political leaders are in place.

They are also looking for the national government to help contribute to the development of this area by creating more government, which means more buildings, more jobs, and more money. There is currently a struggle going on for the reorganization of the province so that Buton becomes its own province, separate from Southeast Sulawesi. They are struggling against nature and their position in life, and striving for a place for their name in the world. With all this struggling and striving that goes on throughout the islands of Indonesia, there is also a very prevalent waiting and watching going on at the same time. People feel like Buton will have an important role in the world, one that will come at its proper time, and they are interested to see how this will come about.

They don't think like those in the West. The best way to describe it is mysticism, which is a way of acknowledging that there are powers at work bigger than us, and regardless of what we do they are going to play a large role in how our life unfolds. Most of us would agree with this, but most of us in the West probably think that we can have a great deal of influence on these factors through our own personal will and determination.

CONTROL

People in the West are generally under the illusion that we are in control of our lives. When it comes to everyday matters we usually decide what we are going to do each day, and many times what we do is based on a long-term commitment or decision we made in the past with continuing consequences. We have jobs, marriages, children, and ways of entertaining ourselves that usually fill up our time. But every once in a while something happens in life over which we have no control. We lose a job, have a car accident, get hurt, experience death, etc. Each time, if we reflect on them, we realize that many of the most memorable things in life were things that we could not control or that we did not plan at all. Those are often the things that stick with us, that determine the direction of our lives, but we usually just respond to them by making some type of decision about what we are going to do in response. Then we think we are in control again, until something else blindsides us. Even if we see it coming, we can't do anything about it.

These types of things happen to all of us, but in different ways and at different times. Maybe we were abused or made fun of as a child. Maybe it was through our parents; the genes they gave us or the way that they raised us. How coordinated we are at playing sports, or the ability we have to learn. Things like having a desire to learn or just a desire to have fun and play around. The people that we date and eventually marry are usually the result of a mystical process that cannot be forced no matter how hard we try. We have accidents that can scar or cripple us for life. We experience sickness, disease, the death of our loved ones, and eventually we each come face to face with our own death. We know these things could happen, but we have no control over when or how. We may try to take control or try to manage the circumstances around these events by force of will or other means, but the truth is, it is ultimately out of our hands.

Now the difference is what we do with the knowledge and how it affects our daily lives. In the West we try to do all we can to give our children the best genes possible, with the rich even combining sperm and eggs from other people in order to breed their children. Abortion seeks to get rid of those children that are undesired or seen to have some type of "defect." We try to manage how our children are born. Many have C-sections so they can plan the time and place of the birth. Big money is spent on toys and education for children and we are indignant if our children are not given the attention by their teachers that we think they deserve. We take self-help classes and buy the best education that we can afford. When we are young (and old) we pursue those that we choose, and some even try to use money, status, and profession to convince others to love them. We spend large amounts of money on our health, try to stay up on the latest health information, and live in a place where many diseases have been controlled (except cancer). We have plastic surgery to change the features that we have been given or hide misfortunes that we have experienced. Some even try to determine the time and place of their death by suicide, even physician assisted, or by taking large amounts of medicines and being hooked up to machines. We try to live lives as insulated as possible from disease and death.

In Buton, the children are the result of the genes of the mother and father and there is nothing they can do about it. When you give birth you are usually in the hands of the lady down the street that, hopefully, knows what she is doing, but if something goes wrong, that is just the way it was meant to be. They are face to face with poverty and may even feed their babies the water they used to wash their uncooked rice if they are too busy to nurse them. They often see people die, and their families wash the bodies of their dead relatives personally. Good education is usually hard to come by, and who gets food to eat by sitting around reading books? In the villages many just sit around staring at the walls for hours on end or take frequent naps, because they don't have books and wouldn't know what to do with them if they did. Sometimes marriages are arranged or forced by parents depending on beliefs, status, and timing. There is not much money for health care, so you need to heal from accidents by getting some massages and just letting things work themselves out no matter how disfigured. Disease comes and often ravages people. When you die, you die, and you don't know when it's going to happen.

The Butonese are at the mercy of many things beyond their control and they know it. Those of us in the West are at the mercy of many things beyond our control, but we pretend like we don't know it. And things usually work out better for us in many ways because we refuse to just sit back and let things happen to us without our say, and we have the money and means to do something about it, even if it is just a small measure. I think this is a better way to live, but in many cases this just isn't an option for the Butonese. So they take a very resigned, even fatalistic view of life, and let the chips fall where they may. This surrendering to the powers and forces greater than themselves is not only in their response to tragedy, but also the way that they receive and recognize their destiny. They patiently wait and watch, and take note of little details and things that cannot be planned to see if it is fate giving them a clue or guidance.

MYSTICISM

Mysticism is allowing yourself to think of each situation and encounter as something that has somehow been determined by fate, and you just need to do what you would usually do and feel what comes naturally. There is a high value placed on letting things flow naturally and not forcing them too much. You should have a sense for when the time is right to do something and there will probably be little indicators that this is the right thing. Maybe words are said that ring true with something your father said when you were a child. Maybe the person you are talking to or the circumstances are similar to something they saw in a dream. Maybe a passing breeze, strong wind, or a passing bird sends some type of omen about the situation. These things cannot be planned, and truly do just happen a certain way out of our control. This mysterious way of interpreting events, making decisions, and interacting with people reminds me of trying to be romantic and getting caught up in those special moments with the ones we love. Our mistake is usually that we try and force them.

If you have a certain point you are trying to get across, then it seems like these people will be putty in your hands. They will usually sit there, watch you, and wait for you to say what you are going to say, then keep looking at you. The Butonese will always walk by and look at you. They seem so passive verbally, but I think they are just sizing up the situation. They know what feels natural and what doesn't, so even though you may say what you wanted to say, it probably isn't really sinking in even if they keep looking at you. They usually aren't measuring what you have said according to logic, they are just watching and waiting for some type of sign. They just want to be polite, but often aren't listening to a word you are saying. The same thing if you are trying to force a romantic situation and it just isn't working out. You can talk all day long and that won't necessarily solve the problem. You have to do it in a way that is natural, and in many cases you just have to do your part and wait and see what happens. See what signs appear or what lights come on in their head. Fate may have it that you impact this person's life, but then again it may not.

Don't get me wrong, if a Westerner comes and visits their village they will probably remember it forever and want to put a picture of you up on their wall. But that doesn't mean you have really impacted what they think and believe. They have learned somewhere that Westerners are something special and should be treated well, maybe because the Dutch in the past demanded this, maybe because they know you have money and think they might get some of it, or maybe they are just nice. But I think part of it is that they are watching to see if you are going to change their lives. They are watching for all the signs. They are looking at you, feeling the wind, watching the birds, and seeing where things lead. They all have stories in their minds that their fathers have told them, and know the world is moving in a certain direction. They feel like Westerners will have a part in taking them there or bringing that time in the future to them. So they will welcome you with open arms. And you never know, fate may have it that you are the one they have been waiting for, and you may have something to share with them that will change everything. So you can try to force it, but don't be suprised if the most memorable things just happen and are out of your control.

Along with this feeling that things progress naturally, the Butonese value the guarding of knowledge and gradual revealing of secrets. If you ask someone a question, especially one about privileged information that only the "old people" know about, don't expect an answer. At least don't expect a full answer. If you want to find the important things it usually means being there for years before they let you know about them. And if you are not truly seeking the information you will probably never find out. And if you are seeking it too hard, you may never find out. It has to come in a way that is natural, full of meaning, and worthy of the knowledge you are going to receive. If the old people tell you everything that they know, what makes them special? They will probably try to hold onto whatever special or unique knowledge they have (usually something passed down from their forefathers) until they know their time is short. They want to preserve this oral information for the future generations, but don't want to treat it haphazardly. So they are watching for the signs, listening to their heart, and waiting for the right moment to divulge what they know. And it won't be all at one time. It will be piece by piece until you are eventually able to put it together. So don't expect to bust into a place and get all the answers. You may get the silent treatment, or you may get some answers but they may just be telling you what you want to hear. Never ask a yes or no question, because "yeah, yeah" from someone in Buton is usually meaningless and just a way to change the subject or get you to go away. You are going to have to invest some time and prove trustworthy, genuinely interested, and having the best intentions if you want to find out what they know and what they perceive as true "knowledge." This is the mysticism that you will find in Buton.

This is the mysticism that is found in animistic societies throughout the world. Each has its own brand or style, but there are those that have the knowledge and those without. Those with the knowledge tend to guard it. There are many from which it is kept a secret. The way I have spoken about it sounds like it is a beautiful thing, but I think most of the time it is to maintain some type of power over people. The intent is to raise one's own importance and get other people to do what you want. It can be very manipulative. It may be as extreme as is seen in the movie "The Village."[190] There is also wisdom in sharing things at just the right time and to people that you judge will treat it respect-fully and take it to heart. In the Bible, Jesus says "Do not give dogs what is sacred; do not throw your pearls to pigs. If you do, they may trample them under their feet, and then turn and tear you to pieces."[191] People will probably appreciate something more if you don't share it with everyone. In Buton it is usually just part of the mystical way of life, and doesn't seem to have ill intent. They just want to keep the knowledge among those

---

[190] "The Village" is a movie about a group of leaders in a village that control the information flow in and out of their community, and even generate acts of terror, in order to manipulate the behavior of the residents.
[191] Holy Bible, Matthew 7:6.

that have been chosen or have important positions as a result of fate. It will not go to those who come and try to force it without unseen forces working in their favor.

BLESSING AND CURSE

Though manual labor is usually a daily reality for the Butonese, they usually try not to work any more than is required. Throughout the islands of Indonesia there is a slower walk and pace of life out in the villages. Since the farmers usually depend on seasons there are long periods of time where there is not much work happening. The fishermen often go out at night, and are usually not very busy during the day. In general, there are a lot of people sitting around wherever you go. They are usually friendly and inviting, are not slaves to a schedule and can usually pick up and go along with you at a moment's notice, if invited. Time is something that they treat with flexibility, because they understand that the timing for many of the important things in life is out of their hands. They are always watching for special blessings and opportunities to come along.

The small and significant blessings that drop into people's lives are known as *rejeki*. People look for a lucky financial break here and there and will always take advantage of it. They try to find ways to "call the *rejeki*" as if there are blessings out there waiting to be had to those smart enough to find them. They see and respect people with money that seem like they don't have much work to do. If you are bargaining with them, they may give you a higher price because if they take advantage of the situation they may just be able to "call the *rejeki*" and make some extra money. This concept was taken to the extreme in places like Papua, with the cargo cult.[192] The people there believed that the white man had the special knowledge to be able to "call the cargo" out of the sea, because they saw ships appear by the thousands over the horizon during World War II. In Buton "call-

---

[192] Observation noted by Rene van den Berg.

ing the *rejeki*" is usually on a smaller scale. They are also trying to "*tolak bela*" or turn the evil away or turn back those disasters and evil things that may befall them. All of their rituals usually boil down to calling the good and blocking the bad.

I have also seen and heard about the ability that some women have to wield power over a man and "put him under her spell." I hear stories of how women control a man's life and have easy access to his money because of a special power or spell that she has. In the West it is understood that some women do have this power over men, but we usually don't think of it in these terms. I have even noticed at times, personally and with friends, that some women stare at men with especially big eyes like they are trying to pull you in with some type of tractor beam. I have always thought these women were trying to put men under their spell.

The timing of Butonese deaths seems to be something that they feel is out of their hands, so they are just waiting for it to happen. They are usually not too distraught when it happens. Of course they mourn, but there is a fatalistic feel to how they think about death. This could be the way that they pull their motorcycles out into traffic without looking. It could also be the way that they usually disregard safety measures. Possibly the infant mortality rate in the past and the lack of solid medical care have contributed to this fatalism. If something terrible happens, they are just resigned to the fact that you won't be getting much help.

They are waiting for their stories to be fulfilled in the perfect time. They want to be ready when the time comes, so that they can take advantage of it. The local leaders and the *adat* are going to be the means by which they recognize fulfillment and respond to it. Not everyone still pays close attention to what the traditional local leaders are saying, but throughout Buton this is still pretty strong.

This time, like all the others throughout the history of these people, is one of opportunity. There are many things in their culture that still maintain a strong presence that has taken root among these people, but they are also still looking for opportunities with the ring of truth to them. They want outsiders to come and befriend them. To really have an impact it must be in their way, with respect to the way that they know things. But they want to hear our message, and they are waiting and watching. Come, visit the islands of Buton and try to discover the answers to some of its mysteries. Who knows, you may even play a part in fulfilling some of them.

Part II – The Land and Sea of Buton

IX
NATURAL RESOURCES, TOURISM, AND INFRASTRUCTURE

The people of Buton have long memories of times throughout their history when groups of tourists from different parts of
the world have visited their land. It leaves quite an impression.
There are stories of foreign cruise ships that passed through
many years ago, foreign students that would show up and challenge the locals to a soccer game, as well as people from countries all over the world coming to do research or explore Buton
for what natural resources it offers. Most of these past visits
are not documented, except for the occasional article that can
be found in tour and travel resources that provide information
about remote places of the world.[193] Parts of Buton are getting
more and more attention, but it is still considered a very remote
destination. This chapter will try to explain the current state of
things that I have experienced and heard in my travels throughout the islands.

Rocky limestone and coral near the coasts and areas that
are fertile enough to grow rice and support jungles farther inland, dominate the island of Buton. Despite this rough terrain,
corn, cassava, cashews and certain types of yams can usually
grow. Buton, Muna, Kabaena, and Wawonii are all large enough
to have fertile soil inland. Buton and Kabaena have also been
blessed with a variety of minerals and ore within their moun-

---

[193] "Go East to Buton: Sea Safari to Southeast Sulawesi," *Travel Indonesia*
11, no. 10 (October 1989): 16.

tains. There are already a couple of nickel mines that are operating on Kabaena, and a hike up its mountains will find the trails littered with various ore-looking rocks. Buton is especially famous for its large deposit of natural asphalt. There is also at least one manganese mine and a large exploration effort to locate oil and natural gas reservoirs. The Japan Petroleum Exploration Company (Japex) obtained the rights to explore southern Buton and are taking seismic readings from thousands of places throughout the island.[194] The other islands surrounding Buton are primarily composed of rocky limestone and coral. There is no place that grows rice among the Wakatobi islands, and this is one of the main reasons cassava and corn have traditionally been the staple crops, because they can grow just about anywhere.

The rich Lambusango National Forest is located on Buton and is managed and publicized in large part by the Wallacea Trust, the same organization that works on the island of Hoga in Wakatobi.[195] The jungle is home to several species of birds and other animals that are exclusively native (endemic) to Sulawesi, and some that can only be found on the island of Buton. Among the rarest and most beautiful are the anoa, hornbills, maleo bird, tarsier, and cuscus. The jungle is also full of great waterfalls with awesome views and cool water. Kabaena and Wawonii also still have vast tracts of uninhabited jungle, while the other islands have unexplored and rarely visited terrain, though the land is not as rich as these larger and more fertile islands.

There are caves throughout the islands, with each island having its own distinct features. Some caves are full of white, crystal-covered walls with networks of tunnels, while some are the primary source of fresh water for the people that live nearby. Many of the caves are brackish- water filled caves that can be great spots to explore for divers, as the tunnels keep reaching towards the coast (whether they reach the ocean or not, no one

---

[194] Japan Petroleum Exploration Co, Ltd. "Buton Block," www.japex.co.jp/english/index.html (accessed 22 Feb 10).
[195] Operation Wallacea Trust, "Lambusango," www.opwall.com (accessed 22 Feb 10).

knows). The floor of one brackish-water cave near Bau-Bau is covered with a great pile of big rocks that reveal ancient ceramic bowls, plates, and vases when moved around. Most of the ceramic is broken, but almost every dive there is more than one piece of ceramic discovered intact.

It does look like on some of the islands that the land used to be covered by ocean. Especially on Wangi-Wangi, one can find fossilized coral far inland. This is also true near the coast of many of the islands. Because cassava has no problem growing in this rocky ground the staple food in Wakatobi is cassava, and it is also prevalent throughout the areas of Buton, though now rice is easily found in stores. The cassava tubers are grated and pressed into either cone-shaped little mounds (called *kasuami*) or the Wanci type that is beaten into bars and mixed with garlic and oil for some flavor (*kasuami pepe*). Cassava has not always been around these islands. Cassava originates from South America. It was first introduced into Indonesia in 1810, and only began to be widely cultivated in Indonesia at the beginning of the 20th century, owing both to promotional efforts by the Dutch government and to failures in rice and corn crops.

The characteristics of crops grown on the island can also affect the name. It is said that the name Wangi-Wangi (*wangi* means "smells good") is from when clove growing was more prevalent on the island. The city of Bau-Bau (*bau* means "smells bad") may have a similar, but opposite, story from the past but no one is sure how it got the name. "Bau" is also similar to the Wolio word for "new," which is "*baau*" and could give clues to the origin of the city's name.

As far as natural disasters, I have only heard of one earthquake that has struck the area in the last ten years and it did not do much damage. There have been a few tremors that could be felt if you are really still, but this rarely happens. Back in the 1970's there was a village along the coast of Buton that was the victim of a tsunami when the face of an opposing cliff of nearby Muna island dropped into the sea and created a giant wave that wiped out their homes. A smaller rockslide had caused a wave large enough to act as a warning to the people, so when the big one hit everyone had already fled inland. There were no injuries from this disaster, though it did convince the village to relocate. There are no stories of volcanoes in the region, and the visible geothermal activity is limited to some hot springs.

TOURISM

The big push in Bau-Bau and Wakatobi is tourism (also starting in Muna). So the mayor and regent are doing what they can to lure investors to build hotels and other tourist necessities in the area. Right now there are hotels with air conditioning and hot water in each of the capital cities, but they are not up to international standards. They are still pretty basic, and can be used for a good night's sleep, but that is about it. There are no other nice amenities at the hotels and none of them have a nice restaurant on the grounds. Hopefully this will change in the future.

In general the transportation routes are picking up throughout the islands, with flights operating between Bau-Bau and Makassar four times a week. Merpati airlines flew a plane that carried around 40 passengers three times a week for almost two years (Oct 07-Jul 09). Because of financial reasons they stopped flying, and a couple of months later Express Air begin flying four times a week. They also added a route to Kendari from Bau-Bau for awhile, but now they go from Makassar to Bau-Bau to Wangi-Wangi to Kendari, and then retrace that route back to Makassar each day. Susi Air (June 2009, about 10 passengers seating capacity) started flights around the same time as Express Air came in. The daily flight route began as a triangle, originating in Kendari, heading to Bau-Bau, Wangi-Wangi, then returning to Kendari. Eventually, it just flew from Kendari to Wangi-Wangi, and at the end of 2009 ceased flights. The word on the streets is that, once again, because of financial reasons, the local governments are not paying the airlines the subsidy that they promised for the flights to continue. This is called shooting yourself in the foot. In spite of this, Wings Air (Lion Air) began flights to Bau-Bau in early 2010 because the demand was so high. The competition created between Express Air and Lion Air helped make the price of flights to Bau-Bau more affordable. Wakatobi Divers has been operating flights for their guests with their own plane between Bali and Tomia (Wakatobi) for years with occasional flights from Kendari to Tomia. The boat transportation between major cities such as Kendari, Raha, Bau-Bau, and Wanci is conducted daily. In addition there are connecting boats to some of the more remote locations. Every inhabited island has some type of regular public boat service, though maybe not everyday, and usually on a boat that would make most Westerners uncomfortable and want a life jacket. The roads in general are not very good inland on the larger islands of Buton, Muna, Kabaena, and Wawonii, but closer to the larger cities they are in decent shape. The smaller islands are hit or miss regarding the condition of the roads, though the more remote you are, the less likely you are going to find anything larger than a motorcycle for public transportation and transportation starts getting pretty expensive compared with the more populated areas.

As far as guides are concerned, there are people throughout the islands that know a little English, but apart from Wallacea and Wakatobi Divers there is no guarantee that you are going to find someone that has a good grasp of English. I do know that at least in Bau-Bau there are several college students and teachers trying to get ready for any tourists that may come. Linking up with them will probably just be done by word of mouth, because at this point there is no prominent, steadily operating travel or touring agency for local sites currently in operation. The only exception to this is the Hill House (noted in Lonely Planet), which is usually a good place to relax in a simple setting with a fantastic view over the city of Bau-Bau, with the food being prepared on the premises. The same people that own the Hill House operate a resort on the island of Hoga and will escort tourists out to Hoga if desired. They have also developed a nice place to stay in the Balinese Hindu village of Ngkaring-Ngkaring which is near Bau-Bau. The accommodations at these places are somewhat spartan, but have a nice charm to them and the hosts generally do a good job of taking care of you.

The traveler to Buton is going to have to be a certain type of person, one looking for adventure or someone that already has good connections in the area. At this point Buton is not just a place to show up and have a great time together as a family. First of all, it may take some doing to figure out the best way to get here, and then you will have to make your way by asking around and getting linked up with the right person. This does not always work out, but it can be a lot of fun trying. If you have read this book then you will probably know more about the history of the area than most of the guides, but they will be the ones that will be able to show you the locations (if you're lucky). They can also show you how to take care of transportation, and keep you out of trouble. It may also be a good idea to stop by the tourism office that is located up in the fortress of Bau-Bau for any tourist information pamphlets they may have.

The availability of Western food is pretty sparse and the local little stores may not have everything you want. There is no real "Western" restaurant, but there are a couple of places that make food resembling Western fare. One restaurant makes a local steak, another makes pizza and various pasta dishes but uses sugar in the tomato sauce for some reason. Other than that, there are some good places to get fried chicken, which is actually a popular Indonesian food (as well as a Western food). Something that is always interesting to me is what type of milk is available and the way people think about milk. There are some cows around (especially on Muna), but we have yet to find one that gives milk other than when it has just had a baby. So there is no fresh milk sold, but only the standard powdered and UHT box milk. If you go to a store and ask for milk you will definitely be given either sweetened condensed milk or chocolate or straw-berry flavored milk. If I clarify that I want it the way it comes from the cow, it usually takes them a few minutes to understand. Only a few places have regular white, boxed milk. Most shops just have strawberry and chocolate milk, and from the impression I get maybe they think it comes that way naturally from the cow. There are also long-shelf-life versions of butter and cheese here, but the refrigerated variety is tough to find.

A. **Wolio** – Bau-Bau has a dominate mountain ridge that overlooks the city and is split in half by the Bau-Bau River. There is a relatively new road that has been built on the northern ridge that has a great view of the surrounding area. The ridge south of the river is where the *keraton* (fortress/palace) is located. It is said that the ocean used to reach up to the base of this fortress. There are cannon on the fortress and people wonder how they could have been accurate from such a long distance if the sea was just as far away as it is now. It could be that these cannon were for use against ground forces. There is also a large anchor on display in the fortress and people say the only way the anchor could have got up there is if the ocean was nearby. Not sure about this, but there may be some truth to it. I have heard that the anchor and cannon may have come from the armada of Dutch ships that wrecked on the west side of Kabaena.[196]

The fortress in Bau-Bau is said to be the largest in Indonesia (in terms of perimeter length), and some even say the world. I have seen some that seem larger in Thailand and Myanmar, so I'm not sure what criteria is being used to identify this fortress as the biggest. It is definitely the largest in Southeast Sulawesi, as well as the best known. Each island has some type of fortress remains on it, and it is said that there used to be 120 fortresses throughout the islands of the sultanate. The fortress of Bau-Bau still has a large community living in it, as well as many of the

---

[196] Liebner, "Kecelakaan Armada VOC," 100.

graves of the past sultans.[197] There is an old mosque as well as a flagpole in front of it that is supposed to have been standing since the 17th century. It looks that old. There are also a couple of rocks that played an important part in the inauguration of the sultan and Butonese cultural rituals of the past. One of them is a hole where the inauguration took place that is said to symbolize (and looks similar to) a woman's private area. The other rock is known as the "crying rock" and it is said that if you do not touch this rock then you haven't visited the fortress. This rock has a little spot on it where water gathers, and this "holy water" was also used in the inauguration of the sultan. The shape of this rock is similar to a man's reproductive organ. This type of sexual symbolism and rocks representing things can be seen throughout the islands of Buton.

The purpose of the fortress is generally considered to be for the defense of the buildings in which the sultanate operated as well as a boundary of separation between the lives of the community within and outside the walls. The fortress is built on Tursina Hill and is 84m above sea level. The fortress is bordered on the east by the Bau-Bau River far below, and is about 3km from the center of the city of Bau-Bau. This is the largest fortress among the islands of Buton and has a perimeter of 2740m. The steeper parts of the fortress walls are around 5m tall and at places it is 3m thick. Within the walls of the fortress can be found: Buton Palace Mosque, two palace buildings (*kamali*) which still remain, an old flagpole called *kasulana tombi*, the grave of Sultan Murhum (first Sultan of Buton), the Buton sultan inauguration rock (*popauna*), and the cave of Aru Pallaka (*la*

---

[197] Some of the sultans have more than one gravesite. For example, Sultan La Karambau has a gravesite in the keraton, as well as a gravesite at the top of Mt. Siontapina. It is said that many of the sultans had the power to die in one place, and then die again in another place a few months or years later. One of the sultans has four gravesites, and supposedly died, and was buried, in each of those different places at different times.

toondo). The fortress wall is composed of three different types of structures: bastion, gates, and the wall.[198]

There are 16 bastions, 4 of which are in the corners (*boka-boka*) and the 12 others are called *baluara*. Each is named individually. Each bastion has windows in which cannon may be placed, and the southwest corner was for storing cannon balls. There are 12 gates on the fortress which are referred to as *lawana* and are each individually named. Some of these gates show evidence of places where guards could be posted, as well as places for the display of those punished for crimes against the kingdom. This could be enemies from within the kingdom or those from outside. Those who received the death penalty by beheading received this penalty with people watching and in the midst of a war dance (*maniu*). After this event the head was usually hung above a gate so that it could be seen by those coming and going, as a warning to those that would want to oppose the kingdom. The wall around the fortress (*Watu tondo*) connects all these bastions and gates together. There are also weapons and pits for defending the fortress. There were a number of cannon (of which a few remain) that were made in Europe. The long cannon fired balls while the short cannon (*endoke-endoke*) used pieces of metal and shrapnel for close range. These cannon are said to have been bought or taken from foreign ships that sunk in the waters of Buton. For example, there are some Dutch ships that sank near Sagori Island (near Kabaena) in 1650. According to the report of V.I. van de Wall in 1931, there were five ships that sunk near Sagori: De Tijger, Bergenop-Zoom, Aagtekerke, De Luipaard and De Juffer. The giant anchor (3.55m long) that can also be found in the fortress may be from one of these ships according to Van de Wall. Next to these cannon there was another lighter firearm (*tarakolo*), along with spears, *keris*, and machete.[199]

---

[198] Haris, 319-321.
[199] Ibid., 321-324.

Van de Wall also said that the walls and bastions of the fortress that face the sea were possibly built by the Dutch, while those facing the land were built by the people of Buton. In the beginning of the 15th century, the city was originally established in the area where the center of the city of Bau-Bau is now, but because of pirate attacks they moved inland and built their community where the fortress now stands. There is also a pit (*parit*) on the west side of the wall about 20-30m from the fortress wall, about 4m wide and 2m deep. Van de Wall said that the fortress was built in 1631 by Sultan Dayanu Ikhsanuddin (La Elangi) under the leadership of the VOC, but was finished by the Butonese. Zahari thinks the building of the fortress took 10 years from 1634-1645, which would have been under the 4th sultan, Gafur Wadudu (1634-45). There are also foreign ceramics, bones, weapons, cannon balls and lead as well as other things that need to be studied further. Other fortresses (*benteng*) on Buton include Sorawolio, Baadia, Bombonawulu, Ereke, Labomba, and on the island of Wangi-Wangi, the fortress of Lia.[200]

A couple of other places other than the fortress are well known for their views of the surrounding area. One of them is *Palagimata* which is the place that the mayor's office has been built. This structure is pretty amazing, especially considering that it was built for a city mayor. It has a beautiful view overlooking the western sky, and it was initially built outside the city, with no houses in the immediate surrounding area, to encourage the city to grow in this direction. From Bau-Bau, looking north past Makasar Island directly across the bay, there is another place. It is just north of the city of Lowu-Lowu and it is a little plateau, which is the highest point in the area. From there you have a 360 degree view of the surrounding area, and can even see Mt. Lambelu to the north. You can see the sun rise and set, as well as a clear view of the city of Bau-Bau. This site is not as popular as the others in Bau-Bau, but the owner is trying to make it an attraction.

---

[200] Ibid., 325-328.

The most popular place in the city of Bau-Bau, where everyone goes, is Kamali Beach (not really a beach). It is a big boardwalk where local vendors sell little toys, set up children's rides, and have children's magnetic fishing pools. There are also little shops along the sea wall that sell various fried foods and the well-known Sulawesi hot ginger drink, *saraba*. In the middle of this area is a big dragon statue with glowing eyes and water pouring from the mouth. This is where most of the concerts and other such events take place. It is also right next to the port, so people passing through on the big Indonesian passenger (PELNI, *Pelayaran Nasional Indonesia*, Indonesia National Sailing Company) ships hang out here while waiting for the ship to leave.

The most popular beach on the island is called Nirvana Beach, and is about 15 minutes south of Bau-Bau (toward Batauga). It has white sand, and is a very beautiful place, especially if the driftwood and trash that comes in with the tide has been cleaned up or washed away. It is fairly well protected from big waves, so the water is usually calm and you have a view of the nearby islands of Kadatua, Liwotongkidi, and Siompu. There are little shops where you can buy snacks and drinks, as well as little benches and bungalows that can be used (sometimes for a small fee). Some of the best, and definitely the most accessible dive sites are at this beach, because there are several coral reefs located in front of the beach. There is also a nice wall dive on the west side (right side) of the beach.

About 15 minutes outside of Bau-Bau on the way to Pasarwajo are three trees near the side of the road that are called the "*batik*" or "camouflage" trees. For some reason the trunk of the trees have three colors on them: green, red, and brown. The brown is the regular bark, and the green and red look to be where the bark has been peeled off and the exposed skin is in different stages of drying out. Regardless of the time of year, these three colors are always present.

About 10 minutes outside of Bau-Bau on the way to Batauga there is a spectacular cave, Lakasa, though difficult to enter. First you need to find someone that can show you where the family of Lakasa lives so you can get the key that opens the gate to the cave. Then you drive towards Batauga and take a turn to the left just before you get to the turn that leads to Nirvana Beach. Take the little road up and around until you eventually get to a little shelter on stilts that is back under a good-sized tree. This cave has a fairly small entrance that goes straight down about eight feet, and eventually leads to an underwater pool whose surrounding walls are covered with little white crystals that will poke you if you bump against them. You will definitely need a lantern and/or flashlights for this cave, and be careful because it is a real maze down there.

There are also several nice waterfalls that can be found in almost every direction leading out of Bau-Bau. Two of the best are in the direction heading to the Bali village of Ngkaring-Ng-karing. One of them is just past the large "BAU-BAU" sign that was built similar to the Hollywood sign in Los Angeles, though not as large and not as well known. On the way to this waterfall you will pass another boardwalk type area farther out from the city where one can watch the sunset and also enjoy some fried foods and *saraba*. This nearby waterfall has several venders selling corn near the right hand turn to the waterfall. There is a nice road that leads directly up to the waterfall, and when it has been raining the falls are quite powerful. There is also a place to swim here.

If you want a more secluded, cleaner, and larger area to swim, then you should head to the Bungi waterfall that is about another 10-minute drive towards Ngkaring-Ngkaring. There is a difficult-to-see right hand turn to this waterfall right after an elementary school. A couple hundred meters down this road you can park your vehicle near a little stilted hut and start the 30-minute walk in the jungle to the waterfall. This trail is fairly well worn and follows a water pipe for part of the way, but it would be best to have a local guide with you because there are a few confusing turns. If there has recently been a hard rain it may be difficult to cross the river, which is required to get to the waterfall. There are actually a series of waterfalls in this location, and each has a pool at the bottom where you can go swimming.

B. **Cia-Cia** – The outlying areas surrounding Bau-Bau are typical of other remote areas in the region, and are primarily inhabited by the Cia-Cia. Their land holds the largest deposit of natural asphalt in Southeast Asia, as every elementary school kid knows throughout Indonesia. The land of the Cia-Cia is rich and they are very wary of those coming and trying to take it from them without asking first. They rely much on the laws and traditions of the past, but some also want to study the law of the present to protect their rights. Some Cia-Cia villages also have old stories in their tradition that they can trust the "people of white skin" above others that may come. They will not sell their land, but can only pass it down to those of their family. They would be willing to allow its use if the right people came along to explore what riches it contains. It will be interesting to see what the results are after Japex's study of the area for oil and natural gas deposits is complete.

On the southern coast there are also a couple of places with historical interest for the island of Buton. In the village of Wabula the remains of a ship can be found that are said to be from when Wakaakaa, the first ruler of Buton, came ashore after sailing from China. Her grave can supposedly be found in Wabula, but a few other villages on the east coast of Buton also claim the grave. No one is really sure which one is hers (if any of them are). Others say it was soldiers from Kublai Khan (people usually say China) that were supposed to have landed at this site on the southeast coast of Buton. The bottom of the hull of their boat is still supposed to be in Wabula. It is also said that this village was where the first mosque was found on Buton. The mosque, along with an old fortress, is supposed to be located above this village and not in the village's current position, which is closer to the coast. Up above the city of Pasarwajo there are also the walls of an old fortress that is supposed to be the place where the first village was located that later became Pasarwajo. It is probably the one identified earlier regarding trading between the Bajo people on the sea and the village that grew crops in the interior. In the Cia-Cia village of Lapandewa there are also the remaining walls of a fortress, an old rock and graves that have great significance for the people. They are the center of harvest and planting rituals that take place several times every year.

There are also some good dive sites in the area inhabited by the Cia-Cia. In Pasarwajo bay, near the old port, there is some good muck diving.[201] On the southern side of the bay near where it opens to the ocean there is some good diving that is very similar to that out in Wakatobi. You can rent a long, skinny wooden boat in Dongkala (just south of Pasarwajo) that can take you out about 20 minutes along the coast to some great dive sites with bigger fish than can generally be found in Bau-Bau.

There is a little hot spring about halfway between Bau-Bau and Pasarwajo on the main road. It is on the east side of the only real bridge on the road that goes over a river, then a little dirt road leads down to the river, where you cross it and find the spring.

C. **Kulisusu** – The northern part of the island of Buton is not quite as connected with the sea lines of communication as much as Bau-Bau and Raha in the strait of Buton, and Kendari in the north. This mountainous land is the remote home to a people who have been making their way in the world for a long time. Ereke is their primary port city. The roads in this regency (North Buton) are definitely the worst on Buton and the trip by land from Bau-Bau to Ereke has always been known as long and

---

[201] Muck diving gets its name from the sediment that lies beneath most dives, which is normally a muddy or "mucky" environment. The muck is the perfect habitat for unusual, exotic and juvenile organisms that make their homes in the sediment and "trash" that compose a muck dive.

treacherous. It is often not passable if there has been any rain recently, which is usually the case from December to June. This regency broke off from Muna and became independent in 2006. I took the trip there with my family in March 2009 (the heart of the rainy season) with a 4-wheel drive vehicle and we did make it, after getting stuck several times. Everyone except one guy in Burangan said that a vehicle could not make it this time of year. Along the way we met people that had spent three days in their vehicle in the jungle because they could not get free from the mud. Eventually about 14 men were called and lifted their truck out of the mud. They then got stuck at a bridge construction site on the way back south when returning and we pulled them out. They insisted no one could make the trip, but the key factor is definitely 4-wheel drive, because we did in fact make it. It is approximately 10 hours from Bau-Bau to Ereke by land. There are plans to improve the roads and bridges, but that will probably be a long process.

Most people opt to take the trip by the bus that departs Bau-Bau daily for the village of Kambowa in the southern part of the regency of North Buton, which is a three-hour drive. There is then a fiberglass speed boat every day at 11 a.m. that will take you to Ereke on a two-hour boat ride. About 45 minutes north of Kambowa is Kioko where you can take a three-hour wooden boat ride to Ereke that leaves every day around 6 a.m. About 45 minutes north of there is the village of Ngapaea that has a 6 a.m. boat ride to Ereke on a wooden boat with two engines that takes about one and a half hours. Along this road we saw a cuscus, a troop of macaques, and some wild pigs. The next village north is Burangan, which is the supposed capital of the district.

The politics behind why Burangan was chosen as the capital shows how politics can negatively impact an area. This village was in no way considered the natural choice for a capital, because it really is not very big and even two years after being chosen is severely underdeveloped. The bridges on the road leading from the main road to the pier at Burangan are generally made up of loose planks of wood and few government buildings can be found. There is one little, self-titled "simple restaurant." Ereke, on the other hand, is the natural capital as it has always been more populated, as well as the heart of the Kulisusu culture. Transportation to surrounding areas is also more readily available there. It seems that the *bupati* of Muna did not like losing this regency from under his grasp, but did have enough influence to determine that the capital be placed closer to the geographical heart of the land of North Buton, and also more easily reached from the city of Raha (in Muna). It is clear that the leadership of North Buton is dragging their feet in building any type of infrastructure in Burangan because they know that the capital is probably going to end up in Ereke. Some of the regency government buildings have even begun to be built in Ereke even though the capital is officially in Burangan. Most of the government officials live in Ereke as there are no offices or anything else to go to in Burangan.

The road between Burangan and Ereke is where you need to have a four-wheel drive vehicle if there has been any rain at all. The key problem is deep and slick mud that will swallow a vehicle's tires. There are also mud covered hills that can cause one to slide off the road. It is generally smart to follow the primary ruts of the vehicles that have gone before, even if they are under water. If there are two or more choices of ruts to follow, it is smarter to have someone check the depth first by walking through the water, which is a dirty business. The problem with trying to take the path less traveled is that the mud is usually slicker and looser, and if it has been raining it is a lot easier to slide off of the road, which can have very serious consequences, especially if you are on a hill or mountain. The well-worn ruts will usually keep you on the road, though you may get bogged down.

If you get stuck, it is best to make sure nothing is lodged underneath like a big rock or piece of wood. Then if there are any rocks around put them in front of the tires in the hole that the tire is sitting in. It can also help to add some wood, but wood can also get slick and make things worse. There may be some pushing required if the car needs just a little help, but always be careful to not let the truck roll back on you. You always need the path in front of you clear, and be especially cautious if there are other people or motorcycles in front of you because they may not understand that if you get moving you are not stopping until you make it to dry ground. They also probably do not understand that as you are sliding around in mud and if they get anywhere close, they have a high probability of getting knocked down and possibly run over. As usual, the one driving the truck is responsible for taking care of the people on motorcycles, because they do not understand the meaning of defensive driving and will often make decisions that would lead to their death or maiming if the driver of the truck is not watching them carefully and able to react quickly. While getting stuck and spending a few hours or nights in the jungle is not a fun thought, there are some other circumstances that could also lead to long stays in the jungle for your vehicle.

The bridges are one of these major factors, the long ones and the short ones. Some of the little culverts or bridges can have gigantic holes in them that could swallow a tire whole. There was also one large hole in the middle of a muddy mountainous road that could have swallowed a tire easily and was hard to avoid. The bridges range from some eight-foot 4x4 pieces of wood stretched across a gap, to metal frame bridges with wooden planks across them, to concrete bridges, often with steep and treacherous inclines on the approaches to the bridge. On the metal frame bridges the planks that run along the steel girders are those that your tires should follow, and at times this crossing may require someone to stand in front of the truck and help guide your tires. Following the steel girders is important because the cross planks of wood are not near as strong and are often broken or not there. There is little room for error in many of these circumstances. If the bridge does have a metal frame it may be tilting to the left or the right and look like it's about to drop, but it's probably been that way for years! At times a bridge may be impassable or under construction and a little detour road may pass down to the creek or river, which has to be forded. These detours can be very muddy and slick adventures, and if it has been raining a good bit could even become impassable. I had one friend that got stuck in one of these little creeks that soon turned into a torrent when the rain started and his vehicle was almost swept away. Nearby in mainland Sulawesi (South Konawe regency) it is said that there was a Canadian man that was washing his car in a river and a damn broke and he and his car were washed away. There are many things to be concerned about on this road, but just stay optimistic and never let your guard down if driving.

In the middle of this nightmare road there are a few villages and also the capital of the district of West Kulisusu. There is a market that takes place here and some of the surrounding villagers come to shop. There are many surrounding transmigration communities from Java, Bali, and the eastern Indonesian islands near Flores and Timor. All of these villages have their own names but are also referred to as SPs 1 to 5 (*Satuan Permukiman*). The Javanese and Balinese that inhabit these villages, and others throughout Buton, produce higher yields (with their rice paddies) than the locals (with their traditional dry rice fields).

A few more hours down the road, in and around the city of Ereke, there are a few neat places to see. After going to the market and seeing what types of things are available in the city, you can then head out to the *keraton* to step on the "kulisusu" shell. This is the shell that one must step on in order to say one has truly visited the land of the Kulisusu. You may be told to stand on the shell and say a prayer to the spirits. It is said the other half of the shell is in Ternate. Outside the walls and slightly downhill in the direction of downtown Ereke is a well. Drinking water directly from this well is said to aid one in learning to speak the

Kulisusu language. This fortress still has people living inside of its walls similar to the one in Bau-Bau and on Wangi-Wangi. The Kulisusu themselves refer to the fortress itself (and the area it encloses) as Wapala.

The largest fort and the one which most visitors will see, is the large kraton at Wapala. This fort is said to have been built around the time that Kapita Maranua from Tobelo attacked the Kulisusu people. The Tobelo were the fighting forces (naval) of the Ternatan ruler. As the story goes, there were two Kulisusu people who wanted the fort built: Kodangku and Gau Malanga. The former wanted to build a large fort, stretching from Kadacua in the north, to Lasora on the west, Linsowu on the south, and Mata Oleo on the east (this is the old Mata Oleo, not the Mata Oleo near present-day Waodeburi). However, Gau Malanga, who apparently had the upper hand in the matter, went ahead and built a smaller fort around the outskirts of Wapala (the present-day fort) without Kodangku's agreement. Because his idea was not accepted, when he died Kodangku ordered that he not be buried inside the kraton. His grave lies outside it, somewhere between Linsowu and old Mata Oleo. There is also said to be another stone fort, about an hour's walk east of Wapala (that is, near the Banda Sea), called Pangilia. This is a holy place for the Kulisusu people, where the trees have not been cut down. The only way to reach it is by foot. There is also a stone fortification on a small bluff west of present-day Lantagi, called *lawa i Pande*. While it has a commanding view of the the southern tip of the mainland (looking toward Tanjung Goram), this fort apparently was never completed. There is also a much smaller fort (perhaps 'outpost' or 'lookout post' would be a better word) directly on the coast at Rompio. The walls of *lawa i Rompio* are about 75 cm thick, and said to measure about 50 meters square. One of the stones facing the sea has a round hole in it, said to be proof that a cannon once stood here, but the hole seems entirely too small for this purpose. If one talks about the stone fort at

Ngapa i Tonga, this refers to the fort at Rompio; Ngapa i Tonga is just to the north of Rompio.[202]

The Wapala fort is also close to the only place to get diesel in town, an APMS (*Agen Premium Minyak dan Solar,* Gas, Oil and Diesel Agent). There is no fuel pump, but just large drums of gasoline and diesel that are available. Sometimes this fuel is not available so it is safest to bring some extra along especially if you have a diesel engine. The trip from Bau-Bau to Ereke and back is a little less than 400 km, but more fuel is burned when on the rough terrain using four-wheel drive. You can always find little shops along the road that have one liter jars of unleaded gasoline for motorcycles, but it is harder to come by diesel fuel out in the villages.

Continuing on past the *keraton* you will eventually come to the village of Bone that is right along the western coast of the peninsula, just like Ereke. If you follow the coast south through the village there will be two options for taking a left and heading to little caves or pools that are great places for swimming or just hanging out. They are salt water, so there is apparently some underground connection to the sea. They are both deep enough to actually swim in and the spot farthest south has a great spot to jump into the water. Out of the other spots like this I have seen throughout the islands these looked like a couple of the best. I have heard there are four more pools like this in the same area.

There is also a very rough road that leads to the eastern side of the peninsula directly from the main intersection (with the monument in the middle) in the city of Ereke. This beach is called Membuku and is known for its large waves that break off in the distance. This is the Banda Sea, and we saw little kids running along the beach with small oars that they used to dig into the sand looking for worms that they could later use for fishing. This is also a place where several small boats are stored, which can be taken along the coast to cassava, coconut or corn fields that are only accessible by boat.

---

[202] Kulisusu stone fort information in this paragraph is from an unpublished work by David Mead.

There is one tourist site that has just recently been developed at Rombia Spring. This is about 30 minutes (should be shorter when the road work is completed) from Ereke in the direction of Burangan. There is a clear freshwater spring here that is a spot for swimming and offers a nice place to relax in the jungle. There is also a wooden pavilion type structure that is just past Rombia Spring and up a hill that offers a nice view of the area off to the west. This site was opened with an environmental awareness event in early 2008 with all of the government leaders in the province present and where each of them planted a young tree (mango, rambutan, sandalwood trees, etc.).

There is also a nature reserve in North Buton, which may be one of the few places on the island to find anoas. An anoa is a small buffalo- or cow-like animal that has straight, sharp horns and is endemic to Sulawesi. People are afraid of them because they have a reputation of being especially mean. It is said that they will charge you with their horns, and if you climb a tree to get away they will wait for you at the bottom of the tree. The only way to get away is to throw your shirt over their head, then make a run for it as they are violently jabbing their horns through your shirt. These animals were first hunted on Buton when the Balinese came, because they weren't scared of the anoa like the Butonese. It is said that when you eat them you feel a fire in your belly and you become more fertile.

D. **Muna** – This island is full of interesting caves and lakes, including the well known Napabale lagoon south of Raha. The land is not as rocky or mountainous as Buton, and has long been a source of teak and cashews. It is famous for being subject to harsh deforestation and illegal logging as a result of its abundant teak trees. There is not a large amount of wildlife on Muna, and it is reported that in 1989 a group of 150 Military Police bagged over 5,000 babirusas on the island and buried them. With a Muslim majority they would not eat the pigs, though I have heard technically these fall in the category of ruminants and they are *halal*, which means they are permitted to be eaten under Islamic law.[203] The roads on Muna are generally not very well maintained. There is even an airfield on Muna that has had flights in the past, although I think that it operated only a short time, many years back. Most people don't even know there is an airfield on the island nowadays. There are several beautiful places on the island, of which a prime example is Napabale lagoon. This secluded saltwater "lake" enclosed by land is actually connected to the Strait of Buton by an underwater tunnel that is exposed at low tide. During this window of time, small boats are able to exit the lake into a cove open to the ocean.

The lagoon is about 30 minutes south of Raha, and the signs alone are not enough to get you there, so ask around. When heading south on the road that follows the coast from Raha it is one of the first major left turns that can be taken. This is followed by a drive of a couple kilometers and a right hand turn, which will lead you through some sparsely populated land until you get to the lagoon. There are a few little shops down by the lake, along with a building and some concrete terrace-type things that have been filled with sand to be similar to a beach (I'm guessing). The shops are probably only open on Sundays. There are quite a few small boats that are parked in this lagoon when the tide is in, but when it goes out many of the little boats make their way out the tunnel. There is a limited window of time to exit and enter and the time I went we sat in front of the tunnel waiting until the water was low enough for us to pass through. Then we had to lie down in the boat to get through and propel ourselves by pushing on the ceiling. The guy with the boat said never to try that when the tide is coming back in because you and your boat could easily get trapped underwater in the tunnel. Scary thought, because the tunnel is probably about 50 meters long. Once through the tunnel there is a cove that winds its way out to the ocean just opposite the islands of Bakialu, Munaente, and Fare, which are close to Buton, just south of the village of

---

[203] Muller, "Buton," 215.

Pure on Buton. There may be a little beach area to stop on the coast of Muna but I haven't seen it. Most of the terrain around the cove is coral rock cliffs with holes in them full of chirping birds or bats. They are easy to hear when you pass by closely. In case your boat does not make it back through the tunnel in time, there is a place to moor them in the cove then walk back to the lake on a trail.

Not too far from Napabale lagoon, the caves of Liang Kabori and Metanduno can be found about 30 minutes southwest of Raha on a small road that winds through hilly country of Muna. Take the same coastal road south from Raha that you would take to Napabale lagoon, but take the first major road to the right once outside of Raha, then a few kilometers later take a left that will take you out into the hilly area where the caves are. Once again, ask around for directions or go with someone who knows the way. Metanduno contains the largest number of paintings. It is said there are over 300 cave paintings, which include pictures of deer, pigs, horses, men with spears, etc. Liang Kabori has a smaller number of similar paintings.[204] The ingredients for the paint include a type of clay along with some type of local leaf. People also claim that blood is mixed into it. It is amazing that the pictures have survived this long and most of them can still be seen quite clearly. The painting of the man flying a kite is about an hour hike through rough terrain from the more accessible Liang Kabori and Metanduno. Seeing the more remote cave is best done in the morning, and can be found by following a trail heading east from the Liang Kabori cave. In late 2008 several improvements to the pathways and stairs leading up to these caves were being made out of cement. The earliest paintings of horses have been dated to hundreds of years ago, while the paintings of people flying kites have not been dated yet (and in fact may be relatively recent). There are a total of 18 caves that have paintings, nine of which are readily accessible. Throughout

---

[204] Judyth Gregory-Smith; photography by Richard Gregory-Smith, *Southeast Sulawesi: Islands of Surprises* (Jakarta: Balai Pustaka, 2000).

these caves are pictures of horses, people, deer, pigs, suns, men on boats, and insect-like figures. There used to also be human bones and carved coffins in these caves, but archaeologists from Jakarta came and took them between the years of 1984-86.[205]

Farther south, in the central eastern part of the island, Kota Muna, in the district of Tongkuno, is probably where some of the oldest villages on the island are. This area is not along the newest main road running through the center of Muna. It is closer to the old road running on the eastern side of the island, but is actually on a road that connects the two. Some very interesting historical sites can be found here as well as one of the better views on Muna. There is a large mosque that was built there within the last 50 years is supposed to be at the site of the old village. There is a grave of an important figure from the past located in the terrace of the mosque on the left side when looking at the mosque from the main road. About a five minutes' drive past the mosque going towards Lasehao on the left is a dirt road that leads up to the "ship run aground that has turned into a rock" and the "rock that flowers."

This "rock ship" can clearly be seen from the road and it is about a ten minutes' walk to the top of this "ship" where little crevices that look like "rooms" are often used as a place to sit down and rest. On top of this hill is probably one of the best views on Muna, as you can see the island of Buton to the east, the island of Kabaena southwest and mainland Sulawesi to the west. It also looks like there are a couple of good places to sleep or set up a tent at the top if you wanted to spend the night. If you go back down the rock, take a right at the main dirt road at the base of the rock, walk another ten minutes, and then you will come to the "rocks that flower." I have been told that there are three of these rocks, but I have only seen the "flowers" on the more popular one. The rocks are large monoliths that have vegetation growing all over them. On one side of the more promi-

[205] Muller, "Buton," 215-216.

nent rock (the side of the rock opposite the trail) there is a large
section of the "flowers" that are growing from the rock. The
"flowers" actually look like a type of white moss. There are also
several interesting places to dive in and around Muna.

A friend and I went scuba diving in a lake that he spotted
while flying over the island of Muna, on the middle peninsula
out of the three that form the southern end of the island. We
wanted to see how deep it was, so we used our GPS and eventually made our way to it. The village at the foot of it said no one
had been up there for the last few years. Everyone was "scared
of snakes." So we paid a couple of guys to carry our scuba gear
for the hour of slashing through brush to reach the lake. On
the hike we managed to have just about the whole village join
us, complete with four or five people up front with machetes
clearing the path. One of them was a woman old enough to be
my grandmother, but there she was, hacking away. We made it
to the lake, and entered the water through the roots of the surrounding mangrove trees. Immediately, we noticed that this did
not look like a lake teeming with life. It was a little murky in
the water and the only fish we saw were near the roots and were
about a centimeter long. We decided to swim out a little farther
from the edge and just drop to see how deep we could go. As
we were descending we hit about ten meters and it was black as
night. My friend had a flashlight, but he could shine it right in
front of his face and not see the light. I grabbed onto him so we
did not get separated in the consuming darkness. Then all of a
sudden we could see! And our lips and skin were burning! My
friend thought it was primarily heat, but I remember how my lips
were stinging and thought it was some type of acid. Needlessly
to say, we immediately gave the thumbs up as a signal to ascend
to the top. When we arrived at the surface we smelled like sul-
fur. We advised the locals that it was probably best they avoided
swimming in that lake. I did not have any idea what kind of lake
this was for two years until I read an article in National Geo-

graphic on "Bahamas Blue Holes." This lake fit the description exactly. It's a blue hole![206]

In southern Muna, there are a couple of fortresses, one near the peak of Mt. Kaligula, which is the highest point that can be seen on Muna from Bau-Bau. The village of Wadiabero is the gateway for the two-hour hike up this mountain. Wadiabero is also home to around six caves from which the people pull their water and wash themselves and their clothes. While scuba diving, one of the caves can be followed pretty far in the direction of the sea, to where some type of guideline is required so that one doesn't get lost when trying to find the exit again. A friend and I also found a large fish in another of the caves, so someone either caught it and put it there or it found its way through a series of tunnels from the ocean (which is about 400m away). There is also supposed to be another fortress on a hill overlooking the city of Lakudo.

There are several islands on the northwestern side of Muna which form the Tiworo Archipelago. There is a pearl factory among these islands as well as Indo Island, which the Muna department of tourism is trying to develop as a tourist attraction. They have built a few buildings out there with several rooms equipped with air conditioners, along with several little structures to go sit and relax on. The little island has one other large family that lives on it in a nearby house, and the head of that family is responsible for maintaining the facilities. There is no running water on the island but they can fill a tank with water from the mainland and a generator provides electricity. It seems like a nice place to get away to a certain extent, though there would always be the local family nearby. There is also a boat that can take you to visit some Bajo communities on nearby islands, or to an uninhabited island, where you could go fishing. Visiting this island can be arranged through the Muna regency tourism department.

---

[206] Andrew Todhunter, "Deep Dark Secrets," in *National Geographic* 218, no. 2 (August 2010): 34-53.

E. **Wakatobi** – These islands are also known as the Tukang Besi (Metal Worker) Islands, but it is now more common to refer to them as Wakatobi. Wakatobi is actually an acronym (using the first two letters of each primary island's name) for Wangi-Wangi (Wanci), Kaledupa, Tomia, and Binongko. All of the islands in this regency are relatively small and have extensive coral reefs surrounding them. The Wakatobi National Marine Park is the second largest marine park in Indonesia. These islands are not very fertile for crops and are made up of rock and coral. No rice is grown on these islands. There are large areas of jungle, but there are also quite a few grass fields that take up large areas of the islands. In this grass you can look down and see the fossilized remains of coral and clams.

The islands of Wakatobi are surrounded by steep underwater cliffs and dropoffs that eventually plunge to around 4000m deep off the western side of the island chain. There are also several large areas of coral that do not rise above the surface of the water, and are separate from the islands. West of Kaledupa, the coral covers an area larger than some of the islands of Wakatobi. There is a large effort coordinated by different organizations aimed at preserving the coral reefs and fish within the borders of the National Marine Park. Operation Wallacea (OpWall) tries to educate the local people and teach them how to protect the coral themselves, while conducting its own education and research with European college students. The World Wildlife Fund (WWF) as well as The Nature Conservancy (TNC) act as the police around the marine park and arrest those fishermen that are engaging in acts that could harm the reef. The Wakatobi Divers Resort has bought out areas of water to provide fish room to breed and also try to teach local leaders what they can do to promote general eco-friendly cleanliness in their communities.[207] The Coral Reef Management Program (COREMAP), which is funded by the World Bank, has three local Indonesians going out to each *kecamatan* (district) throughout Southeast Su-

---

[207] Wakatobi Divers, www.wakatobi.com (accessed on 23 Feb 10).

lawesi in order to promote awareness about protecting the reef and to provide other education opportunities aimed at taking care of the environment.

The roads in Wakatobi are best on the islands of Wangi-Wangi and Tomia. There are asphalt roads on Kaledupa and Binongko also, but many are in poor condition. The boat transportation between the islands is pretty good, with the exception of Binongko, which can be more challenging. The big wave season must also be considered, because not only will it make any ride more uncomfortable, at times the boats will just stop running some of the routes. The water is generally roughest between June and September, but it is hard to predict. The waves between Tomia and Binongko are the most famous for being very big and the transportation to Binongko is the least reliable. The other islands have pretty fast fiberglass boats as an option from Wanci, along with the regular wooden boats.

On Wangi-Wangi there is local transportation in vans that travel certain routes through Wanci, but for the most part on the other islands you have to rely on motorcycles. For places like the island of Hoga, there are not really any roads so you have to walk. There is also a visible sign of how obedience to traffic regulations gets looser as you go down the island chain: the wearing of helmets on motorcycles. On Wangi-Wangi the motorcycle driver always had his helmet on and made sure you were wearing yours. Then on Kaledupa and Tomia the motorcycle driver made sure he was wearing his helmet, but you didn't have to worry about wearing one. On Binongko, no one owned a helmet, even if you had wanted to wear one. The cost for motorcycle transportation in Wakatobi is generally much more expensive than in Bau-Bau and more populated areas, probably because fuel is more expensive and there are less passengers looking for a ride.

The options for lodging throughout Wakotobi are pretty simple and scarce. Wangi-Wangi has some hotels in Wanci (including even some with air conditioning). Tomia has some homestays in its two largest cities (Usuku and Waha). On Kaledupa there is a home-stay in Ambeua. But on Binongko, as well as outside the major cities on the other islands, your best bet is to go to the head of the village and see if you can stay at his house. If you mention you would like to spend the night in the village he will probably invite you to stay at his house.

While Bau-Bau is trying to become more of a tourist destination, at this point in time the Wakatobi islands are the only ones with this distinction in Southeast Sulawesi. However, it is still pretty exclusive. Hoga Island is small, but has been made famous because of Operation Wallacea and all the students from Europe (especially England) that come out to do research and take classes. There is also a very nice (and expensive) resort on the island of Onemobaa off the northwestern side of the island of Tomia, which has had an airstrip built for their private plane that flies guests from Bali. The guests generally sign up for seven to ten day packages complete with food cooked by chefs from Bali, as well as up to three scuba boat dives a day at various dive sites in the area. The newest resort, Patuno Resort, is on the island of Wangi-Wangi, near the airport. It is owned by the *bupati* of Wakatobi and looks to be a nice place, though I'm sure it will be a work in progress for the first year or two after just opening in 2010.

The island of Wangi-Wangi is the most developed of the islands, with the capital of the district in Wanci, the largest city. On the southern outskirts of Wanci (in Lia) there is also a *keraton* or fortress area similar to that of Bau-Bau in which the people from the former Sultan's family lived. Most of the islands have a fortress or two at the higher points on the island, but these are usually uninhabited now or are no longer regarded as special for those descended from the Sultan. The exceptions to this are Bau-Bau, Wanci, and Ereke. There is also a sacred place that can be found at the top of the highest mountain on the island. The graves of the first people that arrived on Wanci are said to be here, and this is supposed to be the area that the earliest village on the island was located. Many things have changed since then, as this is now a pretty remote place on the island.

The tallest mountain, Mt. Tindoi, has a sacred place near its summit. To reach it, from the city of Wanci there is an asphalt road that takes you up the side of the mountain, then after a turn or two there is a cement bike or walking path that winds through the jungle to an old spring that used to be the major source of water for people on the mountain. A few minutes ride past this spring is the village of Wotamuhute, which is just below the peak of Mt. Tindoi. From this village it is best to park your bike and get a local kid to show you the way to the top. Make your way up there as soon as possible because the longer you wait the more likely it is that one of the older men will say you shouldn't go up there now, for no apparent reason. This is also one of those places that you are not to wear red, I think because the spirits or ancestors do not like the color.

One of the big windfalls of development that has recently come to the island (since 2005) is that it became an independent regency. Because Wanci is the seat of the regency there has been a large influx of money for building government buildings, paying salaries for more government workers, and a large number of new vehicles coming to the island for them. The airport has also been a big addition, with daily flights to Wangi-Wangi from Bau-Bau and Kendari. The *bupati* is doing his part in helping tourism by opening the new Patuno Resort near the airport.

If you head north from Wanci and go up the western side of the island you will be going through the most populated side of the island before getting to more remote areas. Besides several nice views and some places where people raise sea cucumbers, there are not many touristy spots along this road until to get to the *bupati*'s resort. There will be a left hand turn that goes down an incline. The resort has a nice little jungle-covered cliff that is behind it, so that it remains secluded. Most of the buildings in the resort are made on stilts, and there is also a restaurant and swimming pool being constructed. The construction of the resort began in late 2008, with an anticipated fifty rooms, an ambitious number for such a remote place. Hopefully it will live up to expectations. The resort is right on the beach, and all of the bungalows have an ocean view and are not more than 30m from the beach. There are a few little rock formations about 50m out in the water, but other than that there is an unobstructed view of the Banda Sea.

Continuing on to the northeast side of the island, Sousu Beach is the primary beach that Indonesians go to on the weekends. From this beach there are a couple of small islands that can be seen in the distance and the surf breaks a few hundred meters away where it turns shallow. Most of the shallow area in front of the beach is covered with sea grass, but there are also a few sporadic coral formations. There is a small village on the beach, but no restaurants or *warungs* (little shops) where you may eat. You can usually order some grilled fish from some of the young men that hang around the beach as well as asking for them to fetch you a young coconut to drink and eat the insides. This beach is about a 30-minute drive from Wanci.

The airport has also been built near the beach, and has a 2km runway which was first used in early 2009 by small aircraft. It now has daily Express Air flights from Bau-Bau and Kendari. When making your way back to Wanci from the beach on the eastern side of the island (taking the clockwise route) you will once again go through several villages before going through a much less inhabited area. In this uninhabited grassy area there is a long hill on the left side of the road. It somewhat resembles the shape of a large ship and it is said that this was a ship that wrecked hundreds of years ago when the waterline may have been farther in than it is now. The ship has turned to stone. Stories like this and hills that resemble ships are found throughout the islands of Buton. I have heard similar stories on the islands of Muna, Buton, and Kabaena.

There are actually three major piers/ports in Wanci. The port that has all the water transportation to the other Wakatobi islands is surrounded by a Bajo village (people whose houses are built on or over the water). This is the southernmost port. The middle port is for the larger ships that bring passengers from Bau-Bau and Kendari every day, along with various cargo ships. The northernmost pier is only used if the tide is too low to take ships in the central pier, especially ships that leave at a certain time each day like those to Kendari and Bau-Bau.

The port for transportation within the Wakatobi islands is also near the main market in town. There are daily boats to Kaledupa and Tomia. The Tomia boat usually stops momentarily on the western side of Kaledupa at a small pier if the tides are right. If not, local fishermen with their little wooden boats ferry passengers to and from the boat as it waits offshore. This Tomia boat is a "speed" or a fast fiberglass boat that costs Rp100,000 per person ($11). The boat to Kaledupa is wooden and goes to the eastern side of the island and will stop at the island of Hoga on the way for about Rp20,000 more a person ($2). This boat was around Rp50,000 a person ($5.50).

Within Kaledupa's political borders is the island of Hoga, which has become quite famous in Buton because of Operation Wallacea (OpWall) and the large number of European students that go there to study every summer. Most Western foreigners that come to Buton will probably be asked if they are going to Hoga, since that is where most Europeans go when they come this way. It is a relatively small island, with one local village, well protected, and is very quiet and relaxing. OpWall has a large number of bungalows for lodging that were built by people on Kaledupa at Wallacea's request, and then rented by OpWall students from June to August each year. OpWall has a sizable compound, located right in front of the pier on Hoga. After arriving on the pier, if you walk down the beach to the left about five minutes there are various houses and bungalows set a little bit back off the coast, many of which are for tourists (specifically backpackers). They are run by a Dutch lady, Geertje, and are a great place to just get lost, relax, and read for a few days or weeks.

A little bit farther down the beach are some bungalows (the Island Garden) built by Mrs. Hanafiya's husband (Pak Kasim), who lives in Bau-Bau. They also own the Hill House and a place in Ngkaring-Ngkaring. Geertje also helps to manage their resort on Hoga when there is no one else around. But usually if someone is going to stay they will be linked up with a lady (Ibu Wia) who will gather enough food for the stay then escort the guests out to Hoga. These bungalows must be reserved ahead of time because the one that coordinates the scuba diving and the people who run the bungalows are not always living on the island, but make special preparations when guests are going to arrive. They also escort guests from Bau-Bau to Hoga if required. Hoga is not only home to various interesting land creatures (like monitor lizards and the maleo, an endangered, ground-dwelling bird endemic to Sulawesi, similar to a kiwi) it is also very close to several great dive sites. The numbers and size of the fish around Hoga along with the large amount of soft coral puts Hoga a step above Bau-Bau for diving. This water is within the National Marine Park, which affords it some protection.

Right across the water from Hoga, before you get to Kaledupa, is a Bajo village that is completely separated from the land. It is complete with a mosque, a pier, and even a house or two where corn is grown. This entire village has been built on top of the ocean (albeit a shallow part). The Bajo people are their own people and are spread across Indonesia and the southern Philippines. They have their own language and culture. The closest city (Ambeua) on the actual island of Kaledupa is a pretty good size and has some local fabric, called *masris*, available for sarongs, which is softer and airier than other cloths. It is originally from Kaledupa. There are not many vehicles on Kaledupa, so travel will probably be by motorcycle. There are a couple more Bajo villages on the western side of the island (including the

original Bajo village among these islands, Mantigola), and another port and bigger city on the eastern side (Buranga, which
shares practically the same name as the capital of North Buton).
Of all the Wakatobi islands, Kaledupa has the most Bajo villages
surrounding it. There are also a couple of villages in the mountains in the middle of the island, one of which, in the center, has
the remains of a fortress. The boat from Bau-Bau to Kaledupa
goes to a village farther south than Ambeua on the eastern side,
while the daily boat from Wanci stops at the village nearest to
Hoga, Ambeua. This village near Hoga (as is Hoga) is difficult
to get into when it is low tide, and impossible for bigger boats.
There is also the inhabited island of North Lintea off the southern end of the island that can only be reached by boat. A few
thousand people live here. Way off to the east is the island of
Runduma, which also has a couple thousand residents, but this
island is much more remote.

The roads on Kaledupa are not very good (though there have
been recent road improvement projects), and this island is in
competition with Binongko for being the least developed. However, the transportation to this island is better, and Hoga gives it
some prestige. It is said that in some areas of Kaledupa violent
men are fearfully respected and it is best to get a security guard
that has already murdered someone because you know that he is
feared in the community. The people on this island also have a
reputation for drinking and fighting, which may just be the opinion of a few, but during our few hours on the island when we
first visited (in the middle of the day) we did run into a group of
pretty drunk young men, who invited us to join them.

The next island south is Tomia, which has a pretty good
reputation and a lot of things going for it. An NGO associated
with OpWall provided a large number of books for a library on
the island, and all of them were soon checked out. I have been
told that the people on Tomia are more concerned with education and cleanliness than the other islands of Wakatobi, which
may or may not be true. It does have a few hostel-type houses

to stay in that are not too bad in the larger cities of Usuku in the southwest and Waha on the north coast. Usuku in the south is where the boat from Wanci docks, and is also the spot to find a boat to Binongko. Your best bet for going to Binongko is on the Tomia market days, when people from Binongko come to shop. This is three times a week, on Wednesday, Friday and Sunday. The boat arrives in Tomia at around 7am and leaves around 9am. Otherwise, chartering a boat yourself is very expensive (maybe 500,000Rp ($50), compared to 50,000Rp ($5) a person on market days). The port on the north end of the island in Waha does have random boats to Bau-Bau and the small island of Runduma, famous for its large turtles that come ashore to lay eggs. The little village of Waiti on the west coast is the best place to get a little boat over to Wakatobi Divers on Onemobaa if you have made arrangements to visit the resort, but are not staying as a guest. You will have to use the little, hard-to-spot trail to the back entrance.

Tomia also has a field on a hill called *puncak* which is where people often go to relax and enjoy the view off the western side of the island. A little farther up is the actual peak of the hill and there is an old fortress there, along with the grave of the man that brought Islam to Tomia. There is another, less-visited fortress nearer to Waha in the jungle. The trip around Tomia is faster than getting around the other islands, as it is the smallest of the major islands. Of the nearby surrounding islands only Onemobaa is inhabited (by local villages which are separated from the resort). South Lintea is an uninhabited island off the southwest side of Tomia, and its southern tip is famous for having large waves crash against it. Overall, Tomia is a nice place to visit. It is more developed and easier to get around than Kaledupa, and it has its own jewel of a resort, which is frequented by Western tourists.

Right off the northwest coast of Tomia is the island of Onemobaa, which has a very exclusive resort, Wakatobi Divers. This resort is fenced off from the rest of the island. The locals know to steer clear of the resort so they do not disturb the guests. This resort is known throughout the world for its diving and is especially known by underwater photographers. The guests are about 45% American, 45% European, with the remaining 10% made up of other tourists from Asia. There are nice bungalows and great meals are provided. The food is flown in from Bali, as well as the chefs. The resort employs local Indonesians as much as it can while still maintaining high standards of service. For most of the service jobs, Indonesians from Tomia are hired. The closest place with a good pool of skilled technicians and mechanics is Makassar, so many are hired from that city. Bali is the closest place with international chefs, so the chefs are from there. Instead of taking the usual long transportation routes through Southeast Sulawesi, the resort has built an airfield (in conjunction with the government) and owns its own plane, which makes direct flights from Bali. For getting around there is a small fleet of boats used for transporting divers throughout the islands, but even the house reef just in front of the resort is identified as "the best in Indonesia and possibly the world."[208] The islands of Wakatobi are surrounded by steep walls, some of which drop to around 400m. The Swiss owner, Lorenz, has bought the fishing rights for over 20 kilometers of water around Onemobaa so that he can protect it from local fishing and provide the fish room to breed. The high price of the resort is due, in part, to the fact that the resort is totally self sufficient (fuel, power, water, food, etc.), and also that Lorenz basically pays the Indonesians more for leaving the waters alone than they would make fishing it. Tourists can also choose to spend their time aboard the resort's beautiful live-aboard boat, the Pelagian.

The last island of Wakatobi is Binongko, which may have the most character of all the islands. It is definitely the hardest to get to, though there is a weekly boat, the Dharma Putra, directly from Bau-Bau every Wednesday afternoon from the Rock

---

[208] Kal Muller, *Diving Southeast Asia: A Guide to the Best Dive Sites in Indonesia, Malaysia, the Philippines and Thailand* (Periplus Editions, 2003).

Bridge harbor next to the Plaza. The Wakatobi islands used to be referred to as the Tukang Besi, which means "metal workers." In all actuality the only metal workers in these islands are found on the island of Binongko, and even then it is not the whole island of Binongko, but the western side centered around the village of Popalia. The market boat to/from Binongko docks at the city of Tolina on the western side. There really aren't any vehicles available for transportation on the island so you will either ride on the back of a normal motorcycle or a motorcycle that has three wheels and something that resembles a truck bed on the back of it. As you head to Popalia you see the Long Sand beach which has a steep wall drop-off in the ocean about 100m off shore. You then pass the only place on Binongko where you can get a cellphone signal, a group of benches set up next to the ocean in the middle of nowhere. On the islands of Tomia and Binongko the only cellphone service available is Indosat, and the tower is located on Tomia. The primary service on Kaledupa is also Indosat, though you may be able to pick up some Telkomsel from Wangi-Wangi.

As you enter the city of Popalia you can hear the clang of metal being beaten. All along the edge of the hill are little shelters where men and women are heating up various types of metal (like the metal from vehicle leaf springs) from Java and beating it into blades. The sound of clanging metal fills the air near the hill inland from the village. The interesting thing about this reputation for working with metal is that the metal does not come from the island of Binongko, it is all imported. So it is not clear how Binongko became famous for having smiths, or how the first metal made it to the island. It is hard to imagine how this little village could have enough influence to determine the name of an entire island chain, but there are plenty of other charming things about it.

There was a constant stream of stories from the head of the community in Popalia (a great guy, Pak Edris) and from the wife of the head of the newly formed district, *Togo Binongko*. Behind the metal workers on the side of the hill is a spring where fairies are said to bathe. There is also a hole in the area where no one goes because of its history of killing foreigners. Some people believe that a power will pull you into the hole, by taking hold of your shadow. They would not take us there because they said the last time a Westerner, a German, went to take a picture his camera exploded in his hands and almost killed him. People also relate how, many years ago, this same power pulled a group of Portugese into the hole.

F. **Kabaena** – This mountainous island looms large on the horizon on clear days, and is quite beautiful from afar and up close. Its mountains are considered by many to be inhabited by spirits and ghosts, which adds some mystery and charm to the island. Even the names of some of the prominent mountains on the island like Sangia Wita and Batu Sangia bring to mind things supernatural for Indonesians. Mt. Sabampolulu is the tallest mountain on the island at around 1550m and has a crevice in it that is said to look like a human mouth (or the chipped blade of an adze), followed by mountains descending to the south that seem to make up the form of a human body lying down. This island is famous for the nickel and other ores that are mined on it, and for the palm sugar sweets that are sold to the surrounding islands.

There is a vehicle ferry that departs from Bau-Bau three times a week and sails for five hours directly to Dongkala, the largest city on the eastern shore of Kabaena. The ferry then sails two hours to Mawasangka, on the southwestern shore of Muna, stays the night, then sails back to Dongkala the next morning, then on to Bau-Bau. This schedule changes during the West Wind Season (approximately January-March). During this time the schedule slows down a little, and the ferry usually spends the night in Dongkala after sailing from Bau-Bau. There are several passenger ferries (wooden boats) from Mawasangka and

Kasiputih to various cities on Kabaena. There is also a vehicle ferry from Bira, on the southeast tip of the South Sulawesi peninsula, which stops at Sikeli on Kabaena (west coast) on its way east to Tondasi on the island of Muna, then stops at Sikeli again before it heads west again to Bira, from where you can then drive to Makassar. This route is plied twice a month, and, provided the schedule is right, it is the fastest way to get your car to Makassar (or get a car from Makassar). The usual route is to go to mainland Sulawesi via the ferry from Tampo on the north side of Muna, then head to Kolaka and cross the Bay of Bone on a ferry that departs every night.

To access the tallest mountains of Kabaena (including Sangia Wita and Sabampolulu) it is probably best to go to Tongkeno (also called Enano), which is the highest village on the island, and also at the base of the tallest mountains. There was originally only one Tongkeno, but now it has split and the official Tongkeno is at a lower elevation, and the higher elevation village is officially called Enano, but everyone still calls it Tongkeno. This village should be your starting point for the hike. The hike to Sabampolulu will probably take about four hours one-way and is best done in the morning or early afternoon with the intent to spend the night at the top. This trail follows a ridgeline with part of it in the jungle. It is possibly safe enough for some strong children to go on, but I wouldn't recommend it. From Tongkeno to the top of Sangia Wita takes about two hours. There is also a spectacular looking sheer rock monolith on the top of a mountain called Batu Sangia, which can be seen clearly from most places on the central western side of Kabaena. To climb this you would need to start from the village that is one lower down than Tongkeno in elevation (but closer to the base of Batu Sangia). The hike is said to be about one and a half hours to its summit.

When driving from Dongkala you will eventually pass through the village of Ulungkura (which has a friendly head of the village that will open up his home to you), and this is where you need to start paying close attention to the roads. A few kilometers after Ulungkura, there is a pretty bad road heading to the left, which is best navigated with a four-wheel drive vehicle. This road climbs up a ridgeline and at some points is like driving through a rocky creek, as some of the road has been washed away. It goes straight to Tongkeno and rarely sees automobile traffic, which is good because it is one lane. This is definitely the fastest way (if you don't get stuck) to get to Tongkeno. Another option is to continue on past Ulungkura to Sikeli on the west coast, then head back inland to Tongkeno on a recently improved road that has some tough spots for vehicles near the bridges, but should be a smoother option in the future. This road will probably add about one and a half hours each way to Tongkeno. It is a much farther distance, though it is a safer option. Ask the locals about the current conditions of the roads. On the main road between Dongkala and Sikeli there are two cities that have tourist spots near them, Ulungkura and Lengora.

Ulungkura is also a possible gateway city to climb Sabampolulu, but it is a longer and much more strenuous hike because instead of following a ridgeline you would be going up the side of a mountain. It would also be a much greater distance. There is a nice waterfall near this village. The walk to the falls is relatively short, and the plunge pool is ideal for a refreshing swim. Many people also bathe here. For a full day of hiking you can get a nice jungle tour with the possibility of seeing a man stirring up a cauldron of palm sugar, along with big bee hives that are the source of the pure honey for which the island is famous (to check if honey is pure you should be able to submerge a match tip in it, then strike the match, and it should still be able to light). After two hours of solid hiking (not including rests) you should reach the lower part of the top of the ridgeline and see the remains of a very old village on the eastern part of the island which is now an area with large, vine covered piles and stacks of old bamboo, all that remains from the former structures. It has been a long time since this village was inhabited. If you follow the ridgeline up for another one and a half hours you will get to the old fortress that was used for defense of the village from bands of raiders from Ternate, Gowa, and other parts. "For the first two decades of the nineteenth century, it (Buton Island, and neighboring islands) was wracked by Iranun-Tobello violence that left thousands of people dead and tens of thousands of others homeless as they abandoned the coastline and fled to the interior."[209] The perimeter of this fortress is probably around 100m and its eastern wall is still intact with a couple openings possibly for cannon. It overlooks Dongkala and is directly between Dongkala and Batu Sangia on the ridgeline. It is the third peak on the ridgeline and just below the highest point on the ridge. There is also reportedly a walled city that this old village of Kabaena lived in, but it has yet to be discovered.

If you leave Ulungkura and keep heading to Sikeli, you will drive past the turn to the mountain Tongkeno, then the lower village of Tongkeno, and finally reach the village of Lengora. In Lengora is a frequently visited cave called Batu Bori. There is a left hand turn right after the soccer field that will lead you to the cave. It is usually good to have one of the locals guide you and it is best if you have a lantern or some flashlights. Inside the cave are a few attractions, such as a little rock formation that looks like a parrot, with another below it that looks like its droppings. There was also a stone in the cave that was a place of prayer for the older people of the past, but the stone was stolen, so just the empty spot remains. The cave can be a little slick inside, so watch your step. There is also a neat spot that has a skylight about 10m up to the ground above. The trail in the cave goes deep, and if you have enough light and time it may be fun to check out.

If you keep driving from Lengora you will eventually reach the western coast of Kabaena. Sikeli is the largest city on the western side of Kabaena and is home to many Bugis and Bajo

---

[209] James F. Warren, *A tale of two centuries: The globalisation of maritime raiding and piracy and Southeast Asia at the end of the eighteenth and twentieth centuries*, Working Paper Series no. 2 (Singapore: Asia Research Institute, National University of Singapore, 2003), 10.

sailors. Sikeli is also the gateway to the smaller islands on the western side of Kabaena, of which there are three close to Sikeli. The northernmost island is the longest (directly west of Sikeli), the middle island is basically a speck with a shack on it, and the best known island is the southernmost, Sagori Island. Sikeli also has a home-stay, which is a place to pay to spend the night, but is usually just someone's large house and doesn't have all the services of a hotel.

Sagori Island is crescent shaped when viewed from above in the mountains and apparently used to be a spot that a cruise ship with Westerners would stop momentarily.[210] The island is quite beautiful, and is inhabited by Bajo people. There is an elementary school and there used to be a place to spend the night, but now it is a boarded up building because there is no one to manage it. There have been some gazebos and places to relax built on the northern part of the island, as more tourists are expected in the future. There are still trees growing wild in this park area and no houses are allowed to be built here. This island is a 30 minute boat trip from Sikeli, and you can take the boat another 30 minutes southwest of Sagori to an ocean tourist site in the area, a sunken ship. There is still a lot remaining of the ship, and what appears to be a smokestack is visible above the water with skeletal remains of the ship body and engine still intact. It is in pretty rough condition as the metal is heavily corroded and the ship is badly broken up in many pieces. Locals suppose it to be several hundred years old, believing it to be one of several Dutch ships that ran aground in this area. The fact that it is primarily metal seems to point to the fact that it is probably not older than one hundred years old. There is also a ferry that sank (reportedly around the year 2000) that is between the northern island and the little sand island. Only half of it still remains, and from its cargo there are several large concrete pylons that were supposedly going to be used to build a pier somewhere near Ambon.

There were also several other shipwrecks reported in the

---

[210] The name of the cruise ship is said to be the "Renaissance."

area. An article written on an Indonesian blog site described it as the "Bermuda triangle" of Indonesia because ships would disappear there so often.[211] The seas are very deep, and then just around the line formed by the three islands west of Sikeli the ocean floor becomes immediately shallow in several places. There is also reportedly an American airplane that went down somewhere in the sea just north of Sikeli, that is supposed to still be completely whole, but no one knows where it is. The pilot is said to have survived the crash and walked to the eastern side of the island where he was eventually rescued. There was reportedly another plane that went down in the water in this area but was broken up on impact.

The wildlife and sealife in and around Kabaena is also interesting. Near the harbor in Sikeli is the skeleton of a gigantic whale that beached there and is referred to as the "King of Baena." It is amazing to see the bones of such a large animal, it is at least 100ft long. The skull alone is incredible. It is on display with a sign next to it. Many people said I might get eaten by a whale if I went diving around the western side of Kabaena. On the land it is interesting to note that the monkeys have long tails. This long-tailed monkey that is dominant throughout Thailand and Indonesia is actually not dominant on the island of Sulawesi (which has several species of monkeys) except on the island of Kabaena. The nearby islands of Muna and Buton also have the short-tailed variety.[212] There have also been some studies of the plant life on the island that can be used for medicinal purposes. The thing about Kabaena's land that is most famous nowadays, especially from an economic viewpoint, is the nickel that is being mined as well as the promise of many other rich ores once the island becomes more accessible.

[211] Hendragoh, "Sagori, Segitiga Bermuda di Kabaena, Sulawesi Tenggara" http://hendragoh.wordpress.com/2007/12/02/sagori-segitiga-bermuda-di-kabaena-sulawesi-tenggara/ (accessed on 15 Nov 09).
[212] Jeffery W. Froehlich, M.A. Schillaci, L. Jones-Engel, D.J. Froehlich, and B. Pullen, "A Sulawesi beachhead by longtail monkeys (Macaca fascicularis) on Kabaena Island, Indonesia," *Anthropologie* 41, no. 1-2 (2003): 17-24.

G. **Wawonii** – The primary way to get to Wawonii is by car ferry or wooden boat from Kendari to the village of Langgara, on the west coast of Wawonii. It is 3 ½-4 hours by ferry and costs Rp 20,000 for adults, and the wooden boat is supposed to be the same price and may be a little faster. This is not from the main port (Nusantara port) in Kendari, but from another smaller port built for the ferry to Wawonii. It is just a little west of the main port. There are also boats from this port to the Central Sulawesi island of Menui that can be seen in the distance off the northern coast of Wawonii. The big wave season usually starts around June and lasts until September, but it really just depends on the day whether the waves are big or not. On the ferry be prepared to listen for hours to some loud Dangdut videos (Indonesian dance music with an Indian flavor).

Wawonii is still very undeveloped, especially the roads. The port city of Langgara (West Wawonii) does have electricity from a government generator that also reaches up to the city of Lansilowu (North Wawonii). I think the only place that has running water is Langgara. This island is made up of five or six districts that are under the regency of Konawe. From the aspect of land area Wawonii is possibly big enough to be its own regency, but the number of residents is far below the required number. Much of Wawonii is still jungle. The soil is fertile and the major thing growing on the island is coconut trees. There are a large number of coconuts and copra that come from this island.[213] It has a large amount of cacao trees and trees for lumber. You can also find sago palm, cashews, cassava and rice grown in dry fields (possibly some on paddies, too). With this fertile soil and mountainous terrain come some pretty bad roads.

---

[213] Copra is coconut meat that has been dried in the sun or in kilns. It is used primarily as a source of oil, but has other uses as well. In the early 20th century (before the Great Depression), coconuts were referred to as 'green gold' because of the high price people could get for copra. See: Christiaan Heersink, *Dependence on green gold: A socio-economic history of the Indonesian coconut island Selayar* in Verhandelingen van het Koninklijk Instituut voor Taal-, Land- en Volkenkunde, 184 (Leiden: KITLV Press, 1999).

From the city of Langgara, during the rainy season (usually about January to June) you cannot reach South Wawonii by land. You have to take a boat unless you want to carry your motorcycle through some very slippery mud. This road (when it is passable) follows the coast south from Langgara. The road to North and East Wawonii heads east through the jungle and is paved for a couple kilometers, then turns into a dirt and rock road. It takes a little less than an hour to make it to Lansilowu, the largest city in North Wawonii, then this same road continues on to East Wawonii, which is quite a bit farther away. The road to East Wawonii is also very difficult to pass through during the rainy season, but motorcycles can make it. The only vehicles found on the island are trucks used for hauling lumber as well as "hardtops" (jeeps). The roads are pretty narrow, have hills of slippery mud, and often have little ravines in them. In general the road to the south is very slippery, but there are not many rocks in the mud so it is not as bad if you fall. The road to the east has mud, too, but is mixed with rock that would make falling a lot worse.

One of the major sites to see on Wawonii is the Tamburano waterfall. It is reported that this waterfall is 80m tall, but I think this height is including the two lower stages of waterfall that are not as spectacular as the upper falls. From the village of Lonsilowu it is a little less than a two-hour walk to the falls if you are walking at a good pace. You will cross the river three times on the way, the last time just before you climb up to the falls. There are two sections in the lower falls and the part that can be seen from the path is about 5m high. If you continue to climb you will get to the spectacular upper falls that look about 40m tall. This waterfall is fairly wide, looks kind of like a big mushroom, and drops into a pool below that averages about 3m deep. It is great for jumping into from the 6m ledge on the right side of the falls. Whoever gets close to this waterfall will probably get wet as the spray travels a long way. If it's not the rainy season then you can take a motorcycle to within a 30 minutes' walk to the falls.

H. **Bajo** – The Bajo are found throughout Southeast Sulawesi. They live on the water and rely on the sea. There are a
variety of different types of Bajo villages. Some are built on re-
claimed land that is now connected with the coastline and some
are built just off the coast where a short boat ride or a long bridge
can get you to them. Then there are some that can be found several kilometers off the coast on a little sandbar or portion of rock
that only appears at low tide. The foundation of these villages is
usually made with rocks from the sea that have been formed into
piles of various shapes. Then in some cases this rock framework
is filled in with regular dirt. I have seen little corn and cassava
gardens on one of these villages on the sea, but this is not the
norm. Many of the houses have nothing under them but water
and are built on stilts. Going from house to house can be fairly dangerous, especially if you have to walk across on a single
plank. I have personally broken through one of these planks, but
thankfully there were two side by side so I didn't drop straight
into the ocean. I have had other friends break through and one
that caught herself at her elbows just in time to avoid taking a
swim. The boards are usually pretty worn and not always rated
for the weight of a Western body. If you are in the area of a Bajo
village it is always an interesting experience to walk around the
village and see what it is like.

Bajo villages are very popular candidates for receiving community development, and there have been many NGOs involved
in trying to improve their life. Since the Bajo live on the sea and
are usually nomadic (at least in the past), they are often marginalized and even discriminated against. Even now, it is often
the case that the Bajo schools seem to generally be neglected,
and because the families don't usually value education they may
not make the extra effort to get their kids to school. They are
also discriminated against in other ways, including withholding
water or charging high prices for it. They have no freshwater in
their villages, so most of the day for many of the women is spent
going to shore in one of their little wooden boats with a bunch of

jerry cans. They fill these jugs with water from a nearby water source, then boat them back to their village.

The biggest effort I know of in Southeast Sulawesi that has been put into helping a Bajo village would probably be the one near Hoga, Sampela, as a couple of NGOs have done work there as well as providing an opportunity for visiting OpWall students to visit this village for fun service, and education. Geertje, who runs a little resort on Hoga, has provided boat rides to school for a number of Bajo kids for many years. On the northwest side of Muna near Indo Island (that the Muna government wants to develop into a tourist site) there are also several Bajo villages that can be visited in the surrounding area. There is an NGO that has been established to look after the rights and protect the Bajo people in Southeast Sulawesi. *Yayasan Sama* in Kendari is a self-help foundation for Bajo, founded by Bajo.[214] The relatively large towns of Wanci, Ereke, Donggala, Raha, and Langgara all have Bajo villages or at least some Bajo presence connected to them.

I know of one Bajo village where everyone works together to provide *teri* to a company in Taiwan. The little, centimeter-long fish are eaten throughout Asia on things like rice and a variety of other dishes. The village that does this is off the west side of Muna, near Kabaena, and is one of the villages that is a few kilometers off shore and has no visible land at high tide. There is a representative from Taiwan that goes out there every few weeks, checks on how things are doing, and organizes getting the fish to ships that will eventually carry them to Taiwan. The people are generally very friendly. You may want to think twice before spending the night on some of the villages over the water because when rats arrive and multiply they have no jungle to run to, and can form quite a presence in these villages, so I've been told.

---

[214] Hope, 204-238.

Part III – The Neighbors of Buton

X
MAINLAND KINGDOMS IN SOUTHEAST SULAWESI

Though the islands of Southeast Sulawesi are the focus of this book, there is still also much to be discovered on the portion of mainland Sulawesi within the province. The indigenous population of the peninsula consisted mainly of Moronene who lived in the Southwestern peninsula (Poleang and Rumbia), Tolaki living in the central parts (Kolaka, Kendari) and some Toraja to the north (relatively recent immigrants from South Sulawesi). The indigenous tribes were the descendants of prehistoric migrants who originated from other parts of Asia and from Oceania. They possessed a hierarchical social structure, which generally consisted of an elite, a middle class and slaves, and lived predominantly in the interior. About 1830, when they entered written history, they appeared to adhere to some form of ancestral religion. They sustained themselves by means of shifting cultivation, hunting, and some barter trade. With only a few exceptions they were unfamiliar with coastal fishing and seafaring. Sporadically they came to the shores, mainly to sell their forest produce and to obtain human heads, which they needed for their festivities and rituals.[215]

TOLAKI

There are a variety of kingdoms that are said to have existed on this land, though none of them rose to the power of neighboring Buton and the Bugis. Not much has been written about these kingdoms, and the West knew little about this area prior to the

---

[215] Aritonang, 483.

20th century. Up until then, knowledge about the mainland of the southeastern peninsula of Celebes (Sulawesi) was limited to the reports of a few explorers, among them the Dutch sea captain J. N. Vosmaer (who circumnavigated the peninsula in 1831),[216] the Englishman (and later rajah of Sarawak) James Brooke (who paid a brief visit to Kolaka in April 1840),[217] the Dutch sea captain C. van der Hart (Kendari Bay, February-March 1850),[218] the Italian naturalist Oduardo Beccari (Kendari Bay, January-June 1874),[219] and the German brothers Paul and Fritz Sarasin (February-March 1903),[220] who were the first to explore the interior,

[216] J. N. Vosmaer, "Korte beschrijving van de zuid-oostelijk schiereiland van Celebes, in het bijzonder van de Vosmaersbaai of van Kendari; verrijkt met eenige berigten omtrent den stam der Orang Badjos, en meer andere aanteekeningen" [A brief description of the southeast peninsula of Celebes, in particular the Vosmaer Bay or Bay of Kendari; with information concerning the Orang Badjo people and some other notes]. *Verhandelingen van het Bataviaasch Genootschap van Kunsten en Wetenschappen* 17/1:63–184. (Batavia: Ter Lands Drukkerij, 1839).

[217] Rodney Mundy, *Narrative of events in Borneo and Celebes down to the occupation of Labuan: from the journals of James Brooke, Esq., rajah of Serawak, and governor of Labuan*, Vol. 1(London: John Murray, 1848), chapters 11&12.

[218] C. van der Hart, *Reize rondom het eiland Celebes en naar eenige der Moluksche eilanden* [Trip round about the island Celebes and to some of the Maluku islands] (Gravenshage: K. Fuhri, 1853).

[219] Enrico Hillyer Giglioli, "Odoardo Beccari ed i suoi viaggi: I. Macassar–Kandari (Celebes); II. I Papua" [Odoardo Beccari and his voyages: I. Makassar–Kandari (Celebes); II: The Papua], *Nuova Antologia* 27 (1874):194–237. See also: P.J. Veth, "Beccari's reis van Makasser naar Kendari" [Beccari's trip from Makasser to Kendari], *Tijdschrift van het Aardrijkskundig Genootschap* 1(1876): 199–204. See also: Odoardo Beccari, "Nuova Guinea, Selebes e Molucche" [New Guinea, Celebes and the Moluccas] (Firenze: La Voce, 1924), 273-314.

[220] Paul Sarasin and Fritz Sarasin, "Reise der Herren Dr. P. und F. Sarasin in der südöstlichen Halbinsel von Celebes" [Journey of the brothers Dr. P. and F. Sarasin in the southeastern peninsula of Celebes], Globus 83(1903): 349–350. See also: Paul Sarasin and Fritz Sarasin. *Reisen in Celebes, ausgeführt in den jahren 1893-1896 und 1902-1903* [Journeys in the Celebes, conducted in the years 1893-1896 and 1902-1903], vol. 1 (Wiesbaden: C.W. Kreidel, 1905), 334-381.

crossing from Kolaka to Kendari. The people who live in this land are identified as the Bungku-Tolaki peoples, and in general this entire region has been subject to significant acculturative change due to Buginese domination.[221]

The languages of the indigenous people groups that are found on the mainland, and at four places on the surrounding islands, belong to the Bungku-Tolaki language stock. There is the Bungku language family, which includes the languages of Wawonii, Kulisusu, and Kabaena. The Tolaki language is dominant on the mainland and includes the Mekongga dialect spoken around Kolaka.[222] The indigenous people that live throughout most of this land in about a 100km radius of Kendari are the Tolaki. They are 1% Christian.[223] There is a tradition that all Tolaki peoples originate from a place called Andolaki, which was somewhere near the source of the Konawe River. Based on linguistic evidence (as well as geography), another theory is that the Tolaki originated from the "Lake area" of present-day Nuha district in the NE corner of SSul, migrated down the eastern coast of Bone Bay, and then from Kolaka crossed the mountains and conquered the eastern half of the peninsula.[224]

As with other languages on the mainland the prefix "To-" means "people, so "Tolaki," means the "Laki people." "Laki" means male (in Malay *laki-laki*), but this does not mean they are the "male people." According to the linguist David Mead, it probably meant something like "the warriors, the brave ones, the leaders," because of the role males had in the society. There were reportedly two primary kingdoms among the Tolaki, the kingdoms of Konawe and Mekongga. On the eastern side of the peninsula the kingdom of Konawe in Unaaha was the largest, and the grave of one of their kings (Lakidende) can still be

[221] Frank M. Lebar, ed. "Muna-Butung" in *Ethnic Groups of Insular Southeast Asia*, Vol. 1: Indonesia, Andaman Islands, and Madagascar (New Haven: Human Relations Area Files Press), 144.
[222] Mead, 33.
[223] Ibid., 73.
[224] Mead, 184, footnote 21.

visited in Unaaha. He is said to have governed in the middle of the 19th century and was the first to convert to Islam. He helped make peace in a conflict between the kingdom of Mekongga and Konawe. Another famous Tolaki man was Haluoleo. Reportedly, one thing that made him unique was that he traveled abroad to Muna with several families, settled a Tolaki village on Muna, then continued on to Buton where he was to become a sultan.[225] His name lives on today as the state university in Kendari has been named after him. Today, the regencies of the Tolaki all have the name Konawe in them (Konawe, North Konawe, and South Konawe). Konawe is the most developed, with South Konawe coming in second, while North Konawe is a fairly recent addition and borders Central Sulawesi. The Mekongga kingdom, in the vicinity of Kolaka, was on the western side of the peninsula (explained in the next section). Laiwui was the name of another smaller kingdom or district in the area, and the related Tabunku kingdom was farther north in what is now Central Sulawesi. I was also told there was a Sao-Sao kingdom in Wua-Wua (in Kendari) as well as a Lasandara kingdom, though I wasn't able to verify these.

Initial Catholic missionary efforts to Southeast Sulawesi were made by a Jesuit in October 1885 when he opened a *statie* (Roman Catholic mission post) on the shore of the Bay of Kendari on the east coast of the peninsula. They built a school that ended up being entirely for the nearby Bugis and Bajo communities. No indigenous Tolaki children attended the school. He tried to make contact with the Tolaki community, but eventually had to leave the area because of pressure from Bugis merchants. Several children and two Bajo adults were baptized as the result of his ministry. The Catholics later returned in 1964 when Kendari became the capital of the new province of Southeast Sulawesi. At this point a true Catholic hospital was opened in the city as well as the government hospital having a Catholic

---

[225] Abdurrauf Tarimana, *Kebudayaan Tolaki*, in Seri Etnografi Indonesia, no. 3 (Jakarta: Balai Pustaka, 1989), 65.

priest and medical doctor as its director, C. Lemmens, who had previously been on Muna since 1958.[226]

By the second half of the 19th century Islam had gained a foothold among the people of mainland Southeast Sulawesi by way of their contact with Bugis and Butonese merchants. As a result Islam quickly became the religion of the elite because it put no restrictions on their role in traditional religion. In contrast, the Protestant Christianity introduced by the Dutch Missionary Society (NZV) found its adherents mainly among the lower half of society and its influence on indigenous society was much more unsettling than that of Islam. It wasn't until the 1930's that these Protestant congregations had their own trained pastors, which was a relatively late effort (compared to the work in Poso) to reach the indigenous population, and no Tolaki or Tomoronene had joined the Protestant Church. The task of approaching them was left up to missionaries that would follow. Nonetheless, even as the quarter-century of initial Dutch missionary activity (from late 1915 until the Japanese invasion in February 1942) drew to a close, they could count over twenty primary schools and over 3000 converts.[227] Islam still became the dominant religion of the area, though a Protestant Christian community eventually developed and has persisted to this day despite persecution under the Japanese from January 1942 to January 1944, and Muslim rebels (some under Kahar Muzakkar) from 1950-1965. The membership of the Protestant Church of Southeast Sulawesi, Gepsultra, was 25,000 in 2001.[228]

MEKONGGA

The other two regencies on the peninsula associated with the Tolaki, are those of Kolaka (Kolaka and North Kolaka) on the

---

[226] Aritonang, 484-486.

[227] Staf Proyek Survey Menyeluruh DGI and M. C. Jongeling, compilers. *Benih yang tumbuh, no. 10: Suatu survey mengenai Gereja Protestan Sulawesi Tenggara (Gepsultra)* (Jakarta: Lembaga Penelitian dan Studi Dewan Gereja-Gereja di Indonesia (LPS-DGI)), 7.

[228] Ibid., 487-490.

west side of the peninsula. This is the land of those identified with the Mekongga kingdom. In Kolaka, as well as Konawe and Buton, the northern regencies seem to be the least developed. The Mekongga kingdom was supposed to have been founded in 1290 with the crowning of the first king, Larumbangi. This man killed the giant bird, "Konggaaha," and was made king because of this. The Mekongga are a sub-group of Tolaki, and the height of their kingdom was in 1697 when the king Sangia Nibandera accepted Islam. The title "Sangia" meant that he was a descendant from heaven. The kingdom of Mekongga was known to steal/kidnap slaves as well as hunt heads on the nearby island of Muna.[229] It is also said that the people of Mekongga and the Moronene people to the south were mortal enemies, and conducted headhunting raids against each other.

Later in 1906, Bokeo Latambaga, the reigning king, helped develop the city of Kolaka, which is the primary port for goods moving from Makassar to Kendari and throughout Southeast Sulawesi. A vehicle ferry leaves three times a night to cross over to Bajoi (the port in Bone) on the east coast of the peninsula of South Sulawesi. It is about an 8-hour trip. There is also a large nickel factory on the south side of the city of Kolaka. Kolaka is the area that Protestant congregations grew the fastest because the establishment of a mining company brought in Protestants from other areas. As for most of the rest of the coast surrounding the Bay of Bone, the Bugis basically have control of it economically. The Mekongga people usually tend to live a little more inland. This kingdom is also said to have been under the ancient Buginese kingdom of Luwuq to the north. The road from Kendari to Kolaka is probably the best stretch of road in Southeast Sulawesi (about a 3 ½ hour trip).

---

[229] Alb. C. Kruyt and J. Kruyt, "Verslag van een reis naar Kolaka" [Report of a journey to Kolaka], *Tijdschrift van het Koninklijk Nederlandsch Aardrijkskundig Genootschap* 38 (1921): 694.

MORONENE

In the southwestern part of this peninsula is the regency of
Bombana where the Moronene people live. They are 3% Christian.[230] The primary city here is Kasipute, and the previously
discussed island of Kabaena is included in this regency as they
are a sub-group of Moronene. The areas of Poleang and Rumbia
often come up in old documents about the kingdom of Buton
because they apparently had a relationship with Buton at some
point. It is also possible that they used to live farther north in the
Tolaki area because there are still some place names there that
only have meaning in the Moronene language.

Bombana has recently been made famous by having a gold
rush in which thousands of people came to try and make it
rich panning and digging for gold. There were many reports
of people dying as they dug tunnels to find gold, and then had
them collapse. There were also many people that got a great
economic boost from this. One newspaper article reported that
the governor of Southeast Sulawesi had somehow received an
estimate that there was 186,000 tons of gold in this area. It will
be interesting to see how this gets managed in the future. With
a tradition in Indonesia of large foreign companies coming in
and getting rich off of the country's resources, the leadership in
Bombana wanted to give an opportunity for the locals to reap
the benefits directly. Many have benefitted, but it also contributed to destruction of the area because of the uncontrolled gold
prospecting. Six months after the official opening of the area to
mining (Nov. 1, 2008), the administration suspended the mining.
This was to try a figure out how to overcome the environmental
damage, settle land disputes, and resolve the security and economic issues that have arisen.[231] It is sure to be a long process.

[230] Ibid., 39.
[231] Farida Sendjaja, "Bombana: Blessing or Curse?" in "Outreach: Development of Indonesia's Outlying Areas," supplement, *Tempo Magazine English
Edition* (June 9-15, 2009): 2-3.

XI
TRANSMIGRATION AND
INFLUENTIAL COMMUNITIES

There are a number of outside people groups that have communities in Buton, the most prevalent of which include: Balinese, Torajanese, Ambonese, Chinese, Bugis, and Javanese. This is in line with the sense that Buton is a place of safety and refuge for people from outside communities that make their home here. These people have been here for a long time, but originally come from different backgrounds that are still evident today.[232] Generally they came to the area for business and trade reasons as well as a myriad of other reasons, including the government transmigration program (the largest moves around 1978) and refugees from the fighting in and around Ambon (1998-2002). Buton and Muna each have portions of land that have been allotted for these communities that are called SP (*Satuan Permukiman*), with numbers 1 to 10 in central-eastern Buton, others in North Buton, and around five SP's on northwest Muna. Sometimes the numbered community is made up entirely of one people group (such as the Javanese), but at other times it is a mixture of people and may even be split into "A" and "B."

There are also communities of Minahasa (from North Sulawesi, a traditionally Christian area) that can be found in the city of Bau-Bau. They are generally somewhat lighter skinned and have a reputation for having beautiful women. The Javanese

---

[232] See map showing the origin of outside and transmigration communities.

can be found here and there, and I have heard it said that they can be found throughout Indonesia trying to spread and strengthen Islam throughout the archipelago. There are also some just here for business and as part of the transmigration program. And as usual there are a couple Padang restaurants in the city (yum), just as they can be found in almost every other major city in Indonesia; they are Minangkabau people. The Bugis are a well-known people of South Sulawesi from the former Kingdom of Bone that are also known for going abroad and for their sailing abilities. The Bugis can be found living next to and with houses on top of the sea in some areas, but they are not quite as tied to the sea as the Bajo. They can be found throughout the islands of Buton, especially in the coastal areas. The Bugis are traditionally stronger Muslims.

Regarding religion, other than the Balinese communities (that are Hindu) most of the official transmigration communities are from Java and are Muslims. There are also some communities from Ambon that may be interspersed with Christians, but most of the people from Ambon had parents or grandparents from Buton so still hold to their religion. Religion throughout Indonesia is generally based more on culture than adherence to certain professed beliefs because they have been found to be true. The other culturally Christian peoples found in Buton not mentioned below are the Minahasa of North Sulawesi, people from Kupang, West Timor, Catholics from the island of Flores, and maybe a few Batak from North Sumatra. The Batak are a lot more prevalent in nearby Java, while the primary culturally Christian community going abroad throughout Sulawesi is Torajanese (mentioned below). The Protestant Church of Western Indonesia is primarily made up of Minahasans and other newcomers to the area.

Transmigrants have generally received pretty fertile ground and have more varied agricultural experience because of the crops grown in their homelands. Along with the Balinese (mentioned below) the Javanese grow rice in a couple of the SP communities on Buton. The other people groups that can be found throughout Buton that are not mentioned below generally are not tied to a certain piece of land or way of life but are interspersed throughout the cities of Buton.

A. **Balinese** – The Balinese have been in the area since 1978 when they were given a very fertile area of land on Buton, just north of Bau-Bau, called Ngkaring-Ngkaring. I have heard that these Balinese took the initiative and came to Buton looking for fertile land, then made a proposal to the government and were allowed to move. The other story is that the Butonese leadership called them because no one else could get rid of the evil spirits in the area. You can see the temples in front of each of the houses and similar architecture that can be found in Bali. You can also buy pork in this village (Muslims don't eat pork) and enjoy some nice relaxing recreation sites by a nearby river. The man that owns the Hill House in Bau-Bau and Island Garden resort on Hoga is also building a restaurant in Ngkaring-Ngkaring near the swimming site. Balinese transmigration communities can also be found on the northwest side of Muna (mixed among the SPs), on the east-central side of Buton (SP3A and Ambuau), in North Buton (mixed among the SPs), and on the northern tip of Kabaena at Pising.

Another interesting development that came with the coming of the Balinese is that more of the animals in the jungle were hunted. The anoa is an animal that looks like a small cow, but has sharp horns that point straight up. It is endemic to Sulawesi, and is especially well known in Buton. The Butonese say it is evil, and everyone says that you do not want to encounter one because they will try to gore you and chase you up a tree, as mentioned earlier. They will wait until you come down. The only way to escape is to throw your shirt on top of their head, and while they are spearing your shirt you get down and run for it. The Balinese did not have this mystical fear of the anoa and started hunting and eating it when they arrived. They are also currently called into villages throughout Buton to set traps for wild pigs to protect the fields and gardens of the local people. The locals will not eat the pigs, but the Balinese will. Everybody wins.

Just as in Bali, they are excellent rice farmers. They are also known for baking and selling bricks in Ngkaring-Ngkaring and another Balinese village just north of it. The Balinese are well known for their beautiful rice fields and work ethic, so it is not surprising that they are thriving in Buton. There are also some rice fields in Ambuau on the eastern side of Buton that they work along with a couple of Javanese villages. On mainland Southeast Sulawesi it is primarily the Javanese that grow the rice.

The Hindu traditions of Bali are still alive and well in this community. They have a good relationship with the surrounding community, but they definitely guard their beliefs because they still have a community large enough to keep them together. It is said that the land of Ngkaring-Ngkaring used to be a place where people often died unexpectedly, purportedly because of some type of curse or evil spirits in the land. As the story goes, since the Balinese came out to this land in the early seventies it has been at peace.

B. **Torajanese** – During the Torajanese resistance of the Dutch, the village leaders Ua Saruran and Bombing were exiled to Makassar, and some of their associates were sent to "a more unhealthy site at Buton island."[233] This is another example of Buton being a popular location to exile someone. Other than this, the majority of the Torajanese arrived just a little before the Balinese and many of them live just south of Ngkaring-Ngkaring in Liabuku. A large number had left South Sulawesi to work for an asphalt mine in the center of Buton (Kabongka) for a company that ended up going bankrupt. There was a friend of the Torajanese high enough in the local government of Buton

---

[233] Terance W. Bigalke, *Tana Toraja: A Social History of an Indonesian People* (Singapore: Singapore University Press, 2005), 61.

that he gave them a good deal of land that they have been growing rice on since the early 1970's. They were reportedly the first to plant and grow rice in rice paddies on Buton, arriving five years before the Balinese.

The Torajanese have also been blessed with fertile land and are another generally diligent people group that are usually successful when they go abroad. They often go abroad to raise enough money to give a proper funeral for their family members in the Land of the Toraja, complete with the slaughtering of 5 to 140 water buffaloes depending on your wealth and family line. Their culture is identified with Christianity, though there are many rituals and traditional beliefs still practiced today that show some deviation from orthodox Christianity.[234]

The Torajanese usually make up the majority of the members of the Indonesian Protestant Church-Southeast Sulawesi churches that can be found in Liabuku and in the city of Bau-Bau near the bus station. The denomination was originally founded with German influence. There are also some Torajanese that worship with the Gospel Tabernacle churches and were instrumental in originally bringing the gospel and planting the first indigenous church on the island of Muna. This initial group of belivers then moved to Batu Sori on Buton and have now moved to Ambon and scattered to different places on Buton. There is a Gospel Tabernacle seminary in Makassar (Jaffray) and this denomination was originally associated with the Christian & Missionary Alliance (CMA) from America.

I heard from a Torajanese man that there were several instances of a nominal Christian Torajanese man wanting to marry a local Muslim woman and being forced to become a Muslim if he wanted the marriage to take place. This is a convenient way of bringing a "Christian" into the Muslim fold. But it would often turn out that several years later when no one was really noticing the Torajanese man would return back to Christianity and

---

[234] Derek Newton, *Deity & Diet: the dilemma of sacrificial food at Corinth* (Sheffield, England: Sheffield Academic Press, 1998).

bring his Muslim wife and children with him. This was seen as an example of "Christianization," and that the Torajanese were somehow trying to convert the local population through marriage. This looks more like a game to me where people are fighting a type of mini-culture war where the actual doctrines of their religions aren't very important.

C. **Ambonese** – After the fighting between Christians and Muslims in the Malukus, especially Ambon, there was a great exodus to the surrounding areas for safety. As a result, many Ambonese can be found on the island of Buton and the surrounding islands. Villages such as Bolo, found near "Soulmate beach" south of the city of Batauga on the southwest corner of Buton, are made up almost completely of people that fled Ambon and the fighting. It seems that most of them were Butonese people that were raised in Ambon, but returned to the homeland of their parents as things became too violent in Ambon. Some heard of the pending violence and went back to where their parents were. Others have stories of how the violence reached them before they could get away, and afterwards they returned to Buton because their house was destroyed or family killed. Others chose to stay in Ambon. There is a whole section of the city of Ambon that is made up of people from Buton, as well as another one made up of people from Muna. It is hard to distinguish the land and work of the people from Ambon from the rest of the people. Since many of them have blood ties with Buton they usually blend right back in with the local populace.

The people from Ambon could easily be Christians or Muslims, with the majority of those in Buton having fled because of the fighting in Ambon right around the year 2000. The beliefs of the people from Ambon in Buton may be a little more open than others on the island, but they are generally Muslim. Even so, in Ambon there is a large Christian community of people originally from the island of Muna that can be found in the village of Batu Sori near the airport. There are stories that as Muslim attackers started to climb the hill to attack this village they saw a large force of white men protecting this community so they did not venture in to destroy it. In this way the people believe that their God was protecting them from their enemies. This community is the larger part of the only indigenous baptistic Protestant church that has come out of Muna and Buton. Remnants of the Gospel Tabernacle denomination still remain near Pasarwajo and Bau-Bau.

D. **Chinese** – People of Chinese descent have long been a part of Bau-Bau and the other big cities in the province and currently own most of the large stores, factories, etc. It is not as though the Chinese just came in and bought everything, but through hard work and having enough capital they have been very successful and have raised their families here for generations. One exception is that there really aren't many Chinese out among the Wakatobi islands yet.

The Chinese usually stick closer to the bigger cities even though they may have factories or warehouses out in more remote areas harvesting fish to send back to China, running pearl farms or fish factories, etc. They usually have nicer houses and own the larger stores in town. Some of the bigger stores even have their own ships that make runs to Surabaya and Makassar to replenish their stock and find new items to sell.

The Chinese usually make up the more charismatic churches such as the Pentecostal church and the Bethany and Bethel churches (connection with Church of God in America). The main Pentecostal church is now located in Liabuku and from what I have heard is the only church that has experienced outright persecution in Buton. I think it was in the late 1990's that the church building used to be located in the city of Bau-Bau, but the surrounding community thought there was too much noise coming from the church on Sundays so they forced the church to close their church building and would not allow them to return. The abandoned building still remains on Kelapa Road.

In this case since the church was primarily Chinese the members had enough money to build another building outside the city. The noise complaint is ironic coming from a community that is totally at ease with speakers blaring at 4:30 in the morning, every morning.

E. **Bugis** – These people are known throughout Indonesia and are the largest people group in Sulawesi. They also have strong ties with the history of Buton as noted in the stories about the Bugis alliance with Buton and the Dutch through the Bugis prince Arung Palakka. In some places people use the name Bugis and Bajo interchangeably because the Bugis also often build their houses near the coastline on the sea. One area where a Bugis community has built their houses on the sea is near the ferry port of Torobulu on mainland Sulawesi that connects with the port of Tampo on the northern coast of the island of Muna.

The Bay of Bone, which is bordered on the east by the southeast peninsula of Sulawesi, is where the Bugis are dominant and where stories such as the origin of the Bajo arise. It is not that far away from Buton, and many stories in Buton reference this part of Sulawesi. The Bugis have ties throughout the people groups of Buton. I have not seen much evidence of close kinship between the Bajo and Bugis, but many outsiders do group them together. The Bugis are also formidable in business and have very influential people throughout the province.

Other than those communities that live on the sea or are tied together as a small fishing community, the Bugis are usually intermixed throughout the cities of the islands of Buton. They do not seem to live in groups clumped together but intermix and intermarry freely with the various people groups on Buton.

The Bugis have a long reputation of going abroad and settling throughout the surrounding islands, which can be a considerable distance from the peninsula of South Sulawesi. In my interaction with several Bugis families it seems that they are usually more staunch in their practice of Islam and leave off some of the local cultural aspects of their celebrations (like the Butonese have their *haro'a*). They are generally friendly, and I am sure they are proud of their heritage and the large and influential presence of the Bugis throughout Sulawesi and surrounding areas, especially East Kalimantan.

F. **Javanese** – Besides individual Javanese families that may be found throughout the islands, the larger communities are a result of the transmigration program in the 1970's. There are several SP's that can be found around Lasalimu as well as some up in West Kulisusu, which is the area on the island that has the worst roads. As with the Balinese, the Javanese have cultivated their land into rice fields and they remain one of the three primary communities that grow rice on the islands, along with the Torajanese.

They have been given some fertile land, and in many cases have given their communities a name other than the SP number. They have names that use words like "Jaya" and "Sari" that can be found used throughout Java. They also have large stretches of land and large transmigration communities on the mainland peninsula of Southeast Sulawesi surrounding the city of Kendari for several miles.

The Javanese have a very ancient and very developed culture of which they are proud. As most of the leadership in Indonesia has been Javanese, there is a sense that the Javanese are viewed as having a higher social status (or at least perceiving themselves that way) than the rest of Indonesia. But I have to say that the Javanese I have met on the islands of Buton have been very friendly and seemingly humble in the way that the Javanese usually are, as politeness and gracefulness are very important virtues to them.

BIBLIOGRAPHY

NOTES ON LANGUAGE RESOURCES

A large amount of the work done with the people groups of Buton has been by linguists. The Dutch linguistic scholar Rene van den Berg has worked with the Muna people. His dictionary and grammar on the Muna language in English was a monumental task. In the Muna language there is a complete New Testament of the Bible that has been translated and distributed, which is in the southern Muna dialect and is primarily for the Catholic villages in southern Muna. The Wolio language also has a Dictionary and Grammar available that was completed by the Dutch linguist J. C. Anceaux about 50 years ago. Another linguistic expert, David Mead, spent years with the Kulisusu people near the city of Ereke (Bone) in North Buton. He has produced a few works on the Kulisusu language and those related to it, including an Indonesian-Kulisusu-English dictionary and a book on the Bungku-Tolaki language group. Mark Donohue, who spent some time in Wanci, in Wakatobi, wrote a grammar for the language of Wakatobi (Tukang Besi).

A number of local language audio resources available on CD and cassette tape. The Global Recordings Network (GRN), which in Indonesia is called Lembaga Rekaman Injil Indonesia (LRII) headquartered in Bandung, has several recordings of stories starting from the Old Testament through the Gospels in the languages of Wolio, Cia-Cia, Wakatobi and Muna-GuLaMas dialect.

Hiroko Yamaguchi from Japan can speak the Wolio language and has spent some time in and around Buton, as well as climbed Mt. Siontapina for the annual rituals. She has published a document on the ancient manuscripts that can be found in the Wolio museum in the fortress in Bau-Bau.

In 2008 an agreement was reached between the city of Bau-Bau and an NGO in Korea to build and run a place of study to maintain the Cia-Cia and the Wolio cultures. Some leaders of a Cia-Cia community said they would adopt the *Hangul* script for their language since it had never before been fully written down. They have produced books to teach school children to write Cia-Cia using the *Hangul* script.[235] Rene van den Berg has also done some writing on Cia-Cia,[236] but this was the first concerted effort to teach the language in schools. There is a sort of following of Wolio history throughout the world, and in the museum of Butonese culture in the *keraton* in Bau-Bau there are various manuscripts that are written in the old Arabic-looking script (*Jawi*) of the Wolio language.

SOURCES CONSULTED

English, Dutch, and Italian

Abidin, A.Z. "LA MA'DUKELLENG: Precursor of South Sulawesi Unification against the Dutch VOC" *Prisma: The Indonesian Indicator 22* (Sept. 1981): 29-46.

---

[235] Choe Sang-Hun, "South Korea's Latest Export: Its Alphabet," *New York Times*, Sept. 11, 2009.
[236] Rene van den Berg, "Preliminary notes on the Cia-Cia language (South Buton)" in *Excursies in Celebes: een bundel bijdragen bij het afscheid van J. Noorduyn als directeur-secretaris van het Koninklijk Instituut voor Taal-, Land- en Volkenkunde* (Verhandelingen van het Koninklijk Instituut voor Taal-, Land- en Volkenkunde, 147), edited by Harry A. Poeze and Pim Schoorl (Leiden: KITLV Uitgeverij, 1991), 305-324.

Andaya, Leonard Y. *The Heritage of Arung Palakka: A History of South Sulawesi (Celebes) in the Seventeenth Century.* Leiden: KITLV, 1981.

Aritonang, Jan Sihar and Karel Steenbrink, eds. *A History of Christianity in Indonesia.* Leiden: Brill, 2008.

Azra, Azyumardi. *Islam in the Indonesian World: An Account of Institutional Formation.* Bandung: Mizan Pustaka, 2006.

Ballinger, S.W., Theodore G. Schurr, Antonio Torroni, Y.Y. Gan, J.A. Hodge, K. Hassan, K.H. Chen, and Douglas C. Wallace. "Southeast Asian Mitochondrial DNA Analysis Reveals Genetic Continuity of Ancient Mongoloid Migrations." *Genetics Society of America130* (January 1992): 139-152.

Bakker, J.I. (Hans). "Resettlement of Bajo 'Sea Nomads': Rapid Rural Appraisal of an IRD-IAD Project in Sulawesi, Indonesia," In IRDR, vol. 1, edited by J.I. (Hans) Bakker, 129-166. Guelph: Guelph-Wgeningen IRD, 1992."

Beccari, Odoardo. "Nuova Guinea, Selebes e Molucche" [New Guinea, Celebes and the Moluccas]. Firenze: La Voce, 1924.

Berg, Rene van den. *A Grammar of the Muna Language.* Dordrecht/Providence: Foris Publications, 1989.

_____. "Notes on the historical phonology and classification of Wolio." *Language and text in the Austronesian world: Studies in honour of Ülo Sirk* (LINCOM Studies in Austronesian Linguistics, 6), edited by Yury A. Lander and Alexander K. Ogloblin, 89-103. Muenchen: LINCOM, 2008.

_____. "Preliminary notes on the Cia-Cia language (South Buton)" in *Excursies in Celebes: een bundel bijdragen bij het afscheid van J. Noorduyn als directeur-secretaris van het Koninklijk Instituut voor Taal, Land en Volkenkunde* (Verhandelingen van het Koninklijk Instituut voor Taal , Land en Volkenkunde, 147), edited by Harry A. Poeze and Pim Schoorl, 305–324. Leiden: KITLV Uitgeverij, 1991.

Biek, Wolfgang. "Just how old is this kite cave painting?" *Drachen Foundation Journal 10* (Fall 2002): 18.

Bigalke, Terance W. *Tana Toraja: A Social History of an Indonesian People*. Singapore: Singapore University Press, 2005.

Bulbeck, David and Ian Caldwell. "Land of Iron: The historical archaeology of Luwu and the Cenrana valley." Results of the Origin of Complex Society in South Sulawesi Project (OXIS); Centre for South-East Asian Studies, University of Hull; School of Archaeology and Anthropology, Australian National University, 2000.

Caldwell, Ian. "Power, State and Society Among the Pre-Islamic Bugis," in *Bijdragen tot de Taal-, Land- en Volkenkunde* 151, no.3 (1995): 394-421.

Cowling, Anthony. *My Life with the Samurai: How I Survived Japanese Death Camps*. Vancouver: Premium Printing, 2001.

Cummings, William Patrick. *A Chain of Kings: the Makassarese Chronicles of Gowa and Talloq*. Leiden: KITLV Press, 2007.

Daum, P.A. *Ups and Downs of Life in the Indies*. Hong Kong: Periplus Editions Ltd., 1999.

Dick, H.W. "Prahu Shipping in Eastern Indonesia." *Bulletin of Indonesian Economic Studies* XI, no. 2 (July 1975): 69-107.

Dijk, Cornelius van. *Rebellion under the Banner of Islam: The Darul Islam in Indonesia*. Leiden: KITLV, 1982.

Donohue, Mark. *A Grammar of Tukang Besi*. New York: Mouton de Gruyter, 1999.

Ekariyono, Willy and Sugiarto. "Environmental Baseline and Impact Management of Jambu-1 Witaitonga Island – Southeast Sulawesi, Indonesia" at SPE Health, Safety and Environment in Oil and Gas Exploration and Production Conference, 25-27 January 1994, Jakarta, Indonesia. Society of Petroleum Engineers, Inc, 1994.

Friedericy, H.F. *The Counselor* in *Two Tales of the East Indies*. Singapore: Periplus (HK) Ltd, 2000.

Froehlich, Jeffery W., M.A. Schillaci, L. Jones-Engel, D.J. Froehlich, and B. Pullen. "A Sulawesi beachhead by longtail monkeys (Macaca fascicularis) on Kabaena Island, Indonesia" *Anthropologie* 41, no. 1-2 (2003): 17-24.

Giglioli, Enrico Hillyer. "Odoardo Beccari ed i suoi viaggi: I. Macassar–Kandari (Celebes); II. I Papua" [Odoardo Beccari and his voyages: I. Makassar–Kandari (Celebes); II: The Papua]. *Nuova Antologia* 27 (1874): 194–237.

"Go East to Buton: Sea Safari to Southeast Sulawesi." *Travel Indonesia* 11, no. 10 (Oct. 1989): 16-26.

Gregory-Smith, Judyth, photography by Richard Gregory-Smith. *Southeast Sulawesi: Islands of Surprises*. Jakarta: Balai Pustaka, 2000.

Grimes, Barbara Dix. "Mapping Buru: The Politics of Territory and Settlement on an Eastern Indonesian Island." In *Sharing the Earth, Dividing the Land*, edited by Thomas Reuter, 135-155. Canberra: The Australian National University E Press. 2006.

Hart, C. van der. *Reize rondom het eiland Celebes en naar eenige der Moluksche eilanden* [Trip round about the island Celebes and to some of the Maluku islands]. Gravenshage: K Fuhri, 1853.

Harvey, Barbara Sillars. "Tradition, Islam, and Rebellion: South Sulawesi 1950-1965." PhD, Cornell University, June 1974.

Heersink, Christian. *Dependence on green gold: A socio-economic history of the Indonesian coconut island Selayar* in Verhandelingen van het Koninklijk Instituut voor Taal- Land- en Volkenkunde, 184. Leiden: KITLV Press, 1999.

Henley, David. "A superabundance of centers: Ternate and the contest for North Sulawesi." *Cakalele* 4 (1993): 39-60.

_____. *The idea of Celebes in history*. Working Papers on Southeast Asia, 59. Victoria: Monash Asia Institute, 1989.

Heynneman, Ron. *Ibu Maluku: The Story of Jeanne van Diejen* Hartwell, Victoria: Sid Harta Publishers, 2002.

Hoga Resort. http://www.tukangbesidiving.com/ (accessed on April 3, 2010).

Hope, Sebastian. *Outcasts of the Islands: The Sea Gypsies of South East Asia.* London: HarperCollins, 2001.

Hubert Th. Th. M. Jacobs, S.J., *A Treatise on the Moluccas* (c. 1544) (Probably the preliminary version of Antonio Galvao's lost Historia Das Molucas. Edited, annotated, and translated into English from the Portuguese manuscript in the Archivo General de Indias, Seville. Sources and Studies for the History of the Jesuits: Vol. III. Rome: Jesuit Historical Institute, 1970.

Japan Petroleum Exploration Co, Ltd. "Buton Block." http://www.japex.co.jp/english/business/overseas/india.html (accessed on April 3, 2010).

Kruyt, Alb. C. "Lapjesgeld op Celebes [Cloth Money on Celebes]." Translated by David Mead and edited by Rene van den Berg, June 2010. *Tijdschrift voor Indische Taal-, Land- en Volkenkunde 73* (1933):172-183.

_____ and J. Kruyt. "Verslag van een reis naar Kolaka" [Report of a journey to Kolaka]. *Tijdschrift van het Koninklijk Nederlandsch Aardrijkskundig Genootschap* 38 (1921): 689-704.

Lebar, Frank M., ed. "Muna-Butung" in *Ethnic Groups of Insular Southeast Asia,* Vol. 1: Indonesia, Andaman Islands, and Madagascar. New Haven: Human Relations Area Files Press.

Liebner, Horst H. "Traditional boats, Forum Makassar Straights: A website about maritime South Sulawesi," 2004. http://www.forumms.com/traditional_boats.htm (accessed on September 27, 2010).

Mead, David E. *The Bungku-Tolaki Languages of South-Eastern Sulawesi, Indonesia.* Canberra: Pacific Linguistics, Research School of Pacific and Asian Studies, The Australian National University, series D, vol. 91, 1999.

_____ and Myung-young Lee. *Mapping Indonesian Bajau Communities in Sulawesi.* SIL International, 2007.

Milton, Giles. *Nathaniel's Nutmeg*. New York: Penguin Books, 2000.

Morvan, F. *Legends of the Sea*. New York: Crescent Books, 1980.

Muller, Kal. *Diving Southeast Asia: A Guide to the Best Dive Sites in Indonesia, Malaysia, the Philippines and Thailand*. Periplus Editions, 2003.

_____ and Dinah Bergink. "Buton" in *Sulawesi: Island Crossroads of Indonesia*. Singapore: Passport Books, 1995.

Mundy, Rodney. *Narrative of events in Borneo and Celebes down to the occupation of Labuan: from the journals of James Brooke, Esq., rajah of Serawak, and governor of Labuan*. 2 volumes. London: John Murray, 1848.

Munoz, Paul Michel. *Early Kingdoms of the Indonesian Archipelago and the Malay Peninsula*. Didier Millet, 2007.

Newton, Derek. *Deity & Diet: the dilemma of sacrificial food at Corinth*. Sheffield, England: Sheffield Academic Press, 1998.

Noorduyn, J. "Makasar and the Islamization of Bima," in *Bijdragen tot de Taal-, Land- en Volkenkunde* 143, no.2/3 (1987): 312-342.

_____. "The manuscripts of the Makasarese chronicle of Goa and Talloq; An evaluation" *Bijdragen tot de Taal-, Land- en Volkenkunde* 147 (1991):454-484.

_____. "The Wajorese Merchants' Community in Makassar," in *Authority and Enterprise Among the Peoples of South*

Sulawesi, edited by Roger Tol, Kees van Dijk and Greg Acciaioli, 95-120. Leiden: KITLV Press, 2000.

Operation Wallacea Trust. http://www.opwall.com/ (accessed on April 3, 2010).

Overstreet, Paul and Don Schlitz. "When You Say Nothing At All." Universal: MCA Music Publishing, 1988.

Reid, Anthony, ed. *Slavery, Bondage and Dependency in Southeast Asia*. St. Lucia: University of Queensland Press, 1983.

Reuter, Thomas, ed. *Sharing the Earth, Dividing the Land*. Canberra: The Australian National University E Press, 2006.

Ruhe, Ben. "Time Will Give More Answers: Muna Cave Painting Is Hard to Date." *Drachen Foundation Journal* (Fall 2003): 15-17.

Sarasin, Paul and Fritz Sarasin. "Reise der Herren Dr. P. und F. Sarasin in der südöstlichen Halbinsel von Celebes" [Journey of the brothers Dr. P. and F. Sarasin in the southeastern peninsula of Celebes]. *Globus* 83(1903): 349–350.

_____. *Reisen in Celebes, ausgeführt in den jahren 1893-1896 und 1902-1903* [Journeys in the Celebes, conducted in the years 1893-1896 and 1902-1903]. 2 volumes. Wiesbaden: C.W. Kreidel, 1905.

Sather, Clifford. *The Bajau Laut: Adaptation, History, and Fate in a maritime fishing society of South-Eastern Sabah*. KL: Oxford University Press, 1997.

Schoorl, J.W. "Belief in Reincarnation on Buton, S.E. Sulawesi, Indonesia" *KITLV Journal of the Humanities and Social Sci-*

ences of Southeast Asia and Oceania 141, no. 1 (1985): 103-134.

Schutte, G.J., ed. *State and Trade in the Indonesian Archipelago* Leiden: KITLV, 1995.

Schwartz, Stephen. *The Other Islam: Sufism and the Road to Global Harmony.* Doubleday: New York, 2008.

Sendjaja, Farida. "Bombana: Blessing or Curse?" in "Outreach: Development of Indonesia's Outlying Areas," supplement, *Tempo Magazine English Edition* (June 9-15, 2009): 2-3.

Sidel, John T. *Riots, Pogroms, Jihad: Religious Violence in Indonesia.* Singapore: National University of Singapore Press, 2007.

Smith, Holly S. *Adventuring in Indonesia: Exploring the Natural Areas of the Pacific's Ring of Fire.* San Francisco: Sierra Club Books, 1997.

Southon, Michael. *The navel of the perahu: meaning and values in the maritime trading economy of a Butonese village.* Canberra: Department of Anthropology, Australian National University, 1995.

Stacey, Natasha. *Boats to Burn: Bajo Fishing Activity in the Australian Fishing Zone.* Canberra: Australian National University E Press, 2007.

Steenbrink, Karel. *The Spectacular Growth of a Self-Confident Minority 1903-1942,* vol. 2 in series "Catholics in Indonesia 1808-1942: A Documented History." Leiden: KITLV Press, 2006.

Sutherland, Heather. "Trepang and Wangkang: The China Trade of Eighteenth-Century Makassar, c.1720s-1840s" in *Authority and Enterprise Among the Peoples of South Sulawesi* edited by Roger Tol, Kees van Dijk and Greg Acciaioli, 73-94. Leiden: KITLV Press, 2000.

Taylor, Jean Gelman. *Indonesia: Peoples and Histories*. New Haven: Yale University Press, 2003.

Todhunter, Andrew. "Deep Dark Secrets." *National Geographic* 218, no. 2 (August 2010): 34-53.

Touwen, Jeroen. *Extremes in the Archipelago: Trade and Economic Development in the Outer Islands of Indonesia 1900-1942*. Leiden: KITLV, 2001.

Velthoen, Esther. "Mapping Sulawesi in the 1950s" in *Indonesia in transition: Work in progress* edited by Henk Schulte Nordholt and Gusti Asnan, 103-123. Yogyakarta: Pustaka Pelajar, 2003.

_____. "Sailing in dangerous waters: piracy and raiding in historical context" *IIAS Newsletter*, no. 36 (March 2005): 8.

Vermonden, Daniel. "Reproduction and Development of Expertise within Communities of Practice: A Case Study of Fishing Activities in South Buton (Southeast Sulawesi, Indonesia)." Chapter 9 in *Landscape, Process and Power: Re-evaluating Traditional Environmental Knowledge*, edited by Serena Heckler, 205-229. Vol. 10 in Series entitled "Studies in Environmental Anthropology and Ethnobiology" New York: Berghahn Books, 2009.

Veth, P.J. "Beccari's reis van Makasser naar Kendari" [Beccari's trip from Makasser to Kendari]. *Tijdschrift van het Aardrijkskundig Genootschap* 1(1876): 199-204.

Vlekke, Bernard H. M. *Nusantara: A History of Indonesia*. The Hague: Van Hoeve, Ltd, 1965.

Vosmaer, J. N., "Korte beschrijving van de zuid-oostelijk schiereiland van Celebes, in het bijzonder van de Vosmaers-baai of van Kendari; verrijkt met eenige berigten omtrent den stam der Orang Badjos, en meer andere aanteekeningen" [A brief description of the southeast peninsula of Celebes, in particular the Vosmaer Bay or Bay of Kendari; with information concerning the Orang Badjo people and some other notes]. *Verhandelingen van het Bataviaasch Genootschap van Kunsten en Wetenschappen* 17/1: 63–184. Batavia: Ter Lands Drukkerij, 1839.

Vuyk, Beb. *The Last House in the World* in *Two Tales of the East Indies*. Singapore: Periplus (HK) Ltd, 2000.

Wakatobi Divers. www.wakatobi.com (accessed on 23 Feb 10).

Warren, James F. *A tale of two centuries: The globalisation of maritime raiding and piracy and Southeast Asia at the end of the eighteenth and twentieth centuries*. Working Paper Series no. 2. Singapore: Asia Research Institute, National University of Singapore, 2003.

Weatherford, Jack. *Genghis Khan and the Making of the Modern World*. New York: Three Rivers Press, 2004.

Wicarawati, "Gowa, on the Crossroads to the Spice Islands." *Garuda Magazine* 9, no. 3 (1989): 15-22.

Winstedt, R.O. *A History of Johore* including the work by Professor Dato' Ismail Hussein, *Hikayat Negeri Johor: A Nineteenth Century Bugis History relating events in Riau & Selangor*. Selangor, Malaysia: The Malaysian Branch of the Royal Asiatic Society, 1992.

Indonesian

Alifuddin, M. *Islam Buton: Interaksi Islam dengan Budaya Lokal.* Indonesia: Badan Litbang dan Diklat Departemen Agama RI, 2007.

Baja, Sumbangan. "Strategi Pengembangan Wilayah dan Manajemen Sumberdaya Menuju Kemandirian Buton Raya." Paper presented at the graduation of Dayanu Ikhsanuddin University, Bau-Bau, Southeast Sulawesi, Indonesia, 30 May 2009.

Couvreur, J. *Sejarah dan Kebudayaan Kerajaan Muna.* Trans. Rene van den Berg. Kupang: Artha Wacana Press, 2001.

Darmawan, M. Yusran, ed. *Menyibak Kabut di Keraton Buton (Bau-Bau: Past, Present, and Future).* Bau-Bau: Respect, 2008.

_____, ed. *Naskah Buton, Naskah Dunia.* Bau-Bau: Respect, 2009.

Haliadi. *Buton Islam dan Islam Buton: Islamisasi, Kolonialisme, dan Sinkretisme Agama.* Yogyakarta: Yayasan untuk Indonesia, 2000.

Hamid, Abd. Rahman. *Spirit Bahari Orang Buton.* Makassar: Rayhan Intermedia, 2010.

Haris, Tawalinuddin. "Benteng Keraton Buton," in *Monumen: karya persembahan untuk Prof. Dr. R. Soekmono*, eds. Edi Sedyawati and Ingrid H.E. Pojoh, pp. 325-328. Depok: Fakultas Sastra, Universitas Indonesia, 1990.

Harisun. "Kedudukan Nilai Kearifan Lokal di Indonesia Kaitannya dengan Hukum Adat Buton di Siotapina," Skripsi, Universitas Dayanu Ikhsanuddin, Bau-Bau, 2009.

Hendragoh. "Sagori, Segitiga Bermuda di Kabaena, Sulawesi Tenggara,"http://hendragoh.wordpress.com/2007/12/02/sagori-segitiga-bermuda-di-kabaena-sulawesi-tenggara/(accessed on November 15, 2009).

Ibrahim, Irianto. *Buton, Ibu dan Sekantong Luka.* Yogyakarta: Framepublishing, 2010.

Ikram, Prof. Dr. Achadiati. *Istiadat Tanah Negeri Butun: Edisi Teks dan Komentar.* Jakarta: Djambatan, 2005.

Kasim, A. Sultan. *Aru Palakka Dalam Perjuangan Kemerdekaan Kerajaan Bone.* Makassar: CV. Walanae, 2002.

La Ode Rabani. *Kota-Kota Pantai Di Sulawesi Tenggara.* Yogyakarta: Penerbit Ombak, 2010.

La Ode Sidu. *Cerita Rakyat Dari Sulawesi Tenggara.* Jakarta: PT Gramedia Widiasarana, 1995.

Laporan Peninjauan Tim Direktorat Jenderal Perhubungan Laut dan Koordinator Angkutan Aspal Buton ke Nusa Tenggara Timur: 22 Januari to 5 Pebruari, 1986. Jakarta: Southeast Asian Material Indonesia, Filmed by The Library of Congress Office, 1989.

Liebner, Horst H. "Sebuah Naskah Belanda tentang Kecelakaan Armada VOC di Pulau Kabaena, Maret-Mei 1650," in *Naskah Buton, Naskah Dunia,* ed. M. Yusran Darmawan, 73-112. Bau-Bau: Respect, 2009.

Melayu Online. "Kerajaan Paling Demokratis Di Nusantara." Opinion article. http://melayuonline.com/ind/opinion/read/59/kerajaan-paling-demokratis-di-nusantara (accessed on April 3, 2010).

"Popaua Dan Gambaran Keraton Siotapina." *SKU Berita Keraton*. Edition 60, 2001.

Schoorl, Johan Willem (Pim). *Masyarakat, Sejarah, dan Budaya Buton*. Jakarta: Djambatan bekerjasama dengan Perwakilan KITLV Jakarta, 2003.

Sedyawati, Edi and Ingrid H.E. Pojoh, eds. *Monumen: karya persembahan untuk Prof. Dr. R. Soekmono*. Depok: Fakultas Sastra, Universitas Indonesia, 1990.

Southeast Sulawesi tourist booklet. "Selamat Datang di Sulawesi Tenggara." Kendari: Dinas Kebudayaan dan Pariwisata, Sulawesi Tenggara, 2009.

Staf Proyek Survey Menyeluruh DGI and M. C. Jongeling, compilers. *Benih yang tumbuh, no. 10: Suatu survey mengenai Gereja Protestan Sulawesi Tenggara (Gepsultra)*. Jakarta: Lembaga Penelitian dan Studi Dewan Gereja-Gereja di Indonesia (LPS-DGI).

Tarimana, Abdurrauf. *Kebudayaan Tolaki,* in Seri Etnografi Indonesia, no. 3. Jakarta: Balai Pustaka, 1989.

Udu, Sumiman. *Perempuan Dalam Kabanti: Tinjauan Sosio-feminis*. Yogyakarta: Penerbit Diandra, 2009.

Unknown. *Assajaru Huliqa Daarul Ba'tainy Wa Daarul Munajat.*

_____. *Pengenalan Diri Pada Maha Pencipta.*

Usaha Peningkatan Pemanfaatan/Penggunaan Aspal Buton. Indonesia: Departemen Pekerdjaan Umum Dan Tenaga Listrik, 1971.

Yamaguchi, Hiroko. "Naskah-naskah di Masyarakat Buton; Beberapa catatan tentang Keistimewaan dan Nilai Budaya," in *Menyibak Kabut di Keraton Buton (Bau-Bau: Past, Present, and Future)*, ed. M. Yusran Darmawan, 97-104. Bau-Bau: Respect, 2008.

Yunus, DR. H. Abd. Rahim. *Ajaran Islam Yang Dominan Dalam Naskah Peninggalan Kesultanan Buton*. Ujungpandang: Pusat Penelitian Iain Alauddin, 1996/1997.

_____. *Posisi Tasawuf dalam Sistem Kekuasaan di Kesultanan Buton pada Abad ke-19*. Jakarta: INIS.

Zahari, Abdul Mulku, ed. *Adat dan Upacara Perkawinan Wolio*. Jakarta: Departemen Pendidikan dan Kebudayaan, Proyek Penerbitan Buku Sastra Indonesia dan Daerah, 1981.

_____. "Islam di Buton: Sejarah & Perkembangannya." Unpublished manuscript. Wolio Museum, Bau-Bau, 1982.

_____, ed. *Sejarah dan Adat Fiy Darul Butuni (Buton)* I, II, III. Jakarta: Proyek Pengembangan Media Kebudayaan, Depdikbud, 1977.

Zuhdi, Susanto. "Berpikir Positif Orang Buton," in *Bunga Rampai Berpikir Positif Suku-Suku Bangsa*. Jakarta: Departemen Kebudayaan dan Pariwisata RI bekerja sama dengan Asosiasi Tradisi Lisan (ATL), 2005.

_____. *Sejarah Buton yang Terabaikan: Labu Rope Labu Wana*. Jakarta: RajaGrafindo Persada, 2010.

MAPS AND TIMELINE

Map 1: Sulawesi

Map 2: South Sulawesi Kingdoms

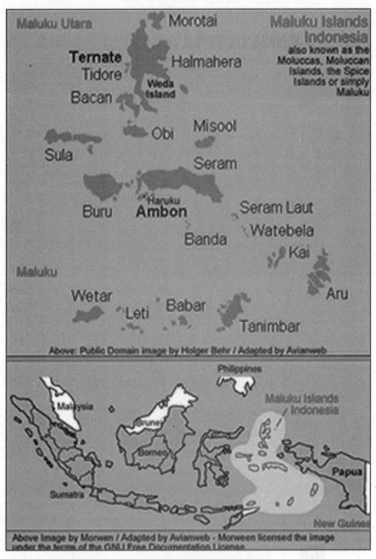

Map 3: Maluku Islands

PETA BAHASA SULAWESI TENGGARA

Program Kerjasama SIL International & Direktorat Jenderal Pemberdayaan Masyarakat dan Desa
Departemen dalam Negeri Republik Indonesia
di Kendari, Sulawesi Tenggara
2006

Map 4: Bahasa-Bahasa Sulawesi Tenggara
(Languages of Southeast Sulawesi)

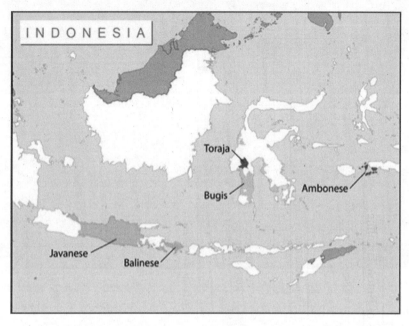

Map 5: Origin of Outside and Transmigration Communities

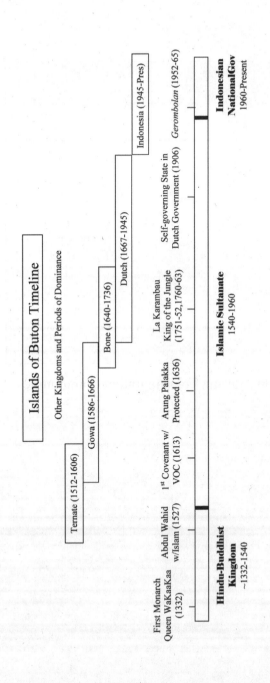

Islands of Buton Timeline

Other Kingdoms and Periods of Dominance

Ternate (1512-1606)

Gowa (1586-1666)

Bone (1640-1736)

Dutch (1667-1945)

Indonesia (1945-Pres)

First Monarch
Queen WaKaaKaa
(1332)

Abdul Wahid
w/Islam (1527)

1st Covenant w/
VOC (1613)

Arung Palakka
Protected (1636)

La Karambau
King of the Jungle
(1751-52, 1760-63)

Self-governing State in
Dutch Government (1906)

Gerombolan (1952-65)

**Hindu-Buddhist
Kingdom**
~1332-1540

Islamic Sultanate
1540-1960

**Indonesian
NationalGov**
1960-Present